D1552573

WRITING IN ONLINE COURSES

WRITING IN ONLINE COURSES

 How the Online Environment

Shapes Writing Practices

EDITED BY PHOEBE JACKSON

AND CHRISTOPHER WEAVER

Myers
Education
Press

Gorham, Maine

Copyright © 2018 | Myers Education Press, LLC
Published by Myers Education Press, LLC
P.O. Box 424
Gorham, ME 04038

Myers Education Press is an academic publisher specializing in books, e-books and digital content in the field of education. All of our books are subjected to a rigorous peer review process and produced in compliance with the standards of the Council on Library and Information Resources.

Library of Congress Cataloging-in-Publication Data available from Library of Congress.

13-digit ISBN 978-1-9755-0009-2 (paperback)
13-digit ISBN 978-1-9755-0008-5 (hard cover)
13-digit ISBN 978-1-9755-0010-8 (library networkable e-edition)
13-digit ISBN 978-1-9755-0011-5 (consumer e-edition)

Printed in the United States of America.

All first editions printed on acid-free paper that meets the American National Standards Institute Z39-48 standard.

Books published by Myers Education Press may be purchased at special quantity discount rates for groups, workshops, training organizations and classroom usage. Please call our customer service department at 1-800-232-0223 for details.

Cover design by Sophie Appel

Visit us on the web at **www.myersedpress.com** to browse our complete list of titles.

Contents

Acknowledgments

The authors would like to thank Louis Palmer for his professional advice during the writing of this book. We also wish to acknowledge the release time granted to us by William Paterson University in support of this collection.

Introduction: Why Do You Teach Online?

EVEN THOUGH ONLINE CLASSES HAVE proliferated and have become a mainstay of teaching on most campuses from community colleges to research institutions, it's not unusual for those of us who teach online to get this question: Why do you teach online? For those who have not taught online, it's difficult to imagine how learning can effectively take place without the spontaneous give and take of class discussion guided by the teacher's presence. What is difficult to explain to naysayers about the promise of the online classroom is the positive impact that technology can have on teaching and writing.

The aim of this collection is to examine the ways in which online instruction enhances and informs student writing and learning. As more of us from different disciplines begin and continue to teach online, an ever-growing conversation is taking place about how the new medium changes what we do and how students learn. When instructors make the transition from teaching in the traditional classroom to teaching online, they soon discover, if they didn't already know, that the process involves more than exchanging one type of instruction for another. To that end, we examine the ways teaching online has enabled us to rethink how writing functions in our classes, allowing us to pursue educational goals and student outcomes that may have been more difficult or not even possible in the traditional classroom.

Because writing is at the heart of learning online, it is particularly important to understand how it differs from writing in the traditional classroom. In the online environment, writing provides the medium through which discussion takes place. That being said, writing does not merely provide a medium for communication; it also constructs all of the relationships that determine learning: relationships between teachers and students, among students, and between all of the participants and the textual material that makes up the course content. The central role that writing plays in online courses constitutes one of the main reasons that faculty gravitate toward teaching online.

The writers in this collection choose to teach online because doing so has led them to insights about the way that writing informs student learning that they would otherwise never have reached. The bottom line is that writing online creates more effective opportunities to reach specific student outcomes than might be possible in the traditional classroom.

Although the essays in this collection offer many ideas for readers to consider, this book is not primarily concerned with giving advice about the practical aspects of teaching online. Excellent books already exist that offer advice on "best practices" and on teaching pedagogy (Harrington, Rickly, & Day, 2000; Hewett & Ehmann, 2004; Warnock, 2009). Instead, the assembled authors take the necessary step forward in the evolution of online instruction to reflect upon what they have learned, specifically how writing helps to shape online instruction and how online instruction helps to shape the writing process.

Finally, our collection purposefully engages instructors from across the disciplines. Including these colleagues in our book has engendered different ways of thinking about the process of writing, as they have important and unique observations to make about a student's engagement with writing. In their respective chapters, the authors examine what they have learned about online student writing from the standpoint of their particular disciplines. The contributors also consider how writing online has helped them to achieve specific academic goals and has opened up and created new opportunities for writing expression in their academic disciplines. We expect that these multiple perspectives will enable all the readers of this collection to reflect on their own online practices in new ways.

Teaching Writing as Process: Writing as a Collaborative and Social Act

In considering how the online environment affects the writing process, it is important to understand that many of the issues that engage those of us who think critically about the use of writing in online courses are not new. The authors in this collection continue to address issues of composition pedagogy that arose in the writing process movement of the 1970s and that were influenced by the work of social constructionist scholars of the 1980s. Their approaches are also clearly informed by the Writing Across the Curriculum movement that emerged in that same time period and which is well established on most college campuses today. In particular, our interest in how we use writing when we teach online is predicated on two ideas which have roots in these movements: writing to learn and writing as a collaborative and social act. Before we examine how these ideas play out in the online classroom, it is worth noting how these movements and the past practices associated with them inform our assumptions about writing in the online environment.

In the early 1970s, the paradigm of teaching writing shifted from a focus on writing as a set of features that could be identified and imitated by students to a focus on the processes that writers used as they composed. In "Teach Writing as a Process, Not a Product," Donald Murray explained that most writing teachers were trained to analyze literature and that this training did not serve their students well, because "dissecting" writing did not help students to create writing. As an alternative, Murray called for a new focus on teaching the writing process. As to what such a process would look like, Murray (1972/1997) wrote: "It is the process of discovery through language. It is the process of exploration of what we know and we feel about our world, to evaluate what we learn about our world, to communicate what we learn about our world" (p. 3).

The shift in attention from product to process also changed the role that writing played in the composition classroom. Previously the primary purpose of writing had been to demonstrate knowledge that the writer already had; now the goal of writing was, in Murray's words, "discovery through language." For the process advocates who followed Murray, writing was the form of language most likely to lead to discovery because it allowed the writer to move back and forth between composing and reviewing (Emig, 1977). Many of these process advocates also argued that the goal of writing to learn required new modes of writing. They would come to be known as "expressivists" for their emphasis on expressive writing, which fostered voice, growth, and discovery, over transactional writing, which conveyed information. To achieve this goal, expressivists argued for narrative, dialogue, letters, and even "creative" writing as supplements to traditional forms such as the essay and the research paper.

Some of these new forms would help to shift the view of writing from a solitary act to a collaborative one. Process advocates argued that the writer did not discover meaning on his own but through extended interaction with readers—preferably readers also engaged in the writing process themselves. Perhaps no one articulated this idea more forcefully than Peter Elbow, whose influential book *Writing Without Teachers* (1973) went so far as to suggest that writers needed each other as readers and responders far more than they needed formal writing instruction. This need gave rise to the workshop model of writing, where students read works in progress to each other and used readers' feedback to measure the impact of their words and to inform the revision process.

Scholars who advocated for a collaborative model of writing argued that students needed to take a more active role in the writing process—measuring their drafts' effectiveness by sharing them with a group of readers rather than relying on an instructor's comments. Writing groups and peer feedback, they argued, would fundamentally change the source of authority, resulting in a more student-centered classroom. In fact, process-advocates such as Elbow believed that *authority* could only be found once students began to identify themselves as *authors* and that elusive qualities in writing such as "voice" and "power" were only available to them once they took control of their own writing. Authority came from ownership, and writing teachers were admonished to resist the temptation to appropriate students' texts (Brannon & Knoblauch, 1982).

In the decade that followed, social constructionist scholars argued for a slightly different understanding of the relationship between collaboration and authority, pointing out that writing was socially and institutionally situated. For these theorists it was not just writing that was a social artifact, but knowledge creation in general, and they advocated for teaching strategies that demonstrated to students how communities produced knowledge through discourse. Kenneth Bruffee (1984) wrote that teachers should foreground the role of discourse in the writing process so that by seeing writing as embedded in conversation, students could begin to "negotiate their way into that conversation" (p. 647). Social constructionists such as David Bartholomae (1986) also emphasized the role of discourse communities, arguing that each community had its own set of discourse conventions that outsiders must learn before they could speak with authority to that community. While composition scholars debated the best way for students to enter that community (Bartholomae, 1995; Elbow, 1995), there was no doubt that the idea of writing as communal discourse was now central to the composition classroom and that writing was no longer a neutral skill to be mastered in the service of learning but a central part of learning itself.

Writing to Learn and Writing as Collaboration in the WAC Classroom

In the 1980s, the Writing Across the Curriculum (WAC) movement embraced the shift that had occurred in composition studies from viewing writing as a product to viewing writing as a way to learn. At the same time, the WAC movement sought to encourage instructors to think about the importance of writing and its role in critical thinking. Looking back on the movement years later, WAC pioneer Art Young (1994) would explain that one of the first WAC programs at Michigan Tech arose because the university "wanted students to become more active and engaged learners, critical thinkers, and problem-solvers—and they believed that providing students with increased opportunities to use writing as a tool for learning would help meet these goals" (p. 60). This new model of writing instruction was crucial to the development of the WAC movement, which would make the goal of writing to learn and the process of writing as collaborative discourse central features of its agenda.

WAC programs also adopted the concept of writing to learn as a social and collaborative act, acknowledging that writers need others to read and to respond to their words to move the writing process forward. The WAC movement seized on collaborative writing both as a model of instructional discovery and as a means to facilitate learning. Toby Fulwiler (1986) wrote of the importance of peer groups "to motivate and educate each other" (p. 27), and WAC workshops suggested various assignments and activities where students write to each other in order to pose questions, solve problems, or begin discussions. By giving students these kinds of writing assignments and asking them to engage in debates about a discipline, WAC-informed courses emphasize that it is not merely writing that is collaborative but the nature of disciplinary knowledge itself.

The ultimate goal of WAC practices was to initiate students into a new community—the discourse community of a particular discipline. In order to enter such a community, students would have to see discourse not merely as a way to learn or to communicate disciplinary knowledge, but also as the way in which knowledge was constructed. Traditionally, both students and faculty may have viewed knowledge as something to be transmitted in readings and classroom discussions and then demonstrated in tests and written assignments. Such practices failed to acknowledge the fact that knowledge in a discipline is the result of a "conversation" that has evolved over time (Bruffee, 1984) and that involves dialogue, disagreement, and significant rethinking of previously held positions. Armed with this new perspective, students would, in theory, be better prepared to engage in critical inquiry through writing.

These two core elements of composition pedagogy—writing to learn and writing as a collaborative act—were influential in shaping the WAC movement and current-day writing practices used in courses in different disciplines. The writers in this collection that come from disciplines other than English owe much to strategies developed from WAC programs, particularly strategies based on collaboration and writing as a mode of discovery. As we examine the effects that online courses have on the writing process, it is particularly important for us to note how these elements found fertile ground outside of writing programs. The fact that core elements of composition pedagogy might actually work better when transplanted to a different environment is something that ought to be of particular interest to us as we prepare to think about how writing works differently online than it does in the traditional classroom.

Composition Pedagogy and WAC: Encounters in the Online Classroom

Both composition and WAC pedagogies were instrumental in re-conceptualizing the way that instructors thought about writing. Instructors who began to teach online quickly realized the possibilities afforded them in this new environment, allowing them to pursue the twin goals of writing to learn and writing as a collaborative act in a more effective manner than was possible in a face-to-face class. In this latter environment, instructors all too often encountered a myriad of challenges that hindered the successful articulation of these pedagogical goals. With online teaching, however, instructors have found that these goals are easily within reach. There are a number of factors in the online classroom that allow for this important change.

Of particular significance is the change in the teacher–student relationship. The "de-centered" classroom that process-pedagogies envisioned was difficult to create in the face-to-face environment because this setting reinforced students' expectations about the teacher's authority. The online environment, however, provides better opportunities for realizing the ideal de-centered class that process-writing pedagogues advocated in the 1970s and 1980s. As many of the chapters in this book affirm, teachers often discover that online it is easier to guide activities and discussions without dominating them. The instructor becomes yet another participant in the class, thus putting more responsibility on students to participate and perform. This change in authority, as our authors suggest, has a positive effect on teaching and on learning in the online classroom.

Because of this change in authority, students come to view learning as more of a collaborative process. Areas such as group sites and discussion boards occupy a more central space in the online classroom than student groups do in a face-to-face environment, and when students write in these online spaces, they are more likely to view their teacher as part of a wider audience that includes other students than when they write in the traditional classroom. In working collaboratively online, students learn to ask each other questions, to build on discussions, and in some instances to use student material as references. This dynamic among students shows them the importance of an audience and emphasizes the significance of engaging in a written conversation that encourages critical inquiry. As a result of reading, writing, and responding to each other's work on the discussion board, they are in effect building spontaneous discourse communities.

The building of discourse communities in an online classroom enables students to share knowledge in a supportive atmosphere. In the face-to-face classroom, it is frequently not possible for all students to talk because of time limitations. Moreover, students in a face-to-face classroom are sometimes reluctant to speak up, fearful of saying the wrong thing or fearful that they might appear stupid. However, because of the implicit anonymity of the online environment, instructors have found a greater willingness on the part of all to "speak up" and to participate in student group discussions.

These conversations on the discussion board differ from those in a traditional classroom where the discussion can seem rather scattershot, moving from one idea to another without delving deeply into a topic. On the discussion board, students have the opportunity to spend time reading and responding to others in a thoughtful way. Instructors who teach online have found that when students are able to take more time to think and write, the result usually is a more thoughtful and productive discussion. Unlike the traditional classroom where there might be little carryover from one class to another, the discussion board becomes a permanent record of student responses and comments that allows students to return to the discussion for further reading, writing, and reflection.

Finally, both process writing and writing across the curriculum pedagogies emphasize the importance of collaborative writing as a way for students to share ideas and knowledge. In a face-to-face classroom environment, working in a collaborative manner for students is much more difficult to achieve. External factors, such as the physical arrangement of a classroom and time limitations, present challenges for groups to come together to work successfully. The online environment, as many of our contributors attest, enables students to work collaboratively with more effective results and with greater satisfaction than is typical in a face-to-face setting. Through the discussion board, students ask each other questions, debate points, and offer up suggestions. This process of writing online enables students to see that learning through collaboration can be an effective and productive endeavor.

Many faculty embrace teaching online because it allows them to rediscover and reinvigorate such core practices as writing to learn, collaborative learning, and critical thinking. But many also come to find that the online classroom leads to other discoveries about writing, teaching, and learning. Because the online environment calls into question the "givens" of the traditional classroom and opens them up for interrogation and analysis, writing in online courses provides a wonderful opportunity to reconsider and reimagine what we do as teachers. The chapters that follow explore different aspects of online writing from a variety of disciplinary perspectives. What the authors have in common is a sense of optimism about the power of online courses to help them and their students understand teaching and learning from different perspectives and the central role that writing plays in this discovery.

Part I: Technology and the Writing Practice

As Nick Carbone writes in our collection's first chapter, "Technology changes what we see and how we work. Or it can if we let it." The authors in our first section discuss how the use of technology has enabled them to rethink their own pedagogical practice in the online environment. In his chapter, Carbone explains why the online classroom affords teachers the opportunity to realize the community-based pedagogies advocated by composition scholars. Next, Chris Anson looks at the use of screen capture response software and suggests how this technology changes the relationship between teachers as responders and students as writers. For Christopher Weaver, the use of audio and visual media has had a direct effect on how he now conceives of the relationship between writing and speaking, thus helping his students to better understand the composing and editing process. In the section's final chapter, Andy Buchenot advocates pushing back a bit on technology to get students to think about the way that online tools and spaces construct them as writers.

We begin our first section of the individual chapters with Nick Carbone's article, "Past to the Future: Computers and Community in the First-Year Writing Classroom." In his chapter, Carbone astutely observes that because of the Internet and social media, we are currently living "in a 'golden age' for writers and writing teachers, an age where writing matters and more people want to write." Online courses, he argues, fit this new paradigm that writing matters to students because it helps to create a community of writers. He believes that the online classroom offers us an opportunity to better realize the community-based pedagogies that have evolved over previous decades of composition scholarship. If writing teachers foster authentic, student-centered discussions, they can help students to take the first step toward participating in academic discourse communities where the focus is on sharing and acknowledging writing. Actively engaged in these academic discourse communities, students come to learn the excitement of online discussions and the power of working within a larger community as a way to learn.

In his article "She Really Took the Time": Students' Opinions of Screen-Capture Response to Their Writing in Online Courses," Chris Anson outlines the results of a "small-scale study" that involved professors using screen-capture response to comment on student papers. These researchers were specifically interested in analyzing the "affective dimensions of teachers' comments" from the student's perspective. The study looked at screen-capture responses given to both face-to-face and online courses and compared them to professors responding to papers electronically. Anson's study concluded that online students found screen-capture comments more helpful than their counterparts did in face-to-face courses. Most notable, students in online courses reported more positive results when it came to a discussion of the affective dimensions of screen capture, namely their perceived expectations and perceptions of how teachers delivered their comments. Anson's study underscores how the online environment changes aspects of the teacher–student dynamic and how new tools and technologies can have a positive impact on the writing process, which offers a promising alternative to using written commentary.

Christopher Weaver's article, "Shifting Again: Electronic Writing and Recorded Speech in Online Courses," explores how the use of technology in writing classes can help instructors reimagine and rethink their pedagogy. Counter to the argument that technology should not drive teaching, Weaver's article demonstrates how technology can open new ways of thinking about it. In his first-year writing course, Weaver had his students compose in two different media: writing and video. He found that composing in both media helped them to better understand the significance of audience and the relationship between form and content. Moving between print and video texts enabled students to gain important insights into the composing and editing processes involved in both.

The contributors in our collection attest to the way that technology can enhance teaching and in turn enable instructors to rethink the writing process. Often, however, we don't look closely enough at the technology itself. In his article, "Revising the Defaults: Online FYC Courses as Sites of Heterogeneous Disciplinary Work," Andy Buchenot problematizes the use of course management systems (CMS) in teaching writing online, specifically the "default arrangements" on CMS, which tend to distance students, thus making them passive consumers of technology rather than active ones. His project is to reengage students by having them consciously think about the limitations of CMS like Blackboard and Moodle and to work against them. He demonstrates that by questioning and reflecting on CMS, students can "rework technologies to serve different ends."

Part II: Negotiating Identity Online

In assigning writing in our online courses, we need to consider not only what students need to know, but also who we want them to be. Indeed, the two issues—knowledge and identity—are often intertwined. When students write, they don't merely communicate knowledge; they also assume a stance, a voice, and a persona. Online courses are particularly well suited to the kinds of transitions that we hope to see students make as they begin to grapple with academic knowledge and to position themselves in relation to that knowledge. The authors in this section, "Negotiating Identity Online," discuss the ways in which the online environment establishes a space for students to create different identities that are not possible in a face-to-face classroom. Patricia Boyd, Linda Di Desidero, and Mark Ellis look closely at the ways students construct themselves through their online interactions and the manner in which online classes afford opportunities for observing and managing identity-creation through monitoring what is effective and what is not. By structuring their respective classes to have their students move through different phases of identity-creation, Boyd, Di Desidero, and Ellis demonstrate the manner in which the online environment helps them and their students to achieve specific affective goals, ones that would be difficult to attain in a face-to-face course.

In "Creating and Reflecting on Identities in Online Business Courses," Patricia Boyd examines how business students learn how to construct professional identities. Boyd considers how problem-based writing assignments, a hallmark of most business classes, often fail because they ask students to "put on masks" rather than to build genuine professional identities that start from their experiences as students. Boyd demonstrates the unique opportunities that online classes provide for teachers to guide students through the transitional stages that mark the shift between personal and professional identities, specifically "the transition between school and a job." Using her business-writing courses as examples, Boyd argues for thinking of the online classroom as a space where students can try on and then reflect on the professional identities they create online through their writing.

Linda Di Desidero's chapter, "Facework and the Negotiation of Identity in Online Class Discussions," is also concerned with the stages that students go through as they construct online identities through writing. In her chapter, however, Di Desidero examines the rhetorical choices that students make as they create personas, interact, and manage relations and negotiations with each other and with the instructor. She identifies three stages of identity construction in her senior capstone class in communications: personal, academic, and scholar-professional. To negotiate these various phases of identity construction, Di Desidero argues that students use facework. Because

xxii   Introduction

students aren't able to pick up on visual cues online, the facework that they employ through writing takes on a different dimension. Students have to be more attentive to the written text on Blackboard to pick up nonverbal cues in order to build alliances within the online classroom and to create agency for themselves as individuals trying out different identities. Di Desidero's essay explores how students use different rhetorical strategies in writing to "construct a range of personal and academic identities." Their ability to effectively deploy facework strategies ultimately informs their writing and how they come to view themselves as writers.

While the two previous chapters focus on facilitating identity construction through writing online, Mark Ellis approaches the issue of identity through a discussion of dispositional change, "the transformation of student behaviors, ideas or attitudes." In "Free to Speak, Safe to Claim: The Importance of Writing in Online Sociology Courses in Transforming Disposition," he argues that writing online is better able to effect dispositional change as a student outcome than it is in a face-to-face classroom. For Ellis, identity is both individual and social. His role, he argues, is to help students expand their own concept of identity, moving from limited, individualistic viewpoints to an appreciation of the complex social forces shaping societal problems. As he notes, there are many challenges that are present when an instructor attempts to discuss and examine "hot-button" issues in a face-to-face class, such as the issue of "hidden" diversity and issues of "safety" and "anonymity." However, in an online environment, students can participate fully without compromising the safety of their own identities. "As such," Ellis argues, "the online environment can better facilitate the discussion of controversial material." Ellis's chapter will be of interest not only to sociology teachers, but also others whose coursework involves sensitive or high-affect subject material.

Part III: Learning Academic Discourse Online

The connection between writing and identity continues to be of interest in our third section; however, here the authors focus on writing online as a medium for entering the discourse community of a particular discipline. In this section, the contributors address the topic of academic discourse communities that Carbone identified in the opening chapter. They discuss the ways that the online environment allows students to move into academic discourse communities and what can be gained by students when they do. The articles by Jackson, Robertson, and Larsen argue that online courses can open up opportunities for students who formerly felt excluded from academic discourse. As Robertson comments in her article, "online courses ask students to approach their learning in ways they have not previously experienced."

Phoebe Jackson's chapter, "The Reading–Writing Connection: Engaging the Literary Text Online," examines the way that online courses enable students to learn differently about academic subject areas, in this case literary studies. As she notes, too often in literature courses, reading and writing about literature appear to be disconnected and discrete activities with reading frequently trumping the writing process. In this chapter, Jackson examines how this misunderstanding causes students to view literary interpretation as a quest for finding the correct meaning of a text. As Jackson explains, the online course allows for multiple viewpoints from other students and other critics. Writing and reading online thus put the student in a position to see the study of literature as a dialogic process—one that yields multiple interpretations. Students ultimately come to learn that literary interpretation is a continuous process of reading, writing, and a rethinking of one's ideas. Through this recursive process in an online class, students have a better understanding of how they are participants in creating a text's meaning rather than being passive consumers of one.

In her chapter "Teaching for Transfer Online: Insights From an Adapted Curricular Model," Liane Robertson focuses on a new model for learning academic discourse through writing, Teaching for Transfer (TFT). With the Teaching for Transfer model, students learn to construct their own theory of writing, which in turn can guide them in writing for other courses. Through her study of Teaching for Transfer online, Robertson found that the online environment inherently challenges students to take more responsibility for their own learning, leading to greater student agency. Because online students spend more time working alone on their computers, Robertson noted that they also spent more time reflecting on their writing, a central component to the TFT model. Both of these learning attributes (student agency and reflection) inherent in the online classroom align with the goals of TFT. While the success of TFT is dependent in part upon a student's ability to develop a theory of writing, the online environment manifests certain advantages that promote a student's capability to "think about and understand writing."

In attempting to enter an unfamiliar discourse community, students are often hindered by myths and misunderstandings they have about that community. In "Getting Down to Earth: Student Writing in Online General Education Science," Kristine Larsen demonstrates how this is a particular problem for non-science majors taking general education science courses. She argues "that online science courses provide a unique opportunity for non-science majors to engage in scientific discourse." While many in the science field would argue that there is no place for personal writing in science, Larsen's article turns that argument on its head. Larsen argues that the use of personal writing on the discussion board helps students to develop a sense of community. By interacting online with their peer group, non-science students are more likely to engage in a different type of inquiry through asking all types of questions and by reading what others have to say on a given subject. Through this type of engagement, students learn that science is not just a question of rote learning but involves "critical thinking, reflection, and questioning." As Larsen concludes, this type of activity comes "closer to actualizing a more authentic scientific inquiry than non-majors are usually able to achieve in a traditional face-to-face course." Writing about science from their own perspectives and engaging with peer groups online, non-science majors learn that science and scientific discourse are more accessible than they might have otherwise realized.

We end this collection with Christopher Justice's chapter, "Hybrid Spaces and Writing Places: Ecoliteracy, Ecocomposition, and the Ecological Self." In his article, Justice brings us full circle and takes us back to a question that haunts the margins of this collection: Why can't what's being done in an online course be done in a face-to-face classroom or, in other words, what makes the online classroom so very different? Justice upends this either/or dichotomy through a consideration of the hybrid classroom. Using the theoretical lens of ecocriticism, he analyzes the ways that changing places from the physical classroom to the digital classroom and vice versa puts students in a position to rethink the ways that they interface with writing.

By choosing to teach in the hybrid classroom, Justice argues that there are specific advantages that can accrue for the student in combining both environments. Among the many benefits that Justice notes is the ability of students to interact with their peers in two locations, online and in person, and how both locations help students to think about "how exactly these places influence their composing processes." The hybrid classroom also makes students aware of different types of "discourse communities" that they occupy. Depending on their location and the assignment, students can be working individually and communally. The requirement to move locations in the hybrid course challenges them to negotiate the different needs of each environment and in turn of each discourse community. Justice's chapter ultimately suggests that teaching online as opposed to teaching face-to-face need not be an either/or choice. Rather, by seeing each class environment through the lens of the other, instructors stand to learn a lot about the practice of teaching overall.

Justice's chapter brings our collection to an end by engaging with our original question: Why teach online? We hope that this chapter in particular and the collection in general delivers a satisfying answer. By changing the environment in which writing takes place and by changing the act of writing itself, teaching online invites us to re-examine the role that writing plays in the classroom both in English and in other disciplines. It also invites us to see our teaching practices anew, reconsidering, among other things, how we and our students use writing to construct ourselves in our classes, the nature of writing groups and discourse communities, the impact of media and technology on writing, editing, and responding, and the effects of teacher presence in the classroom. We teach online because we believe that online courses open up the potential for discovery, agency, and change. We also believe that we stand at an exciting moment in time, when we can begin to reflect on and analyze our teaching practices and to ground them in a sound theoretical understanding about the writing process and about how the online environment affects writing and teaching. We hope that this collection is an early step in a rigorous discussion on that topic.

References

Bartholomae, D. (1986). Inventing the university. *Journal of Basic Writing,* 5(1), 4–23.

Bartholomae, D. (1995). Writing with teachers: A conversation with Peter Elbow. *College Composition and Communication, 46*(1), 62–71.

Brannon, L., & Knoblauch, C. H. (1982). On students' rights to their own texts: A model of teacher response. *College Composition and Communication, 33,* 157–166.

Bruffee, K. (1984). Collaborative learning and the "Conversation of mankind." *College English, 46*(7), 635–652.

Elbow, P. (1973). *Writing without teachers.* Oxford, UK: Oxford University Press.

Elbow, P. (1995). Being a writer vs. being an academic: A conflict in goals. *College Composition and Communication, 46*(1), 72–83.

Emig, J. (1977). Writing as a mode of learning. *College Composition and Communication, 28*, 122–128.

Fulwiler, T. (1986). The argument for writing across the curriculum. In A. Young & T. Fulwiler (Eds.), *Writing across the disciplines: Research into practice* (pp. 21–32). Upper Montclair, NJ: Boynton/Cook.

Harrington, S., Rickly, R., & Day, M. (Eds.). (2000). *The online writing classroom.* Cresskill, NJ: Hampton.

Hewett, B. L., & Ehmann, C. (2004). *Preparing educators for online writing instruction: Principles and processes.* Urbana, IL: National Council of Teachers of English.

Murray, D. (1997). Teach writing as a process not a product. In V. Villanueva (Ed.), *Cross-talk in comp theory: A reader* (pp. 3–6). Urbana, IL: National Council of Teachers of English. (Original work published 1972)

Warnock, S. (2009). *Teaching writing online: How and why.* Urbana, IL: National Council of Teachers of English.

Young, A. (1994). The wonder of writing across the curriculum. *Language and Learning Across the Disciplines, 1*(1), 58–71.

WRITING IN ONLINE COURSES

PART ONE

TECHNOLOGY AND THE WRITING PRACTICE

ONE

Past to the Future: Computers and Community in the First-Year Writing Classroom

Nick Carbone

The Past and Our Present

THE LITERATURE ON TEACHING WRITING with and by computers—often written by those who are first adopters—includes a strand that describes whatever technology and pedagogy is being discussed as necessary, inevitable, and revolutionary. There's something in us that likes to study and herald change. New writing technologies and computer networks for sharing and using writing excite us, I think, because they allow scholars and teachers to project their best hopes onto those technologies. And so, academic journals such as *Computers and Composition* or *Kairos*, which focus on technology, conferences such Educause or Computers and Writing or the League for Innovation, which focus on technology and teaching, or e-mail discussion lists such as TechRhet, which focus on technology, attract scholars and teachers ever curious about what change makes possible.

And the change is constant. New technologies for writing emerge at what feels like a Moore's Law pace. Moore's Law, based on a 1965 prediction made by Gordon Moore of Intel, the computer chip maker, holds that the processing power of computers will double every two years. So, it is that every two years it feels as if, even if such is not factually true, the technologies for writing double. Working from present to past, and just off the top of my head, the field of computers and composition's gaze has focused on the following: Massive Open Online Courses (MOOCs), Game Theory and Learning via Games, Second Life (A visual role-playing world), mobile learning, mobile writing, social networking theory, digital collaboration and team building, Twitter, Facebook, blogs, e-portfolios, content management systems, wikis, digital video, digital audio, multimodal composing and remixing, course management systems, online learning records, Multi-User Dimensions (MUDs), and MUDs, Object-Oriented (MOOs) as writing and course spaces, students writing HTML and building home pages and joining web rings, the World Wide Web, e-mail discussion lists, discussion boards, news groups, using Gopher, Internet Relay Chat, Bitnet, HyperCard/hypertext, grammar and spell checkers, word processors, graphical user interfaces versus command-line interfaces, teaching on local area networks, and heuristic software for writers.

And within and between the items on the above list, the literature explored related issues: access, copyright, plagiarism, re-mixing and mashing up, collaboration, team writing, research ethics in online communities, funding, and technological support; the role of interfaces, data mining, information tracking, feedback loops, and faculty development and support on learner experiences; the work and role of teachers; and so much more (Hawisher, LeBlanc, Selfe, & Moran, 1996; Krause, n.d.).

One of the key events in the growth of computers and composition as a field began at the same time composition studies celebrated more fully, to borrow from its title, "the winds of change" and the "revolution in the teaching of writing" Maxine Hairston noted in her 1982 article exploring the revolution of composition's pedagogy. In 1983, just a year after Hairston's piece, *Computers and Composition* emerged as a newsletter founded and edited by Cynthia Selfe and Kate Keifer (Computers and Composition, n.d.). Early articles in *Computers and Composition* and other journals explored why word processors and computer networked classrooms were ideal revolutionary tools for realizing the process pedagogies described by Hairston. See, for example, Barker and Kemp for an evangelical view of this goal or Klem and Moran for a look at the struggles on reaching the ideal.

Change must drive our curiosity, our publications, our conference presentations, our discussions, our theories and practices; it is when change happens that theory and the discovery of good practice can do the most to make the best of change. And let's celebrate this: As ceaseless and relentless as the change in writing technologies is, writing's never had it so good. Never in human history have more people been writing in more ways for more reasons than we now see possible. "We're now in the midst of a literacy revolution the likes of which we haven't seen since Greek civilization," said Andrea Lunsford in *Wired* to Clive Thompson. Thompson (2009) adds, "It's almost hard to remember how big a paradigm shift this is. Before the Internet came along, most Americans never wrote anything, ever, that wasn't a school assignment."

To my mind, this means we live in a "golden age" for writers and writing teachers, an age where writing matters and more people want to write. Yet, for all that *joie de l'écriture*, there still exists a gap, a big gap, between the look-at-what's-new/what's-coming-next-in-writing excitement of our journals, conferences, and books, and the daily work of most college writing teachers and their students.

Bringing the Past Scholarship and Teaching Ideas to the Present and Why It's So Very Necessary

In their introduction to their 2003 edited collection, *Teaching Writing With Computers*, Pam Takayoshi and Brian Huot described a truth that has even more relevance now:

> Scholarship which introduces teachers to writing technologies needs to be updated in terms of what we now know about the place of writing technologies in writers' lives and in classrooms. Although more teachers every day are facing the (forced or embraced) integration of writing technologies into their curriculum, current scholarship does not address very well the needs of teachers new to a computerized teaching environment. The field's current scholarship largely assumes an audience familiar with the ongoing debates and issues that shape current conversations in the field. (p. 2)

In the decade since *Teaching Writing With Computers*, the "debates and issues that shape current conversations in the field" have grown faster and further from the discussions most writing teachers need to have. Most writing teachers, nearly 70% of whom are adjuncts or graduate students (Coalition of the Academic Workforce, 2012), work in places where the course goals and outcomes for first-year writing rest still fully on the standard novice academic essay, defined by print conventions as four to five double-spaced pages, in a respectable font, with MLA style manual margins. And most writing teachers are only now, in these past few years, grappling with pedagogies and tools explored 20–30 years ago: how word processors affect student composing; how the Web affects research; how to have effective online discussions; or how to adjust face-to-face practices when supplemented by online practices.

The basis for this assertion that writing teachers are largely focused on earlier technologies comes from surveys we've conducted over the past few years at Bedford/St. Martin's. In 2005 Bedford/St. Martin's conducted a survey that asked 49 questions of faculty about their programs, their teaching, and their use of technology. In 2010, we did another national survey; it was much shorter than the 2005 survey, but did use 26 questions from the 2005 survey. While the two surveys and their data are unpublished, I do want to draw on their findings for the 26 common questions. The 2005 survey had 1,856 respondents, the 2010 survey, 1,181.

Digital technology, based on instructors' report of its use, is more integral in the 2010 survey than it was in 2004. On a scale of four options, we asked instructors to describe the importance of digital technologies in their teaching:

Not Part of classroom practice:	14% in 2005;	2% in 2010
Peripheral to the classroom:	20% in 2005;	12% in 2010
Enhances in-class work:	43% in 2005;	46% in 2010
Integral:	23% in 2005;	40% in 2010

However, institutions differ as to what digital technology is used. Instructors at research institutions self-reported using more trend-setting digital tools in their pedagogy: making video, using Skype, Tumblr, Facebook, and other applications and services.

Instructors at two- and four-year colleges are more likely to use digital tools that help with their workload: plagiarism-detection technologies, quizzes and tests online, publisher-supplied companion sites to textbooks with resources such as e-books, tutorials, bibliography builders, and increasingly instructional video and audio for students to watch/hear.

The most popular digital assignments and pedagogies call for working with prose online: electronic peer review (mid 40%), teacher response (near 60%), research writing using web sources (mid 80%), and online discussions (low 60% range). In 2010 we asked about the student creation of multimodal assignments, and the data revealed that, as in other areas, two- and four-year colleges were doing less of this than universities, but then university professors reported using these assignments at very low rates as well.

We see then a pattern where digital technology use centers on text and prose-based practices that many in computers and composition first explored

20–30 years ago: writing academic essays, peer reviewing them, doing research papers, and so on. A similar pattern emerged in a 2011 survey of instructors conducted by the Committee on Best Practices for Online Writing Instruction.

Our survey also confirms findings that the Committee's survey reveals and that Takayoshi and Huot intuited: Access to pedagogical support and time to learn the technology's pedagogical benefits is more of an issue than access to the technology itself. We didn't survey directly on pedagogical support and time to learn technology, but we did have a question about instructor access to technology in 2010, and it included an open response option. We received 122 written comments (4% of the survey participants). Of those comments, 63 identified the lack of theoretically grounded pedagogical training as an obstacle to using more technology; 26 comments included concerns about finding the time to learn technology.

Given this need, it's important for those conversant with the scholarship and discussions to recall and revalue the earlier work in the field of computers and composition—especially the work that provided a theoretical grounding for good practices in online networks, and the role of online community in fostering writing process pedagogies—for folks who are new to the discussion.

Community, Plagiarism, and Online Writing Spaces: Pulling Some Things Together

What follows are teaching ideas that I've found useful in helping teachers find more joy and promise in online teaching. Three central premises, two born directly out of scholarship and one that emerged from my own instructional trial and error, shape how I see online teaching.

1. The computer-enhanced (whether face-to-face or online) class can be uniquely shaped as a learning community of writers that better realizes the community-based process pedagogies Hairston (1982) described (Carbone, 1993; Handa, 1990; Harrington, Rickley, & Day, 2000).
2. The understandings imparted by thinking about academic discourse communities, with attendant practices in those communities for defining the writing genres and citation systems that shape scholarly

conversation of a community (Bazerman, 2009), can build on community in a way that alters the plagiarism discussion.

3. Technology changes what we see and how we work. Or it can if we let it. The trick is to work smart, and to not make more work than already exists.

Ideas for Using Computers to Create Community

Joseph Harris (2012) warns that "community can soon become an empty and sentimental word" (pp. 134–135). Harris goes on to note, too, that community is problematic because it is sometimes viewed simultaneously as both fixed and changing, something that seeks to invite students in, yet is, as Bartholomae (1985) points out, something so opaque that students have to invent it.

But when speaking directly to students, a more simplistic, even naive, notion of community matters. The idea, as with all teaching, is to start with what students know, and starting naively, or vaguely if you prefer, lets them reference what they know. In *Language and Learning*, James Britton (1993) offers my favorite metaphor for starting from what is known. He describes how he and his brother explored the countryside, making their own crude maps as they went:

> The map was a record of our wanderings, and each time we returned we added to it or corrected it. It was, though a crude one, a representation of the area; we valued it as a cumulative record of our activities there. Furthermore, looking forward instead of back, the map set forth our expectations concerning this area as we approached it afresh each time. By means of it we might hope to move around more purposefully, more intelligently. (p. 1)

Students come to us with cognitive maps imprinted with prior community engagements—whether from school, church, work, neighborhoods, military service, or civic groups, to name a few. And now, unlike 20–30 years ago, their cognitive maps are imprinted with engagements of online social networks. Teaching involves helping students add to their maps, much in the way Britton and his brother added to theirs, by revisiting good routes, by building on what is known, and by layering on new experiences through exploration and reflection.

The use of community here is more metaphorical than theoretical, more to teach with than to teach about. But, like Britton's map, community is also real. Students gathered in a course are in fact a type of community. The questions are: how to purposefully use online writing and learning tools to form a community dynamic that supports process pedagogies; and how to make explicit to students that they are in a community of writers and why that matters. In other words, though we start with a metaphorical idea of community, classroom activities and reflections make the metaphor literal. Being purposeful and explicit lays the groundwork, as a course progresses and writing interactions increase, for moving to activities that promote students' understanding of the conventions and practices of academic discourse communities. What follows are online writing activities that can help make community real.

Making Students the Center of Discussions

Scott Warnock (2009) wisely recognizes that when teachers first move to online teaching, the often necessary and certainly natural step for most instructors is to graft their face-to-face practices into their online learning space. However, in most face-to-face classrooms, the teacher primarily runs a discussion instead of primarily participating. Mehan (1985) describes a process that really is a lecture in disguise, IRE: the Instructor asks a question; a student Responds, and the instructor Evaluates the response. Then another question, another response, another evaluation. Students are not talking to students; they're hearing students talk to their teacher. A digital equivalent of this, and an early mistake many instructors make, is trying to respond to every post in a discussion. This turns a discussion into an expectation of a teacher's attention, putting the teacher at the center of things. Instead an instructor can respond judiciously, sharing new thoughts discovered from participating in the discussion, writing as learner rather than expert. The instructor can skim messages and write posts that draw attention to other students. For example, a teacher might notice three or so students having made a similar point, or having divergent views on the same point, but for some reason they aren't responding to one another. The teacher can write one post that addresses them in way that shifts the discussion to them, instead of three separate ones.

Starting with Low-Stakes Writing Builds Fluidity

I find it especially useful not to require anything too important during the first two weeks of a course. Requiring a completed first "essay" isn't something I do. The word "essay" alone carries weight that can change how a writer approaches the screen, very often moving them to form over thought, a fear of risk over openness to exploration. I just want a lot of writing, writing that serves larger course purposes, writing that feels like conversation (the "discussion" in discussion boards, the "comments" on a blog) but happens to be in writing. I use prompts and discussion starters that do not seek right answers, but invite observation and varied thinking, making it safer for writers to share tentative and initial thoughts.

Because more and more students, increasingly of all ages, use digital social networks that rely on informal writing, using online spaces in our courses to encourage writing builds on what students know. This means accepting writing that might show, to start, features of informal writing, including messaging slang and abbreviations. As long as writers are exploring ideas and themes that will be used later in the course, the instructor should not worry. The goal is to write early and often, to get the word count up. Discussion boards with short and frequent posts, online discussion tools, setting up Twitter accounts, rapid-fire social network posts, and fun options abound. The goal is to talk in written words, to create "continuous, intensive and horizontal communications as students interact around each other's work" in what become "very busy, 'silently noisy' classrooms" (Scholar, n.d.).

Being Explicit About Your Pedagogical Whys and Hopes

Taken together, and with some tweaking and experimenting from course to course, the strategies above go a long way to helping students form a community of writers. I've gestured at reasons why I think these strategies matter, and how important they are; it's necessary to share that reasoning explicitly with students, and to reference it often. A writing course asks students to work hard, and a good one will have them working harder than their teacher (Jackson, 2009); it's important that all work support the goals of the course, and that instructors understand and can explain to students how and why the work matters. This becomes especially true the more online a course is. In face-to-face courses, teachers often can see confusion, hesitation, and doubt when students don't understand why they are being asked to do something. Online that's not visible. So, an instructor should always teach the meta aspects and answer questions like these for students: Why do we do a lot of low-stakes writing? Why do we spend more time in online discussions than is set aside for drafting an essay? How do activities and assignments in a course connect, build, reinforce, and strengthen the writer for assignments yet to come?

Understanding these kinds of things helps students to buy into the course, into the class ethos and goals, into the work. When students know why all the work matters, why it isn't busy work, it helps your writing community to form. The formation of a community of writers in turn makes it easier to address writing in academic discourse communities and makes it easier to teach the rhetorical reasons for using and citing sources. And that makes it easier to address plagiarism.

Moving From a Community of Writers to an Academic Discourse Writing Community

In order to form a community of writers, classes need to "begin with the giving of words" as Wendell Berry (1982) says of marriage. Berry goes on to say, "We cannot join ourselves to one another without giving our word. And this must be an unconditional giving" (p. 92). So too in writing classes. A community of writers cannot form without the giving of words, and while that giving is not unconditional in the sense that Berry evokes for a marriage, words need to be given generously, constructively, fairly, and honestly for a community to form. Those qualities are at the heart of academic discourse communities, communities marked in large part by "giving of words" in articles, monographs, convention talks, and digital postings.

And so, the idea here is simple: By explicitly being asked to become a community of writers, students establish some essential ideas for understanding an academic discourse community: sharing and acknowledging writing. Two of the key differences between the kinds of informal online writing used to form a community of writers as outlined above, and the kinds of writing done by academic discourse communities, center around the formal conventions of sharing and acknowledging. If students do not understand first that those conventions are about community, that a citation in a research paper is no different from quoting a classmate in an informal online discussion, then they risk seeing the conventions as only hurdles and hoops. When students don't see the rhetorical and communal reasons for citation and convention, the risk of both accidental and intentional plagiarism increases.

And all too often students view citation as a mere mechanics. Research by Howard, Rodrigue, and Serviss (2010) shows that research papers tend to have these features: lots of patch writing—longer quotes dropped into the essay, often taken from the first page of the source; accurate in the use of citation and quotation; little in the way of summary and synthesis; and more borrowing an argument rather than building their own. Every first-year writing teacher knows that students all too often turn in research that is mechanically adept and rhetorically tone deaf; in large part, says Larson, because the assignment as done in a first-year writing course takes a form that exists nowhere else, a form focused on mechanics and not purpose nor audience, a form that lacks an understood and felt discourse community.

It is easier to move students to a form of writing that does exist, writing that is rhetorical and grounded in the practices of an academic discourse community. What follows are some strategies that can help you move them in that direction and thus away from plagiarism.

Online Conversations Can Be Exciting and Citable

Kenneth Burke describes a metaphorical parlor that in essence captures the spirit of what academic writing is, with its use of citations and publication in journals that are read by folks who have often read or will perhaps read the sources cited, who read the journal because they may seek to publish in it, who often have met and know personally the authors of the articles they read or the authors of articles being cited. He writes,

> Imagine that you enter a parlor. You come late. When you arrive, others have long preceded you, and they are engaged in a heated discussion, a discussion too heated for them to pause and tell you exactly what it is about. In fact, the discussion had already begun long before any of them got there, so that no one present is qualified to retrace for you all the steps that had gone before. You listen for a while, until you decide

that you have caught the tenor of the argument; then you put in your oar. Someone answers; you answer him; another comes to your defense; another aligns himself against you, to either the embarrassment or gratification of your opponent, depending upon the quality of your ally's assistance. However, the discussion is interminable. The hour grows late, you must depart. And you do depart, with the discussion still vigorously in progress. (pp. 110–111)

My goal with online discussions is to generate discussions that excite in the way Burke describes. Almost always the discussions are around issues and ideas that have previously been discussed and are ongoing in the journals or the culture at large when the class ends. Thus, I might assign two or three short readings, often op-ed pieces that can be read quickly and that take varied stances on an issue. The discussions begin not by asking writers to defend a position nor to answer comprehension questions, but rather to generate different kinds of responses—list one best line from each piece, name the thoughts you read that surprised you the most, what was your strongest reaction, and why? I often use rules for posting then responding designed to make sure everyone gets a few responses, such as, "After posting, read the response of at least three classmates, choosing first classmates with no response or the fewest. Describe to them where they were similar to your thoughts and where they were different. Describe what you learned from the difference and ask a follow-up question. Respond to your responses, and then we'll move to an open discussion."

My role here is to keep the discussion among students going for a week, sometimes longer. The idea is to get them to where they come to the defense of others, qualify their thinking in response to questions, add nuance to a thought to make their ideas clearer—all of the other things Burke's metaphor suggests. When this works—and it doesn't always, I should add, because sometimes I don't ask questions well, or choose the right readings, or all kinds of other variables that make teaching a wonder—students get feedback on their writing, though they aren't usually thinking of it as Writing. They change their minds. They learn what variations and degrees of agreement and disagreement there might be. They see where their words might be confusing as written, where someone else may have said something better, and so they quote or point to a classmate's post and more.

At some point, we'll pause and study the discussion. I'll ask writers to draft a longer response that sums up their thinking, where they cite not only the sources that kicked off the discussion but where they must also cite fellow writers. Here's where the shift from community of writers to academic discourse community begins—in asking writers to cite classmates. Students see an academic essay for the first time, and they see an article followed by a list of articles referenced. They don't see past that very often, but in having a conversation around an issue, in reading and writing back to classmates, and in then writing another piece that cites those classmates, they get the kind of experience most professional scholars don't get until graduate school: the experience of writing from a conversation they know more fully, of citing people they've been reading, of citing people they've talked to, and of citing people who will be reading the works where those citations occur.

Further, because there's a greater sense of audience and a deeper sense of topic, albeit a fairly circumscribed one of classmates, and also a sense of the discussion, it opens up—doesn't guarantee, of course—new avenues (echoes of Britton's map again) of understanding how to use sources rhetorically and how to use them in a way to frame the argument one wants to make. Another feature of this kind of online discussion is that writers aren't reading alone. A challenge for novice writers is reading, taking notes, writing accurate summaries, and finding a place to bounce ideas. Reading alone can be rewarding and necessary; it's a prelude to discussion and writing. But reading knowing you'll be discussing that work with a group changes how one reads, or it can if the assignment is structured to help writers read rhetorically, read in ways that move beyond quote harvesting and authority seeking. As the course goes, conversations can move to longer, more complex readings, but the principles for discussing, citing the reading in the discussion, summarizing, and being accurate all remain. And all on the record, for here's another thing to keep in mind: If you think back to the best face-to-face classroom discussion you ever had, where students were speaking good ideas one after the other, how many students were taking notes? How many of those ideas were ever referenced again, let alone quoted or summarized and cited?

I cannot imagine this kind of experience happening without online writing tools. Charlie Moran says that you simply cannot go back to not using online writing tools once you've made ideas like this work.

Addressing Plagiarism by Writing Early and Often, and by Having Something to Say

In *The Transition to College Writing*, Keith Hjortshoj has a section of advice with a subheading called "Theft, Fraud, and Loss of Voice." In it, he talks to novice writers about the dangers of going to the library and getting a stack of sources and then building a research paper, quote by quote. It's the same danger that Howard et al. (2010) note: The writer risks getting lost in sources, the quotes slip into being unquoted, the summaries un-cited, and the paraphrases too close to the original. One of the benefits of writing online early and often is the chance for writers to start with their own voices.

So, asking students to write about things that you'll ask them to do research on, before doing research, gives them a chance to exercise their thinking, whether in journals, chats, discussions, or e-mail. If students are choosing their own topics, they can write about the topic in a common discussion, sharing initial thoughts. This also, happily, creates a trail, a path of thinking, a history of engagement that does a few things: opens up avenues of inquiry and helps students to better frame a research project based on questions that emerge from their thinking.

As students work, they can weave sources into the writing they started. By posting and sharing online the sources they find and discover and by writing brief annotations as they go, they also share sources with other writers. Common sources, source sharing, and information sharing help hold discourse communities together; they build collegiality. Online writing spaces support this process in ways that simply cannot be done efficiently by paper. Just as discussion boards preserve a record of online conversations, other online spaces such as e-portfolios allow students to upload, thus preserving a record of their writing process.

In the Bedford/St. Martin's survey data cited above, plagiarism concerns and the use of detection software as a solution to those concerns measured highly. No sequence of activities is guaranteed to eliminate plagiarism. But even Turnitin.com admits that strategies like the ones outlined above—keeping drafts, annotated bibliographies, careful reading, doing work in stages—make the "chances of plagiarism . . . vanishingly thin" (Wedlake, 2001). When students discover they'll be read with respect, will be asked to read and respond to fellow writers with respect, will be given space to make mistakes in thinking or form, and will be given ways and help to revise and to grow, then they will be far less likely to dislike and resent the course.

Students, I believe, deliberately cheat for two reasons, broadly speaking: fear and loathing. Fear can come from fear of failing, fear of falling behind, fear of getting lost. A well-designed online course, where writing is done and responded to regularly, helps to dispel those fears. It creates safe spaces where the students' writing process is highly visible in the early stages and where the instructor can assist before the writer falls too far behind. When students disengage, that can lead to loathing, to frustration, and to anger. And it is those conditions—fear and loathing, being afraid of failure or not caring about the course and its aims—that lead students to cheat deliberately.

Which brings me to the final of the three principles that help guide good online writing instruction: balance.

Working Reasonably: Don't Add Too Much, Do More With Less

The three most common mistakes I see in online teaching are these:

1. Slipping into becoming tech support
2. Doing the same things one did face to face plus on top of those new online things, which increases work without benefit and makes it harder for students and the instructor to keep up
3. Trying to use all of a technology at once, which can make things confusing and overwhelming

One of the first mistakes teachers make is seeking to solve every glitch a student has. There are three causes, generally, of technology problems: one, the technology not working; two, the technology working but the student not understanding its logic or purpose; and three, the user making a mistake—mistyped password, forgetting to hit submit on an assignment. The best thing you can do early in your semester is to get students in the habit of asking one another for help when a technical issue arises. Do not answer a technical question (if you know the answer) unless a student's asked at least two classmates for help. Then instruct all three. The other best thing you can do is require students to contact the help desk or technical support hotline and to show you proof that they've done this before you attempt to address an issue. The key thing with technical glitches, however, is that you stay calm. If things go down, and they sometimes will, be ready with a back-up plan or work-around. If a lot of students get stuck at the same step, maybe because it is confusing, and they start to panic, don't reflect their panic back. Teach the group how to address their confusion.

On the second mistake, consider this: If you're asking students to discuss and respond to posts a lot, don't also ask them to write a draft of a four-page essay and do an online peer review. Design the discussion so that it covers and gets students writing around the issues and ideas the draft would be on. The discussion becomes the drafting and the peer review if designed right. The writers are able to focus their thoughts and time, thereby increasing the likelihood that the conversation, and therefore the writing, will be more fruitful than if they split their time and attention. Also, it's better for an instructor, who will be skimming the discussion and coaching students to interaction. If an instructor is reading drafts and also trying to follow a discussion or to review peer work, giving feedback and coaching writers becomes harder. And more frustrating. Design activities that have double or triple the value, but without creating double or triple the activities.

On the third, remember this: Online learning tools are increasingly complicated. Most instructors start teaching online, often by mandate, with the course management system the campus uses. Those can be ungainly beasts, but serviceable. The trick is to think carefully about what you want students to do, and to choose only the tools you need to get you there. Just doing three things—posting the syllabus, having a discussion board, and creating a place for students to upload drafts-—can go a long way toward using technology in a way that supports your teaching. What also helps is getting into routines in the course that students can follow, so that they too are not trying to figure out a new technology every week. Logging in, answering a prompt, having a discussion, uploading a draft, clicking a link to a reading, repeated, will move the class more quickly to doing essential classwork. As a teacher's experience grows with the online tools at hand, it does become easy over time to add new activities and tools in ways that students will understand and be able to follow.

Have Fun

Need I say more?

References

Barker, T. T., & Kemp, F. O. (1990). Network theory: A postmodern pedagogy for the writing classroom. In C. Handa (Ed.), *Computers and community: Teaching composition in the twenty-first century.* Portsmouth, NH: Boynton/Cook Publishers.

Bartholomae, D. (1985). Inventing the university. In M. Rose (Ed.), *When a writer can't write* (pp. 134–165). New York, NY: Guilford.

Bazerman, C. (2009). Issue brief: Discourse communities. *National Council of Teachers of English.* Retrieved from http://www.ncte.org/college/briefs/dc

Berry, W. (1982). On poetry and marriage: The use of old forms. *Standing by words.* Washington DC: Shoemaker & Hoard.

Britton, J. (1993). *Language and learning: The importance of speech in children's development.* Portsmouth, NH: Boynton/Cook-Heinemann.

Burke, K. (1941). *The philosophy of literary form.* Berkeley, CA: University of California Press.

Carbone, N. (1993). Trying to create a community: A first day lesson plan. *Computers and Composition, 10*(4), 81–88.

Coalition of the Academic Workforce. (2012, June). *A portrait of part-time faculty members.* Retrieved from http://www.academicworkforce.org/CAW_portrait_2012.pdf

Committee on Best Practices for Online Writing Instruction. (2011). *Hybrid/blended courses survey results.* Retrieved from http://www.ncte.org/cccc/committees/owi

Committee on Best Practices for Online Writing Instruction. (2011, April). *Initial report of the CCCC committee for best practice in online writing instruction.* Retrieved from http://www.ncte.org/library/NCTEFiles/Groups/CCCC/Committees/OWI_State-of-Art_Report_April_2011.pdf

Computers and Composition. (n.d.). A brief history of *Computers and Composition. Computers and Composition, an International Journal.* Retrieved from http://computersandcomposition.candcblog.org/html/history.htm

Conference on College Composition and Communication. (2013). *A position statement of principles and example effective practices for online writing instruction (owi).* Retrieved from http://www.ncte.org/cccc/resources/positions/owiprinciples

Hairston, M. (1982). The winds of change: Thomas Kuhn and the revolution in the teaching of writing. *College Composition and Communication, 33*(1), 76–88.

Handa, C. (Ed.). (1990). *Computers and community: Teaching composition in the twenty-first century.* Portsmouth, NH: Boynton/Cook.

Harrington, S., Rickley, R., & Day., M. (2000). *The online writing classroom.* Cresskill, NJ: Hampton Press.

Harris, J. (2012). *A teaching subject: Composition since 1966* (Rev. ed.). Logan, UT: Utah State University Press.

Hawisher, G. E., LeBlanc, P., Moran, C., & Selfe, C. L. (1996). *Computers and the teaching of writing in American higher education, 1979–1994: A history.* Norwood, NJ: Ablex Publishing.

Howard, R. M., Rodrigue, T. K., & Serviss, T. C. (2010, Fall). Writing from sources, writing from sentences. *Writing and Pedagogy, 2*(2), 177–192. Retrieved from http://writing.byu.edu/static/documents/org/1176.pdf

Hjortshoj, K. (2001). *The transition to college writing.* Boston, MA: Bedford/ St. Martin's.

Jackson, R. R. (2009). *Never work harder than your students & other principles of great teaching.* Alexandria, VA: Association for Supervision and Curriculum Development.

Klem, E., & Moran, C. (1992). Teachers in a strange LANd: Learning to teach in a networked writing classroom. *Computers and Composition, 9*(3), 5–22. Retrieved from http://computersandcomposition.candcblog.org/archives/v9/9_3_html/9_3_1_Klem.html

Krause, S. (n.d.). A very brief history of computers and composition. English 516: Computers and Writing, Theory and Practice [Course website]. Retrieved from http://engl516.stevendkrause.com/readings/a-very -brief-history-of-computers-and-composition/

Larson, R. L. (1982, December). The "research paper" in the writing course: A non-form of writing. *College English, 44*(8), 811–816.

Mehan, H. (1985). The structure of classroom discourse. In T. A. Van Dijk (Ed.), *Handbook of discourse analysis: Vol. 3* (pp. 119–131). London, UK: Academic Press.

Moran, C. (2000). From a high-tech to a low-tech writing classroom: You can't go home again. *The Quarterly, 22*(3). The National Writing Project. Retrieved from http://www.nwp.org/cs/public/print/resource/782

Scholar. (n.d.). Learning philosophy: New learning. *Scholar*. Retrieved from http://learning.cgscholar.com/about-scholar/learning-philosophy

Takayoshi, P., & Huot, B. (Eds.). (2003). *Teaching writing with computers*. Boston, MA: Houghton Mifflin.

Thompson, C. (2009). Clive Thompson on the new literacy. *Wired Magazine, 17*(09). Retrieved from http://www.wired.com/techbiz/people/magazine/17-09/st_thompson

Warnock, S. (2009). *Teaching writing online: How and why*. Urbana, IL: NCTE.

Wedlake, P. (2001, October 24). Legal issues regarding turnitin.com. Strategies for Teaching with Online Tools. Retrieved from http://bedfordstmartins.com/catalog/static/bsm/technotes/workshops/fullcopyright.htm

"She Really Took the Time": Students' Opinions of Screen-Capture Response to Their Writing in Online Courses

Chris M. Anson

MEGAN, A PROFESSOR OF WOMEN'S studies, is responding to the paper of Brittany, a student in her Introduction to Women's and Gender Studies class. Activating a program on her computer that captures her voice as well as anything she does with the paper onscreen, she greets Brittany by name and begins:[1]

> Your paper, "The Role of a Woman"—overall, I was really . . . I really liked [in] your discussion that you connected with the reading on a personal level. There are a few things that I wanted to just recommend in terms of the next time you do a summary paper, and so let's just get right in there. First, I wanted to comment on your opening paragraph, your introduction [here Megan is sweeping the cursor across the first paragraph of the text], which you appropriately started broad, and then winnowed your way down to a smaller topic. I did want to point out that your statement here [at this point, Megan has used her cursor to shade off a portion of the opening paragraph]—you probably started out a little too broad

Megan is teaching her course entirely online, which means that she will never meet Brittany in person. The preceding text represents about 35 seconds of a five-minute response that she provided for each student's paper using screen-capture technology. The excerpt demonstrates certain interesting characteristics of Megan's oral response style: She recognizes the level of Brittany's personal engagement in the reading; she acknowledges that Brittany was trying to funnel down to her topic rather than jumping into it; and she starts to offer some helpful advice about what level of generality is most appropriate for the introduction of a summary. We also see that although Megan is direct and focused, she uses nonthreatening, conditional language ("I wanted to just recommend" and "you probably started out a little too broad"). We hear her focusing not on minutiae but on important structural and conceptual aspects of Brittany's paper, and then elaborating on some general concerns by visually tying them to specific sentences and paragraphs.

Some of these characteristics contrast with Megan's usual written responses, which take the form of a few sentences at the top of each student's paper (almost always without addressing the student by name). Although Megan is an approachable teacher who likes to give praise and often writes "good job!" at the end of her brief remarks, her written comments usually remain general, without much elaboration or detail, as in the following full comment she provided on a student's paper:

> I really liked the connection with the military. You set up your analysis well in terms of resistance, concerns, and challenge. Be sure to carry your terminology through in subsequent papers. One way to do so is to include the same terminology in topical sentences at the beginning of new paragraphs/thoughts.

Megan's oral commentary far outpaces her written commentary in length. Whereas her written commentary averages about 50–75 words and offers one or two general suggestions, her five-minute oral screen-capture commentary averages around 700 words and provides extended explanations and examples.

With such stark differences between the modes—in style, detail, and length—it's easy to assume that the elaborated oral commentary, spoken directly to the student, must be more educationally supportive than brief written comments. However, we know nothing about how students react to these differences in Megan's spoken and written responses—whether, for example, they prefer terse, easily read comments over the longer, advisory screen captures.

Abundant research exists on teacher response to student writing (see Straub, 1999, 2006). Most of it, however, has focused on the analysis of teachers' practices and not on what students experience in the process of contemplating their teachers' comments (Anson, 2012). More importantly, very few studies have considered the nature of teacher response in online instruction, where relational aspects of teaching and learning often differ from those in face-to-face instruction. As emerging technologies allow us to experiment with multiple digital forms of response, we need more investigations of such experiences in order to develop and refine our practices.

In this chapter, I describe a preliminary mixed-methods study involving two teachers in different content disciplines who were trained to use oral evaluation commentary through a simple screen-capture program. The results of this small-scale study suggest that in online courses, more interactive forms of response, especially using voice, facilitate relationship-building between teachers and students and are more effective in helping students to learn than conventional written commentary.

The Teacher-Focused Legacy of Research on Response

Over the past 40 years, an extensive body of research has accumulated on teacher response to student writing. Although it is beyond the scope of this chapter to summarize that research, some clear trends will help to put the current study in perspective (see Anson, 2012). Throughout the 1970s and 1980s, scholars were strongly interested in the nature of teachers' written marginal and end comments. By creating taxonomies of teacher practices and then applying those to the analysis of written comments, this research was able to show distinct patterns in teacher response, such as lack of praise (Daiker, 1986), the tendency to "appropriate" students' texts (Brannon & Knoblauch, 1982), and the dominance of error identification (Connors & Lunsford, 1988). However, the instructional implications derived from these studies assumed theoretically—without inquiry into effects on student learning—that certain kinds of written commentary are more helpful than others. By the late 1990s, increasing calls were heard for a deeper understanding of how commentary affected, was interpreted by, or actually taught students. Meanwhile, studies of teachers' response practices were moving beyond writing classrooms and into other disciplinary areas (Smith-Taylor, 1997, 2003). Scholars such as Rutz (1999) argued for the recognition of the complex interpersonal nature of response, which had been ignored in the early, text-focused research, and by the 2000s, research on response extended into explorations of race and ethnicity (Inoue & Poe, 2012; McKnight, 2011). But continued calls for more systematic research on the effects of response on students have gone largely unheeded, and writing scholars continue to urge new investigations in this area (Anson, 2012; Knoblauch & Brannon, 2006; Sommers, 2006).

Research on how students interpret and act on comments made in an oral mode is even more scarce. Until recently, oral response that was not provided live, in face-to-face meetings, came to students in the form of audiocassettes that shuttled between teacher and student. In their spoken commentary, teachers drew students' attention to features of their work with reference to page numbers or by reading sentences and paragraphs aloud. Students were assumed to have their papers in front of them, scanning through as the teacher talked.

Aside from occasional concerns about teachers not modeling the medium that they are trying to teach, almost all the literature on teachers' tape-recorded response to student writing points to its advantages. In his self-reflective analysis, Sommers (1989) found that he could provide much more individualized instruction to his students with oral commentary than in handwritten comments. In later articles, Sommers (2000, 2002) argues that tape-recorded commentary provides more efficient, detailed, personal response, helping students to become aware of readers' needs through "movies of the mind" (2002, p. 173). Yarbro and Angevine (1982) believe that students understand teachers' commentary better and are more motivated to write when it is provided on tape. In my own work (Anson, 1997, 1999), I call attention to the way that spoken taped response cuts the "distance" between teacher and student, compels a stronger focus on broad issues instead of minutiae, and can model a way of thinking about writing using important rhetorical and composing concepts. I suggest that reading text aloud can help students identify the processing effects of certain problems, including surface errors. Along with Olson (1982), I also point to the fact that taped response provides far more feedback in about the same amount of response time.

Compelling as these accounts are, they reflect instructional rather than empirical interest, and are mostly anecdotal or based on personal experience. Very little research in the field of writing studies has intentionally studied the effects or reception of tape-recorded response, how teachers plan and deliver that response, or what differences exist between it and conventional written marginal and end commentary. In a questionnaire-based study comparing tape-recorded response to written response in a developmental writing class, Sipple (2007) found that audio responses increased students' self-confidence and motivation, helped them to internalize feedback, provided more detail, reduced misinterpretation, strengthened the bond with the professor, and were more enjoyable than written comments. Mellen and Sommers (2003) describe a simple survey in Sommers's class about a cassette-taped response that yielded positive impressions. Mellen, a coauthor and student in that course, explores why: the taped response made her feel like "the professor's equal," "a fellow writer," providing more detailed, explanatory, helpful, and at times positive comments.

After the gradual obsolescence of cassette tapes, oral response to students' writing experienced a hiatus as floppy disks and early memory sticks lacked the capacity to store the hundreds of megabytes that even a few minutes of recording produced. Most e-mail systems were unable to accommodate such large attachments, and many students used dial-up connections too slow to download such files in any case. With the development of high-speed connections and Web 2.0 technology, voice recording again became possible for a range of uses. Web-based programs like Garage Band and Yack Pack (now defunct) and various podcasting tools allowed users to create voice recordings that were stored at servers or sent and received synchronously through chat functions. Once again, teachers had the technology to comment on students' writing orally. More recently, screen-capture technology has added a visual element: Not only can teachers talk to students about their writing, but they can video-capture the process of scrolling through the students' papers, highlighting various parts of their texts, or even moving between the papers and other documents. Teachers can identify specific places in a paper that need attention, read sentences or paragraphs aloud to dramatize their effects, and offer helpful suggestions and advice for improvement and revision.

An Experiment in Screen-Capture Response

Our exploration of screen-capture technology began with a study of five sections of first-year composition taught by four instructors. To compare students' impressions of oral screen-capture response with written response in courses where there is no face-to-face interaction, we then replicated the study in a subsequent semester to include two teachers in content disciplines—one from Women's and Gender Studies and one from Psychology. Unlike the first cohort, however, these two instructors were teaching their courses entirely online. This chapter will focus on the online courses, with comparisons to the data from the first phase when relevant.

Our studies have explored three dimensions of the teachers' commentary in each response mode: the cognitive, the affective, and the linguistic. From the students' perspective, we're interested in how much they learn about their writing in each mode and how they feel about the comments interpersonally and as a function of their and their teachers' classroom relationships and identities. From the teachers' perspective, we're interested in how they feel about providing response in the two modes and how effectively they feel they are teaching students about writing. From a linguistic perspective, we're interested in the nature of the commentary itself in the two modes: its focus, style, tone, length, and other characteristics.

Although the study provided large amounts of data for analysis, including all the teachers' written and oral commentary, our interest here is in students' comparative assessments of the two modes of response, especially how they felt about the affective dimensions of their teachers' comments. In a typical face-to-face college course, teachers' written responses to students' work carry the significance of much more than the text at hand. As Prior and Looker (2009) argue, response comes to students from multiple sources both embedded in the genre and social systems of a course and from beyond it. In addition to the "prototypical scenes of teaching writing" (classroom interactions, comments on papers, advisory face-to-face office meetings, and a rich array of shared classroom experience) are "multiple semiotic artifacts and acts, operating in and across activity systems" (n.p.). Whatever teachers write on students' papers is tacitly imbricated with the shared knowledge from these activities and sources, but is also continuing to shape identities through the ongoing interactions afforded by the response. Online courses do not always differ in the degree of such interactions, but in kind: The physical embodiment of teaching and learning yields to a more digital experience, often channeled into episodes of synchronous and asynchronous written interaction, still images such as pictures, occasionally brief video clips or even, in more digitally enhanced settings, live video chat, along with less embodied kinds of information. In this context, teachers' written comments on students' writing connect to and invoke a different relationship constructed along different channels and with different interpersonal associations than exist in a face-to-face class. In the context of courses lacking physically embodied presences, would students feel differently about teachers' spoken responses to their writing as opposed to their more conventional written responses?

Our subjects were students enrolled in one section of Introduction to Psychological Research (n=23) taught by Stephanie, a faculty member in Psychology; one section of Women and Health (n=15) taught by Megan, a faculty member in Women's Studies; and one section of Introduction to Gender Studies (n=17), also taught by Megan. Once we had obtained IRB approval for the project and consent forms from the students in all three sections, we oriented the two teachers to the use of screen capture. Our chosen screen-capture program was Jing, a free, downloadable product marketed by TechSmith, creators of the more sophisticated (and edit-enabled) program Camtasia. When activated, Jing creates a recording of all the activity that takes place onscreen: typing or marking up documents, moving between windows, and so on. In response to a student's text, the teacher first drags a frame over the entire part of the screen where the paper appears. A screen-capture session begins with a countdown of five seconds, at which point the recording starts. For practical purposes, the actions teachers make onscreen include scrolling and using the highlight function to mark off words or parts of the texts that they want to discuss, and occasionally inserting comments in the margins. During this time, the program is also recording the teacher's voice. (We gave our teachers headsets with microphones so that their recordings would be of high quality.) In this way, the five-minute video recordings provide a dynamic form of response, in real time, in both a visual and auditory mode.

After five minutes have elapsed, the program stops recording. The user then saves the file or sends it to a remote site. Jing is connected to Screencast.com, a storage center where the screen captures can be uploaded for free up to a capacity limit. When the student accesses the link to the file, the five-minute screen capture plays (and can be replayed multiple times or saved). The student watches, listens, and takes notes as the teacher works through the paper. To avoid problems with space, we provided our teachers with free one-year subscriptions to Screencast.com. Alternatively, a teacher can save a Jing file to her desktop, where the file can be uploaded to a content-management system such as Moodle or Blackboard. Students can then download the file to their own desktops and open it using a browser, thus avoiding the use of the commercial server. (Many e-mail programs still will not convey files the size of most Jing recordings.)

In their courses, Megan and Stephanie assigned "main papers" of several pages. Both Megan's sections required four papers that together counted for 40% of the course grade. Stephanie assigned a research proposal process involving several stages whose deliverables were worth 25% of the course grade. Our study focused on the teachers' evaluations of students' final texts, not comments on in-process work. The teachers returned students' first main papers with their usual written comments. As noted, Megan's comments were typically two to four sentences typed at the top of the student's paper; she included no marginal comments. Stephanie used the Track Changes feature in Microsoft Word to insert comments into students' papers, usually between lines; occasionally she corrected something in the text, which preserved the original in the margin so students could compare the versions. At the end of the paper, she inserted a scoring rubric. Typically, these contained only scores, but occasionally she would add a comment inside one of the cells of the rubric to explain the score, such as "A lot of information about the stimulus material was missing. No information given about how data were obtained or what surveys or tasks were employed."

For the second paper, each student received a five-minute screen capture that recorded the teacher's oral commentary while she scrolled through each paper, highlighting parts of the text she was addressing. Megan included a grade on the paper, and Stephanie pasted her rubric at the end of the paper and talked about it during her commentary.

To gauge the students' impressions of these two modes, we administered a 14-item survey (plus four demographic questions) that asked students how much time they spent reading the written comments and viewing the screen-capture comments; how helpful the two modes of commentary were in understanding aspects of their writing; how they felt, affectively, about the two kinds of commentary; how easy, and with what comfort levels, the screen-capture videos were to watch; and what response method they now preferred for future papers.

From the three sections, we recruited five students to be interviewed in greater depth about their experiences. As online learners, many students were not located near campus, so we conducted these interviews using the video function of Skype and recorded them with Camtasia. Students received gift cards for their participation.

"Way More Approachable": What the Surveys Said

Of the 55 students enrolled in Megan's and Stephanie's courses, 53 filled out the survey, yielding a return rate of almost 100%. No surveys contained missing responses or were incomplete. To analyze the more complex survey questions, we used a Wilcoxon sign test to determine whether students' responses to questions about the screen-capture comments were significantly different from their responses to the same questions about written comments. To assess differences between data in the first and second phases of the study (face-to-face vs. online instruction), we used the Kruskal-Wallis test for equality of populations. Both tests are nonparametric. For the simplest questions, raw percentages sufficed for the analysis.

Previous Response Modes

The vast majority of online students had received responses to their writing in conventional written modes (marginal and end comments). Almost half the students (43%) had received written comments electronically, in the form of inserted comments, but other forms of response were somewhat rarer (see Table 2.1). These data were consistent with the results from the first phase of the study, except that somewhat more students in the face-to-face classes had received comments inserted electronically in their texts.

Time Spent Reading Comments or Watching the Screen Capture

As shown in Table 2.2, the majority (87.5%) of students spent less than 10 minutes reading their teachers' written comments. Because the teachers almost always used all five minutes of the allowable time for the screen-capture recordings, students reported spending about the same amount of time (five or 10 minutes) watching them as reading the written comments. These percentages were not statistically different from those in the face-to-face condition. A few students watched the screen captures more than twice.

Table 2.1. Previous Modes of Response, by Percent

Handwritten comments	90.6
Comments inserted electronically	43.8
Taped/recorded oral comments	18.8
Face-to-face with instructor	31.3
Small-group peer conferences	18.8

Table 2.2. Time Spent Reading Comments/Watching SC, by Percent

Less than 5 minutes	37.5
Between 5 and 10 minutes	50.0
Between 10 and 20 minutes	9.4
Over 20 minutes	3.1
Watched once	47.4
Watched twice	39.0
Watched three times	6.8
Watched four or more times	6.8

Helpfulness of Comments

Figure 2.1 shows students' judgments of the helpfulness of their teachers' comments in both the written and screen-capture modes. Almost 85% of the students judged the screen-capture comments to be "very helpful," and almost all the rest as "somewhat helpful." Those judgments are reversed for the written comments, with over 60% rating them "somewhat helpful" and 28% rating them as "very helpful." The positive results for the helpfulness of the screen captures were somewhat stronger in the online sections than in the face-to-face sections in the first phase.

Helpfulness in Understanding Writing

Our survey asked students to judge whether screen-capture comments helped them understand several rhetorical and linguistic concepts related to their writing: audience, structure, style, purpose, focus, grammar, and content. For every item, 70% or more of the students agreed or strongly agreed

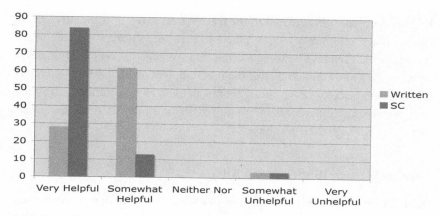

Figure 2.1. Helpfulness of comments in both modes.

that screen-capture commentary was helpful. Differences between their impressions of the helpfulness of screen-capture and written comments were statistically significant for audience (p < .01), style (p < .01), purpose (p < .05), focus (p < .05), and content (p < .01). Students in the online sections rated two of the dimensions statistically higher for the screen-captures than students in the face-to-face sections: purpose (p < .01) and focus (p < .01).

From these more general questions comparing screen capture to written responses, we can see that students in the three online courses behaved similarly in both modes, spending about the same amount of time digesting the written comments or watching the screen captures. However, in the context of this typical investment of time, students reported that the screen-capture comments were more helpful than the written comments and that they were highly effective in helping them to learn about some important features of their writing. Online students were particularly sanguine—even more than face-to-face students—about their learning of purpose and focus from the screen captures as compared with written comments.

In addition to these general impressions, an important dimension of our study concerned how students felt about their teachers *as* responders—what relational characteristics were reflected in their commentary. Although it is theoretically possible for teachers and students to deliberately diminish the strength of their subject positions as mentors and learners, or to try to level their unequal allocations of authority (as task-setter and judge on the one hand and novice subordinated to the teacher's expertise on the other), these differentiated roles are always at play and therefore saturate virtually every interpersonal exchange between teacher and students in every medium, and often varying as a consequence of the medium. If students found the screen-capture responses so much more helpful than written comments, did they also perceive any differences in the underlying attitudes their teachers were conveying through their responses?

Digging Deeper: Response and Affect

In our survey, students were asked to rate on a five-point agreement scale a set of positive and negative terms characterizing how they felt about their teachers' commentary in both the written and screen-capture modes ("supportive," "uncaring," "friendly," "discouraging," etc.). Items were first created in opposed pairs (encouraging/discouraging, distant/engaged, friendly/unfriendly, etc.) and then divided and randomized. These items were designed to measure how students felt not just about the content or focus of the teachers' commentary, but what interpersonal qualities of their teacher accompanied that commentary—*how* it was delivered. We were particularly interested in the relationship between the way teachers' comments were delivered and students' feelings about what their teachers were doing to address their instructional needs and to respond to them as individual learners.

Across all sections in both phases of the study, students reported significantly stronger positive affect and weaker negative affect from the screen-capture responses than the written responses, as shown in Table 2.3. Five qualities ("supportive," "personal," "encouraging," "constructive," and "concerned") were rated more strongly for the teachers' comments in the screen-capture mode than in the written mode (p <.01), and four more ("caring," "considerate," "friendly," and "engaged") reached even higher levels of significance (p < .001). Only one paired item ("disconfirming/validating") was not significantly stronger for the screen-capture mode, perhaps because students had difficulty interpreting the terms.

When the online group's responses were compared with responses from the face-to-face group, five affective dimensions were significantly higher ("personal," "caring," "considerate," "friendly," and "encouraging"). That is, even though all sections reported statistically stronger levels of positive affect

Table 2.3. Significance of Differences in Affect Between Response Modes

Supportive	$p < .01$
Personal	$p < .01$
Caring	$p < .001$
Considerate	$p < .001$
Friendly	$p < .001$
Encouraging	$p < .01$
Constructive	$p < .01$
Concerned	$p < .01$
Engaged	$p < .001$

Table 2.4. Positive Affect Between FTF and Online Groups

Supportive	$p < .08$
Personal	$p < .05$
Caring	$p < .001$
Considerate	$p < .01$
Friendly	$p < .01$
Encouraging	$p < .01$
Constructive	$p < .28$
Concerned	$p < .098$
Engaged	$p < .054$

from the screen captures than the written comments, the online group's responses to these items were statistically even stronger than those of the face-to-face group, as shown in the shaded results in Table 2.4.

Interviews with five students from the online sections help us to understand these results more fully. All five interviewees were female, three from Stephanie's courses and two from Megan's. Interview questions were scripted, asking students how many times they watched the screen capture, how they watched it (e.g., starting and stopping), how they felt about the method, and how it compared with the written comments. Further questions focused on the overall message, or main "takeaway," they thought their teacher was conveying in the screen capture, whether they were surprised by anything in their teacher's response, and what was most and least helpful about the screen capture. A final set of questions focused on how they felt about their teacher, what feelings their teacher was conveying through the screen capture, how

Table 2.5. Thematic Coding of Interview Transcripts

Watched more than once	5
Liked more than written	5
Took away more learning	5
SC better at explaining	5
Learned more about teacher	4
Positive references to voice/tone	5
	2
Positive interpersonal	5
Prefer SC mode (only) now	3
Prefer SC *plus* written now	2

they would describe the relationship the teacher established in the screen capture versus the written comments, and which method they would prefer their teacher used.

A simple coding of the five interview transcripts revealed consistent themes across the interviews, as shown in Table 2.5. First, all five interviewees watched their respective screen capture more than once (Madison watched hers first on her smartphone while walking and then later three more times on her computer). All five students spoke extremely positively about the screen-capture method; Kaylee "*loved* the screen capture," and Kristin thought it was "really good, way more personal." Madison felt that it was "really helpful, especially in an online class, because you don't get teacher face-to-face interaction. It was really helpful to hear her voice and see her comments." Sheena thought it was "very interactive and a great technique for any professor to use whether in an e-class or a regular class on campus."

When we asked the interviewees to say more about what their teachers were trying to convey to them, all the students recalled specific rhetorical or other features of their papers that "made sense" to them as a consequence of their teachers' oral explanations. Madison had received a 100 on her paper, but learned some new ways to format her paper that she wasn't aware of before; the comments "really made more sense and I could use that to fully understand what I needed to do better the next time." Sheena took away a number of suggestions about her style, the use of topic sentences, and a validation of the work she had done connecting the ideas of two authors about whom she wrote; "I understood everything," she said, "and comment was very helpful and it helped me to progress in my papers over the semester."

In further explorations of the students' feelings about the relationships established through the screen captures that were largely missing in the written responses, the students focused strongly on the characteristics of spoken discourse. Sheena mentioned that it was "different to hear her voice, and it seemed to me, it was like it was more intimate, even though I haven't been able to have physical contact with her. I thought it was better than her actually going through a Word document just leaving [written] comments. It was better to hear her voice and her tone and how she spoke about my paper." Kaylee also mentioned tone: "It's hard to understand what a teacher means when it's just written, and so being able to hear her voice, I could tell in the tone exactly what she meant." Madison "really liked hearing the enthusiasm in her voice because it makes you—especially with it being an online class you just don't really know . . . it's hard to get those, I guess, verbal cues from people to see how their emotions are, you know, if they really did like your paper or if they're just trying to be nice about it."

The interviewees also frequently mentioned that they thought the screen-capture method was compelling their teachers to read their work more fully and carefully. Kristin said that she "thought it was cool that she obviously read through my paper because sometimes I feel like a lot of my professors don't read through your whole paper, but she actually read through it for content . . . she went through my paper and she personally reflected on it and then contributed to my topic." Erin commented that "when you hear her voice and hear her diction and her excitement about [the paper] you can really tell that she cares about it and is interested in what we write." Kaylee felt that her teacher was "expounding upon her paper" in ways that she didn't see in her written comments. These results are consonant with what most students said in the dozen interviews we conducted in the first phase of the study; several students believed that their teachers were spending more time with their papers using the screen captures than when they provided written comments, even though the teachers reported spending somewhat less time creating the screen captures.

Interviewees also commented variously but positively about the relationship their teachers established with them through the screen capture that was either absent or less prominent in their written comments. Kristin said that her teacher's response was "more personal . . . even just little things like the fact that she would use my name in the screen capture whereas she may not have in the written comments kind of makes it more personal. . . . You don't really have the opportunity to communicate with your professors through the whole DELTA [online] learning thing. . . . This type of thing [screen-capture technology] really creates more of a connection." Madison also brought up the effect of being directly addressed: "Anytime you say someone's name, it just makes it that much more personal. Even if you don't really know that person, if you can say their name, it means a lot more." Imitating her teacher's response, Erin also praised the personal nature of the screen capture: "It was like, 'Erin, this is what I think about your paper, this is what I read, this is how I reflected on it.' It gave her the opportunity to personalize her comments." Madison found the screen-capture method to be "so much more effective; I think it's more personalized, I felt like I had a better connection with the grading process and more understanding."

Asked to discuss any negative or problematic aspects of the screen captures, the five students had considerable difficulty. Two had no negative comments. One thought that it took more time to watch the screen captures two or three times than to skim through a teacher's written comments—a feature that from an instructional perspective we might consider to be an asset and not a liability. Another student pointed to the lack of opportunity to converse with the teacher, as one would do in a face-to-face conversation, but felt this was not a serious problem given the goals of the method. Another felt that the screen captures did not provide as much "recorded" information on the page as written comments, but admitted that it didn't make much difference.

Overall, then, the five interviewees found the screen captures highly successful as a way to provide evaluative response to students' writing, in a brief amount of time but with great explanatory adequacy and detail. More important, however, they commented enthusiastically on the way the screen capture, compared with the written comments, offered them opportunities to learn about their teachers' feelings toward their writing and to establish a productive, helpful working relationship with them that, ultimately, helped them to learn about their writing in a "personalized" way. In the context of online courses that risk creating further interpersonal distance between teachers and students, the method appears to be highly successful from the learner's point of view.

Moving Forward

In spite of the very positive results of this study, we must be careful about generalizing too eagerly from the students' experience. First, we gauged the effectiveness of the method as it was used by only two teachers who are ordinarily supportive and friendly. Second, our cohort of students was not particularly large and was strongly female-gendered, including all five of the interviewees. We might also consider the survey results showing that fewer than one-fifth of the students had ever received recorded oral comments on their writing, and probably fewer had received comments via screen capture, which raises the possibility that the favorable impressions of screen capture were influenced by a "novelty effect." However, we must also remember that online students are generally used to new technologies, and certainly all of the students have substantial experience with social media and various kinds of YouTube-like videos, among which many are screen captures.

In spite of these limitations, the statistical results were extremely strong, matching or exceeding the similarly positive results in the first phase, the context of which was a required course that not all students approach enthusiastically or with eagerness to learn and with a gender balance approaching 50%. If the anecdotal literature about oral response is based on accurate accounts of students' positive feelings, then our slightly more empirical results argue for the benefits of the method.

In speculating about these results, I am drawn toward sociocognitive models of learning, in which the cognitive ("learning from and about the way I produce text") is interwoven with the affective and interpersonal dimensions of identity ("what my teacher thinks about me through my textual and other contributions to our shared context"), but research and pedagogy have focused more strongly on the former. If it is impossible for teachers and students to pull these identity-based aspects apart from the experiences of learning, mentoring, and assessing, then we must explore them more fully to build models of teaching and learning that can be more productive for students. In addition, focusing on building relationships through more interpersonally dynamic forms of response, such as screen capture, could be especially helpful in retaining at-risk students or students with a variety of learning styles.

Research on oral response to writing is still in its infancy. We know little, for example, about how oral response facilitates positive "face" (Goffman,

1955). For some students, the potential of oral response to heighten face threats is quite real, and far from facilitating learning, we know that the cognitive difficulties of dealing with face threats impede learning: Students are too busy managing the relational aspects of an exchange to focus on its content (Kerssen-Griep, Hess, & Trees, 2003). Our studies suggest that face threat may be diminished through screen-capture response, perhaps because teachers are compelled to address students in person, through their voices, rather than through the potentially distancing mode of written comments. Students consistently called attention to identity cues in their teachers' oral responses that were important to their processes of making sense of the teacher's advice.

However, we know little about the nature of teachers' face-attentive strategies, both conscious and tacit, and the differences between how these are manifested in written and oral comments. In addition to deeper and more extensive analysis of these strategies, further research needs to explore how screen-capture technology influences the teacher–student relationship over time (our study represented a single event, a brief moment during a 16-week interaction). Further, we need to consider aspects of teachers' personalities, instructional ideologies, and attitudes toward students in the analysis of such interactions. Just as oral commentary appears to facilitate students' learning and encourage relationship-building, it could also accentuate negative attributes such as sarcasm, frustration, or tacitly held beliefs about students in general, specific groups of students, or individual students. And just as oral screen-capture technology appears to push teachers toward broader rhetorical concerns in students' writing, in the hands of teachers obsessed with small, surface details of students' writing, it could make even more apparent their lack of attention to students' thoughts and ideas.

Further research on the complex interpersonal aspects of students' and teachers' interactions could also look more closely at the ways that teachers construct students' personae, through their writing and other classwork, and how students respond to the cues left behind about those constructions in teachers' commentary. Finally, our studies have not yet fully explored another important side of the effectiveness of oral screen-capture response: not just what students perceive to be its effectiveness in helping them to learn, but whether it yields statistically more effective learning as manifested in students' work. Such studies would more effectively focus on teachers' comments on students' in-progress drafts than their final texts, after which the potential to learn significantly diminishes.

Clearly, emergent technologies such as screen capture offer new and potentially beneficial ways for teachers to interact with students in online environments. The early results that our studies yielded suggest that there is much room not only for instructional experimentation but for robust research programs to gauge the strengths and weaknesses of these new explorations.

Author's note: This study was made possible with the assistance of a grant from North Carolina State University's Department of Distance Education and Learning Technology Applications (DELTA). I wish to thank Dr. Deanna Dannels, Professor of Communication, and Zachary Rash, Dana Gierdowski, and Meagan Kittle, doctoral students in the Communication, Rhetoric, and Digital Media program, all at North Carolina State University, for their contributions to this study.

Appendix 2.1: Main Questions in the Student Survey

1. Before this study, in what formats have you received responses to your writing from instructors in the past?

- [ ] Written comments in the margins and at the end
- [ ] Comments inserted in electronic versions of your paper (such as Word files sent over the Internet)
- [ ] Tape recorded or other voice-recorded comments
- [ ] Face to face meetings with your instructor
- [ ] Responses in small-group meetings with other students

Other (please specify)

[   ]

2. How much time do you estimate you spent reading through and thinking about the written/typed comments your instructor made on your first paper?

- ( ) less than 5 minutes
- ( ) between 5 and 10 minutes
- ( ) between 10 and 20 minutes
- ( ) more than 20 minutes
- ( ) I did not read the comments

Other (please specify)

[   ]

3. Helpfulness

	Very helpful	Somewhat helpful	Neither helpful or unhelpful	Somewhat unhelpful	Very unhelpful
How helpful were the written comments on your paper or electronic document comments you received on your first paper?	○	○	○	○	○

4. Rate the extent to which you experienced each of the following feelings from your instructor when reading the written (hand written or on your electronic copy) comments on your first paper.

	strongly agree	agree	neither agree nor disagree	disagree	strongly disagree
Supportive	☐	☐	☐	☐	☐
Impersonal	☐	☐	☐	☐	☐
Caring	☐	☐	☐	☐	☐
Distant	☐	☐	☐	☐	☐
Considerate	☐	☐	☐	☐	☐
Personal	☐	☐	☐	☐	☐
Friendly	☐	☐	☐	☐	☐
Disconfirming	☐	☐	☐	☐	☐
Encouraging	☐	☐	☐	☐	☐
Uncaring	☐	☐	☐	☐	☐
Unconcerned	☐	☐	☐	☐	☐
Constructive	☐	☐	☐	☐	☐
Inconsiderate	☐	☐	☐	☐	☐
Concerned	☐	☐	☐	☐	☐
Unfriendly	☐	☐	☐	☐	☐
Validating	☐	☐	☐	☐	☐
Discouraging	☐	☐	☐	☐	☐
Engaged	☐	☐	☐	☐	☐
Unconstructive	☐	☐	☐	☐	☐
Defensive	☐	☐	☐	☐	☐

5. Rate the extent to which the written comments helped you to understand the following aspects of your paper.

	strongly agree	agree	neither agree nor disagree	disagree	strongly disagree
appeal to audience	○	○	○	○	○
structure	○	○	○	○	○
style or use of language	○	○	○	○	○
purpose	○	○	○	○	○
focus	○	○	○	○	○
grammar and/or surface errors	○	○	○	○	○
content or ideas	○	○	○	○	○

6. How easy was the screen-capture video to use?

○ easy

○ somewhat easy

○ not easy

Other (please specify)

[   ]

7. How many times did you listen to/watch the scree-capture video with your instructor's comments?

○ one time

○ two times

○ three times

○ four or more times

○ I didn't watch the screen-capture video

○ I only watched portions of the screen-capture video

8. Did you stop and start or pause the screen-capture video at any time?

○ yes

○ no

9. If you answered "yes" to the last question, please indicate your reasons for pausing the screen-capture video. Check all that apply.

☐ I couldn't understand what the instructor was saying

☐ I wanted to hear the comment again for my own understanding

☐ I was distracted

Other (please specify)

[   ]

10. Helpfulness

	Very helpful	Somewhat helpful	Neither helpful or unhelpful	Somewhat unhelpful	Very unhelpful
Compared to written comments only, how helpful were the comments you received via voice on the screen-capture video?	○	○	○	○	○

11. Rate the extent to which you experienced each of the following feelings from your instructor when watching the screen capture.

	strongly agree	agree	neither agree nor disagree	disagree	strongly disagree
Supportive	☐	☐	☐	☐	☐
Impersonal	☐	☐	☐	☐	☐
Caring	☐	☐	☐	☐	☐
Distant	☐	☐	☐	☐	☐
Considerate	☐	☐	☐	☐	☐
Personal	☐	☐	☐	☐	☐
Friendly	☐	☐	☐	☐	☐
Disconfirming	☐	☐	☐	☐	☐
Encouraging	☐	☐	☐	☐	☐
Uncaring	☐	☐	☐	☐	☐
Unconcerned	☐	☐	☐	☐	☐
Constructive	☐	☐	☐	☐	☐
Inconsiderate	☐	☐	☐	☐	☐
Concerned	☐	☐	☐	☐	☐
Unfriendly	☐	☐	☐	☐	☐
Validating	☐	☐	☐	☐	☐
Discouraging	☐	☐	☐	☐	☐
Engaged	☐	☐	☐	☐	☐
Unconstructive	☐	☐	☐	☐	☐
Defensive	☐	☐	☐	☐	☐

12. Rate the extent to which the screen capture helped you to understand the following aspects of your paper.

	strongly agree	agree	neither agree nor disagree	disagree	strongly disagree
appeal to audience	○	○	○	○	○
structure	○	○	○	○	○
style or use of language	○	○	○	○	○
purpose	○	○	○	○	○
focus	○	○	○	○	○
grammar and/or surface errors	○	○	○	○	○
content or ideas	○	○	○	○	○

13. Screen Capture Comfort Level

	Very comfortable	Somewhat comfortable	Neither comfortable nor uncomfortable	Somewhat uncomfortable	Very uncomfortable
How comfortable are you receiving comments on your work via screen-capture?	○	○	○	○	○

14. Now that you've experienced screen capture video responses to your writing, please choose the method of response to your writing you'd most like your instructors to use.

○ Handwritten comments

○ Screen capture videos

○ Comments inserted into Word or other electronic copies of your papers

Other (please specify)

[   ]

References

Anson, C. M. (1997). In our own voices: Using recorded commentary to respond to writing. In M. D. Sorcinelli & P. Elbow (Eds.), *Writing to learn: Strategies for assigning and responding to writing across the disciplines* (pp. 105–113). San Francisco, CA: Jossey-Bass.

Anson, C. M. (1999). Talking about text: The use of recorded commentary in response to student writing. In R. Straub (Ed.), *A sourcebook for responding to student writing* (pp. 165–174). Cresskill, NJ: Hampton Press.

Anson, C. M. (2012). What good is it? The effects of teacher response on students' development. In N. Elliot & L. Perelman (Eds.), *Writing assessment in the 21st century: Essays in honor of Edward M. White* (pp. 187–202). New York, NY: Hampton Press.

Brannon, L., & Knoblauch, C. H. (1982). On students' rights to their own texts: A model of teacher response. *College Composition and Communication, 33*(2), 157–166.

Connors, R. J., & Lunsford, A. A. (1988). Frequency of formal errors in current college writing, or Ma and Pa Kettle do research. *College Composition and Communication, 44*(2), 200–223.

Daiker, D. (1986). Learning to praise. In C. M. Anson (Ed.), *Writing and response: Theory, practice, and research* (pp. 103–113). Urbana, IL: National Council of Teachers of English.

Goffman, E. (1955). On face work: An analysis of ritual elements in social interaction. *Psychiatry, 18*(3), 213–231.

Inoue, A. B., and Poe, M. (2012). Race and writing assessment. New York: Peter Lang.

Kerssen-Griep, J., Hess, J. A., & Trees, A. R. (2003). Sustaining the desire to learn: Dimensions of perceived instructional facework related to student involvement and motivation to learn. *Western Journal of Communication, 67*(4), 357–381.

Knoblauch, C. H., & Brannon, L. (2006). The emperor (still) has no clothes—Revisiting the myth of improvement. In R. Straub (Ed.), *Key works on teacher response* (pp. 1–15). Portsmouth, NH: Heinemann/Boynton-Cook.

McKnight, M. (2011). *The construction of error in teacher commentary on Latino/a and White students' writing in a first year writing program.* Thesis. California State University, Fresno. n.p.

Mellen, C., & Sommers, J. (2003). Audiotaped response and the two-year-campus writing classroom: The two-sided desk, the "guy with the ax," and the chirping birds. *Teaching English in the Two-Year College, 31*(1), 25–39.

Olson, G. (1982). Beyond evaluation: The recorded response to essays. *Teaching English in the Two-Year College, 8*(2), 121–123.

Prior, P., & Looker, S. (2009, April). *Anticipatory response and genre systems: Rethinking response research, pedagogy, and practice.* Paper presented at the Conference on College Composition and Communication, San Francisco, CA.

Rutz, C. A. (1999). *What does my teacher want me to do? A response-based investigation of the teacher–student relationship in the writing classroom*

(Unpublished doctoral dissertation). University of Minnesota, Minneapolis, MN.

Sipple, S. (2007). Ideas in practice: Developmental writers' attitudes toward audio and written feedback. *Journal of Developmental Education, 30*(3), 22–31.

Smith-Taylor, S. (1997). The genre of the end comment: Conventions in teacher responses to student writing. *College Composition and Communication, 48*(2), 249–268.

Smith-Taylor, S. (2003). The role of technical expertise in engineering and writing teachers' evaluations of students' writing. *Written Communication, 20*(1), 37–80.

Sommers, J. (1989). The effects of tape-recorded commentary on student revision: A case study. *Journal of Teaching Writing, 8(2),* 49–75.

Sommers, J. (2002). Spoken response: Space, time, and movies of the mind. In P. Belanoff, M. Dickson, S. I. Fontaine, & C. Moran (Eds.), *Writing with Elbow* (pp. 172–186). Logan, UT: Utah State University Press.

Sommers, N. (2006). Across the drafts. *College Composition and Communication, 58*(2), 248–257.

Straub, R. (Ed.). (1999). *A sourcebook for responding to student writing.* Cresskill, NJ: Hampton Press.

Straub, R. (Ed.). (2006). *Key works on teacher response.* Portsmouth, NH: Heinemann-Boynton/Cook.

Yarbro, R., & Angevine, B. (1982). A comparison of traditional and cassette tape English composition grading methods. *Research in the Teaching of English, 16*(4), 394–396.

Notes

1. All names in this study are pseudonyms.

THREE

Shifting Again: Electronic Writing and Recorded Speech in Online Courses

Christopher Weaver

ONLINE COURSES OFFER EXCITING POSSIBILITIES for writing teachers because the online environment seems particularly well suited to the goals of a writing workshop. Online tools emphasize collaboration and dialogue, and they also highlight the use of writing as a process of discovery and not merely as an end product to be assessed—key elements of a workshop approach to teaching writing. Moreover, the space accessed by students in an online course is different from traditional classroom space in ways that highlight writing's potential for experimentation and revision and its development over time. In this chapter, I will address how the online environment changes the way that writing works, but I will also explore something more surprising (at least to me): the way the online environment affects how speech works and how it reconfigures the relationship between speaking and writing. I will argue that online courses allow us to exploit the exploratory, dialogic quality of writing while also providing new ways of thinking about speech and even the classroom itself as a kind of a text. Finally, I will suggest how the use of multimedia in online courses can encourage students to switch back and forth between speaking and writing in ways that help them see writing as both a process for exploration and a product to be revised and perfected.

Electronic Writing in Online Classes

Like many others with a background in composition and rhetoric, I began teaching online because I was excited by the possibility that the online environment might work better than the traditional classroom when it came to supporting the active-learning strategies that underpin a workshop-based pedagogy. The workshop approach to teaching writing relies on writing groups where students share drafts and get feedback from readers about how their writing affects them. It emphasizes that students are (or can be trained to be) the best authorities on their own writing processes and should be encouraged to reflect on which writing strategies work better or worse for them, and it focuses on the relationship between the choices writers make and the effects of these choices on readers. Because this writer–reader relationship is a complex one, students are urged to test out their writing on multiple readers. As suggested by the title of Peter Elbow's *Writing Without Teachers* (1973), the workshop model requires a reformulation of classroom space, with the peer response group displacing the centrality of the teacher as primary (or only) responder. Elbow's book urges writers to form their own writing groups outside of school; however, his ideas have had a profound influence on the way that writing is taught in schools. Since the writing process movement of the 1970s, writing teachers have been rearranging desks in the classrooms into circles or small groups to accommodate peer response as the primary class activity. For some teachers, these physical details of the classroom took on an ideological importance, as when Ira Shor pointed out that rows of desks encourage students to hide out in "Siberia," necessitating that the conscientious teacher disrupt the physical arrangement of the classroom by sitting in the back and by moving around (Shor, 1996).

In spite of teachers' desires to disrupt the teacher-centered classroom, many of us have found that traditional classroom space remains resistant to such shake-ups, and this is what makes online classes such an attractive alternative. I had used the workshop model in face-to-face classes for many years, and although I believed in its potency, I was also frustrated by the details of making it work. At times, the challenge was merely practical. Peer writing groups were often difficult to manage. Some groups finished sharing their writing and giving feedback in ten minutes while other groups used up the allotted class time without every member getting a chance to have a turn. Some challenges, however, extended beyond the nuts and bolts of running a writing workshop and went to the heart of the idea of writing as collaborative work. In spite of my eagerness to de-center authority and make the writing process more collaborative, I found that students were often less than willing co-creators of the classroom.

It is true that the workshop classes I taught made sharing drafts with each other and responding to them the primary focus of the class, and it is also true that the reconfiguration of classroom space into circles and small groups emphasized this activity. But this reconfiguration sometimes seemed both superficial and temporary. Students seemed to experience "group work" as a condition that ended when the class was over and they returned their desks to rows and exited the classroom to go to their other courses, almost all of them lecture or discussion-based. While most of them took the work of their writing groups seriously during class time, the sharing that they did and the feedback that they received did not seem to carry over into their revision process as much as I hoped that it would. In spite of various attempts of mine to emphasize the importance of peer response groups (feedback sheets, reflective letters, class discussions of the response process), most students still saw the groups as peripheral to the writing process rather than central. They still valued my feedback much more than their fellow students' and they still remained more focused on the end-goal of a final draft that met with my approval rather than on what they learned about their own writing from the process of drafting and revision.

So, as I began teaching online, I hoped that cyberspace would solve some of the practical problems of conducting a writing workshop while also helping students to value writing as a process of discovery and revision—the tentative and provisional exploration of ideas that come with early drafts and the openness to sharing and rethinking these drafts in collaboration with others. I hoped that the configuration of space in the online classroom would emphasize the importance of writing as a process, since everything in the online classroom would be visible, from early writing to feedback to final drafts. I also hoped that, since the online classroom was constructed almost entirely of words, writing would take on the role that speaking had previously served, particularly as a mode of giving feedback, and that because of this, students might be more willing to see writing as a mode for thinking and learning and not only as a final product to be assessed.

Interestingly, the theoretical basis for this promising new model of an online writing workshop can be found in an article by Peter Elbow entitled "The Shifting Relationship Between Speech and Writing," which was published in 1985, well before the Internet made teaching online possible. Elbow's article argued that the traditional view of speech as ephemeral and writing as permanent might be usefully reconsidered—that it was writing, which could be done privately and then revised, that was really ephemeral, and speech, which once uttered could never be taken back, that was really permanent:

However indelible the ink, writing can be completely evanescent and without consequences. We can write in solitude—indeed, we seldom write otherwise—we can write whatever we want, we can write as badly as we want, and we can write one thing and then change our mind. No one need know what we've written or how we've written it. In short, writing turns out to be the ideal medium for *getting it wrong*. (This evanescence of writing is enormously enhanced by the new electronic media where words are just electronic or magnetic impulses on a screen or disk.) (p. 153)

Elbow's thinking on this topic is closely related to his philosophy of teaching, in which he encourages students to assume different roles, experimenting with opposing ideas and creating dialogues between imaginary characters with different points of view. (See *Writing With Power* [1981] as well as his textbook, *Being a Writer* [2002], written with Pat Belanoff, for examples.) By turning the speech/writing opposition on its head, Elbow carves out a space for writing that emphasizes the importance of impermanence, experimentation, and play, where possibilities can be explored and then, if they don't yield useful material, revised or discarded before a final draft, before the writing becomes "permanent."

Elbow's parenthetical afterthought in the passage above anticipates the role that online classes might play in creating a new kind of classroom—one where words are made not of indelible ink but "just digital or magnetic impulses on a screen." At the time, Elbow was referring to the relatively new emergence of word processing programs. Decades later, however, when online classes began to take hold, we early adopters hoped that this new environment might change students' relationship to the writing process. Given the way that students viewed e-mail (and later, instant messaging, texting, Facebook, YouTube, and the multitude of still-emerging electronic platforms), which borrowed and reinvented oral conventions, wouldn't online classes help them make the Elbowian leap between the playful and the exploratory "oral" nature of writing and the permanence of academic prose? And wouldn't students, who were more likely to be comfortable with these oral conventions than print ones, be more likely in the online environment to claim control over the process of writing? Furthermore, Elbow's vision of the writing classroom as a space in which dialogue shaped writing seemed to fit the online class almost perfectly:

For of course the point of speech is often not to be a final or definitive statement but rather to keep the discourse going and produce more discourse in response—to sustain an ongoing dialogue or discussion. We can easily give writing this quality too by making our course a forum for constant writing-in-response-to-each-other's-writing, that is, by stressing the ways in which writing naturally functions as an invitation to future writing or a reply to previous writing—which is how most writing in the world actually occurs. (1985, p. 158)

What better medium could there be for writing-in-response-to-each-other's-writing than the discussion boards of an online class? Discussion boards, as their name implies, marry some of the best aspects of orality and print. They capture both the conversational nature of discourse in *time* (the "discussion") and the permanent record of writing in *space* (the "board") to which students can return and examine, reflect, and extend the material that is generated.

Discussion boards, then, are not merely a way of adapting the group discussions of face-to-face classes to the online environment. They are more transformative than that. In teaching online, I found that that group "discussion" was deeper and more extensive in online groups or on the discussion board than it was in the peer response groups of my face-to-face classes. And it certainly made managing these groups easier, since I no longer had to worry about some groups finishing long before others and other groups not finishing before the end of class time. But by far the greatest impact of teaching online was the weight that it seemed to give the process of sharing ideas and drafts with other students. The same peer groups that felt peripheral in the traditional classroom felt central to the online one. I believe that the reason for this is that in the online classroom, writing had to carry the weight that speaking had carried in the traditional classroom. Students still offered ideas and responded to each other, as they had always done, but they did so in writing. And, unlike in the traditional classroom, that writing, once it was done, remained visible. Students could return to it both to trace the development of a conversation and to build on such conversations as they revised their writing. When I asked them to write reflective pieces about how their writing developed over time, they were able to scroll through their group pages and quote comments made by members of their writing groups. I could also assign collaborative projects, such as a group discussion of a text. Then, when students wrote individual papers analyzing that text, they were able to cite each other as sources for how they arrived at their analysis through group discussion. While my authority in the class was never close to being displaced (students continued to look to me as the "real" authority about their ideas and their writing, and they continued to value my feedback more than that of their classmates), the role of dialogue was certainly more central and their feedback to each other's writing more extensive than in my face-to-face classes.

Recorded Speech in Online Classes

While writing teachers have been eager to use online classes to exploit the ephemeral qualities of writing, we have been slower to consider how they might affect the other side of Elbow's balancing act: the role of speaking. For if online platforms trade the permanence of ink for the evanescence of electronic impulses, they also trade the impermanence of speech for the permanence of digital audio and video files. This shift in how speech works online has dramatic consequences for how both teachers and students understand the composing process because the digital tools available for recorded multimedia turn speech into a text that can be manipulated and revised in the very way that writing teachers train students to do with print. Moreover, it turns out that the element of play that is so important to Elbow's pedagogy may be more obvious in speaking than it is in writing.

While I had come to online teaching because I hoped it would emphasize the oral qualities of writing, I discovered the textuality of recorded speech accidentally. The very first class that I taught online was the second part of a two-semester writing sequence entitled "Introduction to Literature." While I was excited about how an online course might change the students' perceptions of the writing process, I was also concerned about the loss of the spoken word—especially in a course where students would be reading literature. I wanted students to hear and appreciate the oral qualities of poetry and fiction. Consequently, I recorded a series of ten-minute mini-lectures in the university's recording studio with the aid of a sound engineer who usually worked for the music department. My plan was for students to listen to one lecture a week in which I read some of the literature aloud and called attention to particular sound elements in the writing. The lecture would supplement and inform the writing that students would be doing on the discussion board.

But while I hoped to emphasize the dimension of "voice" in writing, I was unprepared for how the recording process emphasized the textuality of the recorded performance. The process of recording these mini-lectures went like this: I would write out some notes for the lecture beforehand. I would bring these notes to a recording studio where I stood in front of a microphone in a small recording booth with headphones on while the sound engineer watched and recorded from an adjacent booth. I would speak into the microphone, and when I would make a mistake or wanted to re-take a particular part of the lecture, I could tell him through the microphone, and he could communicate to me through my headphones. When the ten-minute recording was done, I would join him in his booth, and we could both listen to the result.

I had taught from notes before, of course, but always face-to-face from my desk in front of a class of students. Here, speaking into the void, I was aware of my words in a way that I had never been before. Speaking into a microphone in a recording booth highlighted a paradox inherent in recorded speech: absence emphasizes presence. When I teach in front of a class, I can't afford to think much about my teaching as a performance. I'm aware of it, of course; I think that all teachers are. But there are so many other things to think about—how to manage time in the class, how the students are reacting, what I hope to accomplish that day—that my own consciousness of how my words sound gets pushed to the back of my mind. In the recording studio, however, I was constantly aware of how my words sounded. Moreover, the very fact that my students were absent called to mind how they would react to my words when they heard them in the online classroom. What would they think? How would they hear me and interpret what I was trying to do? I was aware not only of my choice of what words to use, but also of how I spoke them and how they sounded. In short, I was going through the very process that writing teachers hope to lead their students through—an awareness of the choices they make and the impact their words have on readers or listeners.

This awareness was heightened by the editing process that followed the recordings. I was fascinated to find that the recording and editing software allowed me not only to hear my lectures but also to *see* them. The software rendered the recording visible as a text. In the sound booth with the recording engineer, I could see an image of my voice, represented by sound waves. As the "cursor" swept over this image, I could hear the recording at any point in time, but I could also see the image in front and back of the cursor. I could see my entire vocal performance, not merely the moment that was being played back to me. I could "read" this text linearly in time from front to back, but I could also skip backward and forward to different places in the text. I could, with the help of the sound engineer, edit out hesitations, audible breaths, and "ahems" that cluttered the text. Or I could add pauses for effect. I could also compare two different takes of a lecture and then copy and paste a section from one into another or replace a section in one take with a section that worked better in another. The editing process was like a vocal equivalent of a word processing program, and it encouraged me to understand a vocal performance as similar to a written text. In other words, it captured the very qualities that Elbow had sought to emphasize about writing—that it could be done in private, encouraging exploration, discovery, and play.

In that first class, I tried in my mini-lectures to get my students to hear how important voice is to literature—that a poem or a story read out loud has a very different resonance, and possibly even a different meaning, than a poem or story on the page. In one week's lecture, for instance, I asked them to read a poem through by themselves and to write a brief post to that week's discussion board, noting their reactions. Then I asked them to listen to part of the mini-lecture where I read the poem aloud. Following this, they were asked to once again note their reactions to the poem, paying particular attention to how their ideas and impressions changed in response to my reading. Students reported that their impressions of the poem changed in a variety of ways, including: understanding lines that they had misread because of a difficulty decoding the poem's syntax, a better appreciation of the poem's voice, and a sense of the poem's emotional resonance that hadn't been in their initial reading. Of course, this activity can be done in a face-to-face classroom. Indeed, I had done it many times before. But the students' reactions in the online class seemed to me to be deeper than the face-to-face students who went through the same process. I suspect that this was once again an instance where my physical absence actually magnified the presence of my voice. With no visual cues or distractions, the online students found the difference between the written page and the sound of my voice more dramatic, and they reported more differences in their "before" and "after" reactions.

Ironically, I had initially been attracted to teaching online because it removed me from center stage and allowed students to focus on writing as a communicative act (writing to share, explore, and discover) rather than a performative one (writing as a product for the teacher to evaluate). Investigating recorded speaking, it turned out, brought both presence and performance back into the classroom—except in this context, I was the one "performing." I had come to see an audio text as a performance to be edited, played with, re-recorded, and uploaded. In asking students to respond to my audio text, I was just beginning to experiment with ways that they could experience the interplay between writing and speaking.

I became even more aware of how recorded speech could embody the properties of a written and editable text several years later, this time in a face-to-face classroom. I was one of a handful of teachers at my university to use Tegrity, a software program that could record a class lecture and make it available for viewing and or listening online. The program was being promoted as a way for students to review class material either if they were absent for the class or if they wanted to prepare for a paper or an examination. It did not have the same capacity for editing that I had experienced in my previous recording sessions, but it did have the advantage of ease of use. With very little training, I could record my own classes and upload them to the course website. While I thought that Tegrity might be useful for students as a review tool, I was more motivated to use it by my previous experience recording mini-lectures for my online class. I wanted to experiment with this tool, thinking that I might be able to use it to replicate the experience of recording lectures for online classes without having to visit a recording studio and seek the experience of a sound engineer. I also thought that if I could learn to record audio files on my own, then I might be able, in the future, to incorporate student-recorded audio projects into my classes. My eventual goal was to have the students discover what I already had—that recording one's words changed one's relationship to them, made them a text that could be edited. Once more, I found that the new technology led me in directions that I hadn't expected, and once more I found that the process of recording speech changed the way that I thought about what a text was.

What I began to notice over the semester as I recorded these classes was how the process was reshaping me as a teacher by causing me to think ahead of time about how my decisions would be perceived by my audience—not only the students in the classroom, but also the students who might later play back the class recordings. Tegrity began to change not only the way I thought about the audio aspect of the class, but also the way I structured the class, including visual elements. I was able to set the class recording so that the image that students would see when they later logged onto the website and accessed the recording would be whatever was on my computer screen when I was recording the class. That image could be anything—from the home page of the website to a blank screen. Initially, I didn't give the image any thought. Since the Tegrity recorder was launched from the class website, I simply kept open the home page of that website and used it as a static image over which the recording played. But as the semester progressed, I found myself talking about particular pieces of writing or making points about writing or literature that I would project on a screen. So instead of using the static image of the website, I began recording the audio over these images as we talked about them in class. Since I made extensive use of the Discussion Board in all of my classes, I began pulling the most interesting student comments from their posts and pasting them into documents that I projected onto the screen for class discussion.

Before long, I began planning for this before the start of each class. Now, when I prepared for class, I was thinking not only about the next 75 minutes, but also about what those minutes would look and sound like when they were played back later. In short, I began to see my own classes as texts, thinking about how they looked, how they sounded, and how they were structured. Of course, all good teachers do this to some degree, but I want to emphasize how different it is when the class you are teaching becomes a file to be uploaded, when you can structure the class beforehand and then see it and listen to it afterward. What happens is that you experience the class as both linear, moving forward through time from beginning to end, and as nonlinear, a "space" that can be ordered and rearranged. My experience recording mini-lectures allowed me to see them as texts that could be edited. In a sense then, I was replicating my experience editing mini-lectures in the recording studio, but this time on my own, and with the entire class as a text.

Of course, I couldn't edit the recordings of my face-to-face classes the way that I had with my recorded mini-lectures. The classes had already happened; they couldn't be "rewritten." But in listening to them afterward, I could jump from one point in the class to another. In planning for them ahead of time, I could consider how they would look and sound. And in arranging them and annotating them in a separate area on my course website, I could lay out the

course for both myself and my students in a way that I hoped would emphasize the connections between classes and allow them to see how the course
unfolded over the semester.

Once again, Elbow (1985) talks about the temporal and spatial qualities of
writing, and how managing these qualities is essential to good writing:

> Commentators on orality and literacy tend to stress how speech works
> in time and writing in space. In truth, writing is also essentially time-
> bound. Readers are immersed in time as they read just as listeners are
> when they hear. We cannot take in a text all at once as we can a picture
> or a diagram. We see only a few written words at a time. (p. 161)

The key to good writing, then, is to understand how it embodies the qualities
of both writing and of speech, how it exists both in time as an unfolding narrative and out of time as a document in space. But it turns out that this truth
applies to any text, including an audio recording. One's understanding of the
text changes once one can see it as both a narrative in time and an artifact in
space.

Once again, this is where online classes restructure the way we experience
texts—oral texts as well as written ones. My experience with building recorded audio into both my online and face-to-face classes led me to see them as
texts that could be ordered and reordered but also as narratives that unfolded
over time. What was useful to me as a teacher was the ability to move in and
out of these two dimensions and to see my recordings as embodying both
qualities. The next step was to create assignments that would help students
compose and edit their own texts using this insight.

Composing in Writing and in Video

With my own discoveries about oral and written texts in mind, I began thinking about how to construct assignments which would ask students to compose and edit in both print and multimedia and to move between the two
formats in ways that could help them understand both the narrative and spatial qualities of texts. In my first-year composition class, I had students work
on a project that would result in two different texts: a traditional paper and a
digital video. The assignment required students to choose a topic that would

allow for their own commentary as well as incorporate the opinions of others—any faculty, staff, or other students whom they could find on campus to interview. For the video project, they were assigned to small groups and required to share responsibility for writing questions, conducting interviews, shooting and editing the video, and providing commentary. At the same time, I assigned them to write individual papers where they could draw on the material they had gathered for their interviews, but where they each had to make decisions about what material to quote, how to present that material, and what to say about it. They worked on these projects simultaneously, with "drafts" in both formats due at different times over the semester. I also set up two separate spaces on the class website—one for the groups to post their videos and for students outside of the group to give feedback, and one for individual students to post drafts of their papers and to get feedback from the class. Finally, I set up a third space for students to post their thoughts on composing in both formats and on whether or not one project had influenced the other. My goal was to have insights from one format influence the composing and editing process in the other.

What I discovered was that students responded differently to each format and that these responses sometimes highlighted how the print and video texts themselves worked on readers or viewers. In one case, reviewing the texts online led a particular student to change the way that she edited her work. This student was in a group that interviewed people around campus about what they did and didn't know about politics and current events. When I asked the class to post reactions to the feedback they received and reflections on the process of composing in two different media, she wrote the following:

> In my head, the purpose of the paper was pretty clear, it was about what people didn't know about what was going on in the world. When I was writing, it just kind of made sense to me and I assumed that it would make sense to the reader too. But when we posted the videos and watched them I was a little embarrassed. It took a lot of time editing the interviews together and finding the funny parts. But when I watched the video with the others when we posted them, it seemed kind of pointless. Yes, there were funny parts, but after a while it started to drag. I thought "where is this going?" That made me realize I had to go back to the paper too. Sure, we interviewed all these people, but what does it add up to?

Writing teachers put a great deal of faith in the act of sharing drafts. The workshop model is supposed to help writers see how the choices that they make affect readers. But creating a video foregrounds and dramatizes those choices in ways that creating a piece of writing may not. It's difficult for many students to think about the editing process in writing because they are rarely conscious of making those decisions as they are in the midst of the writing process: "When I was writing, it just kind of made sense to me and I assumed that it would make sense to the reader too." We hope that workshops will demonstrate the effects that a writer's choices have on readers. But this student—who had a chance to workshop her writing in her online writing group—did not conclude that her paper lacked focus until she watched her video along with the others that were posted. It was her own reaction to the video that led her to revise the paper, not any feedback that she received from her writing group.

It's possible to draw two conclusions from this example. First, the process of creating a video foregrounds the editing process in a way that composing in writing does not. The student above was aware of making decisions about what parts of her raw footage to use, where to make cuts, and how to piece them together. Editing may take a greater portion of the time in the process of creating a video than it does in writing—at least for a novice writer: "It took a lot of time editing the interviews together and finding the funny parts." This student was aware of the role of editing in her video and refers to it specifically in her reflection, even as she admits that the editing process focused too much on finding the "funny parts" and not enough on giving the entire video a sense of purpose. Most importantly, her reflection on seeing the video has led her to think about the role of editing in her writing as well. She now realizes the importance of presenting her material in a way that emphasizes a narrative thread and leads to a conclusion, and this causes her to reconsider her paper: "That made me realize I had to go back to the paper too. Sure, we interviewed all these people, but what does it add up to?" Reviewing her video leads her to think about the editing process—something she does not mention at all in the reflective letter that she wrote for her paper. The nature of putting together a video has forced her to think about how her material is organized and to what purpose.

The second conclusion is that audience may work differently for video than it does for writing. We hope that by posting and responding to each other's writing, students see how their words affect readers. This is an important goal, but writing is still an unnatural act for many students, and they often feel awkward about sharing their drafts and inadequate about giving feedback to each other. Viewing video, on the other hand, is something students are usually quite comfortable with, and they tend to be much more aware of how an audience reacts and why. The student above recognized something about her video project right away—even though she had failed to recognize the same problem in her writing. It was easier for her to make the transition from video composer to video viewer than it was for her to make the transition from writer to reader. That's an important lesson for teachers who make extensive use of workshops. Having students reflect on the impact of video on audience may help them to be more conscious of the relationship between writer and reader.

Another advantage of having students compose both in writing and video is how working in the two media dramatizes the relationship between form and content. This became apparent to me when I asked my first-year literature class to create edited videos about some aspect of the horror genre in literature, film, and television. As in the composition class above, students worked simultaneously on an edited video and a written paper. Students were required to include several components in their video: still images, film clips, titles, voice-over narration, an interview with an expert, and a reading from a piece of literature. They were instructed to use as many of these components as possible in their writing as well. I was interested to see whether editing different elements in the process of creating their video would increase their awareness of the editing process in their writing. The video editing tools that they used allowed them to layer on these different elements and to easily move them around in their video "text." I hoped that having to "fit" these elements together in one medium would help them think about how these elements worked in the other.

One thing that became clear when students workshopped drafts in both media was how much more sophisticated and innovative the students were at integrating these elements in their video texts than in their written ones. A dramatic example of this difference appeared in one group's project on how vampires have been portrayed in popular culture. The video version of this project begins without any introduction or explanation as it presents a clip of the two main characters from the 1995 film version of *Interview with the*

Vampire. At the end of this clip, there is a sudden and dramatic moment where the vampire attacks the protagonist. In the students' video, music swells and then the title card is shown. The video segues to a succession of different images of vampires taken from films and television over an 80-year span. At first the music plays over these images, but as it fades out, we get a student's voice-over inviting us to consider how these images embody different elements of the vampire myth. The images are then followed by a film clip from the 1931 film version of *Dracula*. As the clip plays, a voice-over reads a passage from Bram Stoker's novel, describing Count Dracula's physical appearance. This video is strikingly effective at capturing the viewer's attention from the first moment and at blending together examples from different texts—images, video, and literature—in a way that invites analysis.

The video's success at integrating different elements effectively stands in stark contrast to the clunky introduction to a paper written by a student from the same group that created the video:

> Throughout history there have been many different versions of vampires in movies and stories. You can begin with Bram Stoker's novel, *Dracula*, and continue to today's movies such as *Twilight* and television shows such as *True Blood* and *The Vampire Diaries*. There are many different elements to vampire stories. In my paper I will look at different examples of vampires and analyze how each one is different while at the same time there are also aspects of the vampire story that almost always remain the same.
>
> The first vampire that I would like to talk about is the one that most people probably think of when they think of a vampire. It is Count Dracula, played by Bela Lugosi.

One can sense the writer struggling to present the material here in contrast to the effortless feel and confident presentation of the video version. In the video there is an implicit trust that the material will speak for itself and that the audience will stay interested long enough for the video's purpose to become clear. Thus, the authors of the video do not introduce narration until a minute or so into the video, after the introductory film clip and after the sequence of different images. Even before the narrative voice-over, it is probably clear to the viewer that the video's subject matter is the physical appearance of vampires in different stories in different times. Only after the viewer is presented with these images does the music fade out and the voice-over introduce the material to be analyzed.

That implicit understanding between the author and the audience is missing from the written version. Notice the shift in voice in the introductory paragraph from the general, sweeping claim, "Throughout history there have been many different versions" to the direct address to the reader, "You can begin with Bram Stoker's novel" to the explanation of the writer's intentions, "In my paper I will look at . . ." It is almost as though the writer is trying to find a way into her material and is not sure how to do it.

However, while many of the students' videos were better at presenting their material, they tended to be analytically weaker than their written counterparts. The vampire video, for example, presented a gorgeous array of images to analyze, but the analysis itself was fairly cursory and superficial, as though the students who created the video relied too heavily on the images to speak for themselves and did not need to analyze them at length. The same students' papers, though presenting fewer examples and doing so in a much less interesting way, tended to spend more time discussing them. It may be that while students are much more confident about composing in video and more intuitively aware of how elements of composition work in video form, they are less used to videos as a form of textual analysis. As with the student in my college composition class, the students in this literature class focused more on how to arrange their material than on what that material added up to. The videos were more sophisticated and innovative in their *form* while the papers delivered more substantial *content*.

It is not, then, that students are better at composing in one medium than the other nor that one medium is superior to the other for academic work. The point is that students composing in one medium are likely to have blind spots that can be brought to their attention when composing in another— particularly if there is ample time for comparing the projects and reflecting on the process. The students in this Introduction to Literature class were required to present their video projects before an audience in a university-sponsored event on writers and their writing. I asked students to write a discussion board entry, reflecting on the process of composing and editing parallel projects in two different media. While not all of the students reported that they found transitioning between the two projects useful, quite a few did. One student wrote:

In the beginning, I thought that I would end up using my own paper as material for the video, but it turned out to be more complicated than that. As my group met and then as I got comments from you and the other students, I found myself going back and forth between the two projects. Teachers have always told me that I need a thesis in my papers, but it wasn't until we were arguing in my group about which movie clips to use in the video that I realized what the thesis for my writing was. On the other hand, I wouldn't have known what movies to include in the video if I hadn't been writing about them in my paper. So, it was more of a back and forth kind of deal than I would have expected. Overall, I think this helped both our video and my paper.

This student's comments demonstrate the potential advantage of composing in two media. Through moving back and forth between writing and video, different features of the text and of the composing process can be highlighted and examined and students can gain a greater mastery over them in both media.

Conclusions

Like many other writing teachers, I was originally motivated to teach online because I wanted to discover what happened when the writing workshop model moved from a physical classroom to a virtual one. After teaching online for a decade, I offer the following conclusions to that question.

Online Classes Dramatize How Writing Is Both Process and Product

As many teachers have discovered, features such as the Discussion Board are uniquely situated to exploit what Elbow refers to as the "underside" of writing—its tentative, exploratory, and dialogic qualities. Because writing replaces speaking in the online environment, writing takes on some of the features of speech. It is not only the final product that students submit for evaluation; it is also the process that students and teachers use to do the work of the class. Because the online class consists almost entirely of written words, sharing and responding to writing are central to it in a way that they can never be in a face-to-face classroom.

However, online courses also emphasize writing as a text that can be edited and manipulated. While Discussion Boards enact the speech-like activity of discussion and response, they also provide a transcript of that response in a way that is unavailable to the face-to-face writing classroom. Moreover, by expanding the composing process to include audio and video texts, we can encourage students to see authoring and editing as activities that occur in both time and space. By moving back and forth between electronic writing and recorded media, we can make students more conscious of the choices involved in composing texts and of the impact their choices have on audiences.

It's possible to see how asking students to compose in media other than writing represents an evolution in the writing workshop that's created by teaching online. The traditional workshop model used in face-to-face classrooms asks students to become aware of how texts work on readers through sharing drafts and observing readers' reactions. Online writing workshops have some advantages over the face-to-face classroom because they give students more time to read and react to each other's work, and they make writing and sharing activities the main focus rather than a "time out" from the normal teacher-led classroom. However, an even greater advantage of online classes is the way that they encourage teachers and students to think of media other than writing as "texts." Composing in writing as well as audio and visual media allows us to see texts differently—to step in and out of the composing process more easily and, in doing so, to understand the relationships between author and audience and between form and content that are at the heart of the writing workshop.

Online Courses Should Foster a Sense of Play

When I began teaching online, I hoped that the course website would prove a more effective environment for workshop activities that already had a central place in my face-to-face classroom. While this turned out to be true, the online environment also led me to see both writing and speaking differently and to exploit the overlap and the differences in the way that electronic writing and recorded audio and video work as texts. This unexpected result may say something important about the impact of technology on teachers' expectations about writing and teaching. We begin with assumptions that are based on what we know about sound writing pedagogy, but when we begin to apply these assumptions, we find ourselves taken in unexpected directions. In "Fools Rush In," Scott Lloyd DeWitt and Marcia Dickson (2003) caution against limiting online teaching to a technology for better achieving the goals of the traditional classroom:

> Early research in the field of computers and composition strongly suggested that sound pedagogy should always begin with what we already hold to be true about teaching writing: that technology should be secondary and used as a means to achieve our primary goal of facilitating student learning. Not only does this sell short the possibilities for inventing pedagogy that grows out of our experience with various technologies, but it also paints an unrealistic picture of how innovative classroom applications of technology are created. Often, computer-rich assignments and classroom activities grow out of teachers' experiences with the technology itself. (p. 69)

I suspect that this is why most teachers begin experimenting with technology in the first place, whether that technology is used in the traditional classroom, as with recording technology such as Tegrity, or online. We want to see where it leads us and what it can teach us about our craft. The dramatic increase in the number of courses offered online has led teachers and administrators to worry about these courses providing comparable experiences and equivalent learning outcomes to their traditional counterparts. If the profession has learned anything from the assessment mania of recent years, it should be to approach such concerns with caution and not to let them drive our pedagogy. Though we may be tempted to defend online classes as more efficient ways to promote the same goals as our traditional classes, we would be wise to heed DeWitt and Dickson's advice about the way that technology works and to understand that experimentation with online teaching itself leads to new insights about teaching rather than the other way around.

This understanding is particularly important as the writing-across-the-curriculum movement begins to focus more on writing in online courses. The WAC movement's success over the past few decades owes a great deal to its willingness to target faculty who already have an interest in writing and whose collaborations and successes filter down to others in their departments. These faculty engage in WAC workshops and retreats not because they feel obligated to but because writing interests them, and they see that thinking about writing in new ways can lead them to insights about their own teaching. Similarly, faculty who teach online tend to be those individuals who are interested in the way that this technology leads to insights about teaching and learning that they might not otherwise have.

It's important to remember that Elbow's pedagogy, which relies on creating a space that is experimental, tentative, and playful rather than just evaluative, applies to teaching as well as to writing. The old model of writing instruction tended to overvalue planning (advising students to make outlines before they had even begun writing). What writing teachers have learned through the workshop model is that writing itself tends to lead to new insights that could not have been anticipated by such a plan. So too with online teaching. As colleges rush to offer online courses, we should not neglect the impulse that leads many of us to teach online in the first place. As teachers, we need to allow ourselves the space to experiment and to see where the technology will lead us.

References

DeWitt, S. L., & Dickson, M. (2003). Fools rush in. In P. Takayoshi & B. Huot (Eds.), *Teaching writing with computers: An introduction* (pp. 69–78). Boston, MA: Houghton Mifflin.

Elbow, P. (1973). *Writing without teachers*. New York, NY: Oxford University Press.

Elbow, P. (1981). *Writing with power*. New York, NY: Oxford University Press.

Elbow, P. (1985). The shifting relationship between speech and writing. *College Composition and Communication, 36*, 283–303.

Elbow, P., & Belanoff, P. (2002). *Being a writer: A community of writers revisited*. New York, NY: McGraw-Hill.

Shor, I. (1996). *When students have power: Negotiating authority in critical pedagogy*. Chicago, IL: University of Chicago Press.

FOUR

Revising the Defaults: Online FYC Courses as Sites of Heterogeneous Disciplinary Work

Andy Buchenot

I<small>N A MAJORITY OF A</small>MERICAN universities, first-year composition (FYC) courses are positioned in ways that cut across conventional disciplinary boundaries. This cross-disciplinary character of FYC courses stems from the gatekeeping function of these courses. Students who wish to pursue a major in chemistry, for instance, are required to pass through a FYC course housed in a department of English in order to prove their ability to manipulate academic discourse. Because of their gatekeeping function, these courses are populated by students with a wide range of academic foci and interests. As a result, FYC instructors must facilitate reading and writing interactions that, ideally, inform discourse practices from across disciplines. This disciplinary positioning is further complicated when these FYC courses are taught online. By and large, online writing courses are taught using text-based course management systems (CMS) that facilitate asynchronous interactions and frustrate the approaches to student-centered pedagogy that inform the teaching of writing. Put differently, online writing courses are overwhelmingly taught using software like Blackboard or Moodle, which feature text-only or text-mostly interfaces. Guided by these interfaces, students and instructors communicate through messages that are posted and read at different times. In-person FYC courses, by contrast, emphasize the importance of communication in the moment by teaching through class discussion, peer review, and a host of other approaches that turn on participants being in the same place at the same time. These approaches—which emphasize conversation over lecture, guided exploration over direct instruction—either do not apply or require substantial revision to occur in text-only, asynchronous CMS. These material conditions reposition online FYC courses away from, if not outside of, the history of composition theory.

My purpose in pointing out these disciplinary complexities is not to lament the loss of tradition, but to suggest that these conditions should be acknowledged and engaged. Informed by these conditions, I argue that instructors should embrace the unique disciplinary positioning of online FYC courses in order to promote student agency.

To embrace online FYC's disciplinary positioning, I encourage instructors and students to investigate the institutional and technological assumptions that shape their courses. This work might be thought of as "opening the black boxes" of disciplinarity and technology. I take the phrase "opening the black boxes" from science and technology scholars who use it to refer to the efforts of individuals who take an established technology (say, a computer keyboard) and then adjust it to serve different needs (use software to make it write in Arabic). The "black boxes" are the limits placed on a technology by a producer (sometimes literally boxes that keep users away from the working parts) and the limits placed by a user (the inertia of familiar use). Susan Leigh Star (1991) argues opening black boxes exposes the "invisible work" of technology and offers valuable insight in "attempting to represent more than one point of view within a network" (p. 33). A computer keyboard's keys, for example, are not arranged according to an objective logic of keyboard design. Instead, their arrangement is a product of the invisible work of development (In what language is existing software written? Who might buy it?) and the invisible work of use (How can I use this to type accents? To use kanji?). Opening black boxes helps us to identify histories and expectations, features that directly inform student agency.

To promote student agency, I encourage instructors and students to reimagine agency in dynamic, relational terms. Following Marilyn Cooper (2011), I understand agency as "an emergent property of embodied individuals." Cooper suggests that "agents do reflect on their actions consciously; they do have conscious intentions and goals and plans; but their agency does not arise from conscious mental acts . . . Agency instead is based in individuals' lived knowledge that their actions are their own" (p. 421). Put plainly, agency is not an ability that individuals possess and then deploy when they want to act independently; agency is an often unintentional function of living in a social/material world. To borrow a phrase from Cooper, agency is "the process through which organisms create meanings through acting into the world and changing their structure in response to the perceived consequences of their actions" (p. 426). Such a view of agency encourages a consideration of a "writer's surround" that goes beyond fraught discussions of imagined audience and pushes students to understand their work as a nuanced meeting of factors. Cooper takes the term "surround" from Glenn Mazis, who defines it as the constantly changing conditions that shape how an individual experiences the world. Notably this term is "used to suggest that natural environments cannot be distinguished from social ones" (p. 444). The educational implication of this construction agency is a student-centered pedagogy that eschews familiar "think for yourself" approaches in favor of "attend to your surroundings and act responsibly." Students remain at the center of this pedagogy, but rather than imagine the student as independent and empowered, this pedagogy imagines the student as one of many agents, all of whom have a stake in creating meaning.

In this chapter, I present an approach to teaching that encourages student agency by asking students to question the naturalness of their assumptions about disciplinarity and technology. I make this case by presenting the results of a qualitative study of online FYC courses where students assumed an agency that problematized notions of typical online interactions.

Opaque Interfaces and Built-In Pedagogies

In her most recent work, Sherry Turkle (2011) suggests that contemporary human computer interaction is defined by a design that separates users from the workings of their technologies. Turkle points to "the 1984 introduction of the Macintosh [computer]" as a crucial moment in the history of opaque design: "transparency," she argues, "used to refer to the ability to 'open up the hood' and look inside. On a Macintosh it meant double-clicking an icon" (p. 312). In effect, Macintosh's use of icons creates a black box around the software that separates users from the way that computer code works. Instead of entering a string of code that instructs the computer to execute a program, users click the blue "W" on their desktop and a word processing program appears on the screen. For Turkle, this opacity leads to a troubling affective relationship with computers. For online FYC courses, this opacity leads to a troubling complacency regarding writing technologies.

The most prominent technology in online courses is the CMS. Lisa Lane (2009) explains that CMS "were originally designed to focus on instructor efficiency for administrative functions such as grade posting, test creation, and enrollment management. *Pedagogical considerations were thus either not considered, or were considered to be embodied in such managerial tasks* [emphasis added]." ("The Inherent Pedagogies of CMSs," para. 1). This administrative focus creates opacity, fostering what Lane terms a "built-in pedagogy" that encourages an administrative use of CMS. This influence:

> can be seen in the selection of features which are most accessible in the interface, and easiest to use . . . the simplest tasks are uploading documents and creating text in boxes. Although the Discussion Forum is at the top level of access, most other non-traditional features are buried deep in the system. ("The Inherent Pedagogies of CMSs," para. 2)

These default arrangements support a use of the CMS that limits the options by distancing users from all but authorized uses. Asking students (and instructors) to investigate the opacity of this design creates openings for agentive action. If users can identify the ways that their technologies push them toward particular interactions, it is possible to incorporate that force in producing writing. What the CMS "wants" can be considered another agent influencing student text production.

In addition to these technological concerns, FYC courses are shaped by a complex disciplinary position. I contend that a similar investigation of the "interface" of disciplinarity offers another avenue for encouraging agency. Writing about FYC's disciplinary positioning, Bruce Horner (2000) argues that the field is "in some ways removed from the dominant, though not removed from the social" (p. 115). That is, FYC is not positioned as the authoritative site of learning to write, but it is a part of a university's mission to teach writing. An accounting student, for instance, does not learn to write fiscal analyses in an FYC course; the student learns to write these complex documents in advanced accounting courses or during internships. For this student, an FYC course is a requirement to be fulfilled in order to engage in the discourse of accounting. In short, universities position FYC as both present and removed from the work of learning to write. Horner uses this present/removed position to argue that the "realm" of first-year composition is "neither as transparent media for the expression or operation of dominant social forces nor as opaque deflections of the social" (p. 116). Rather, the realm of FYC courses offers possibilities where "a range of work—hegemonic, counter-hegemonic, alternative—might occur" (p. 116). I understand Horner's range of work as an expression of the agency that comes from investigating the disciplinary position of FYC courses. Acknowledging FYC as simultaneously removed from and invested in the dominant obliges (or, at least, *encourages*) students to respond to a broader writing situation. Responding to this broader situation promotes agency by highlighting the embodiment of rhetorical action—embodied in disciplines, in requirements, in courses, in students—and creating opportunities for students to make meaning from this embodiment.

Online FYC courses are a powerful site for exploring this embodiment because they bring together technological and disciplinary complexity. In these courses, students have opportunities to push past opaque interfaces and open the black boxes of CMS. Students also have opportunities to consider the disciplinary complexity of learning to write in a university.

This argument is a continuation of observations conducted from 2008 to 2010 at an urban midwestern university. The data offer valuable ways to discuss the ways critical, production-focused agency might be explored in online spaces. Through my analyses of several teaching engagements, I argue that, by paying special attention to technology, disciplinarity, and their attendant conventions, students might be encouraged to take a more active part in the reading, writing, designing, and learning that makes first-year composition a part of the social imagination of the university—even in the still-contentious space of online instruction.

Contexts for Critical Work

My research centered on a required writing course on academic research. The course asks students to compile annotated bibliographies, to write shorter analyses, and to compose a ten-page research essay. At the end of the semester a committee of FYC instructors review the research essay as part of a portfolio evaluation system. The university offers online sections of the course through Desire2Learn Incorporated's Enterprise eLearning Suite, a popular CMS that includes an asynchronous discussion forum, e-mail, a test-making/taking platform, an online grade book, and options for students and instructors to upload/download files. Desire2Learn Inc. (2013) promotes its software as "a seamless experience for creation, delivery, and management of courses" featuring a "comprehensive and easy-to-use toolset . . . [that] provides everything you need to design, develop, and deliver quality courses."

Notably, this official language echoes some of Turkle's warning about opaque interface design. In an effort to create a "seamless experience," the eLearning Suite simplifies the creation of a website to clicking "create site" and filling in some basic information; it makes formatting text in a discussion board a matter of selecting a style from a pull-down menu; it even streamlines sending e-mail into a series of preset options. It is possible to customize some elements of the interface, but only by selecting from a list of options. With a few exceptions, it is not possible to edit the interface at the level of coding language. For example, a student cannot add a string of HTML code into a message board post to embed an interactive PDF into a message. These limitations are often extended by university technology staff who administer the eLearning Suite. At my current university, many of our CMS' features are "turned off" in order to prevent faculty from accidentally damaging the software while trying to customize the interface. My purpose in pointing out these limitations is to suggest that the typical use of CMS distances students and instructors from their technology. This distancing limits the possibilities for action by only allowing users to affect their learning environment in superficial ways. Further, this distancing reinforces Lane's concept of the "built-in pedagogy" of CMS. By restricting what students and instructors can do with their technology, the eLearning Suite quietly enforces a pedagogy concerned with "presentation and assessment" (Lane, 2009). Put plainly, what the eLearning Suite does extremely well is facilitate the uploading and downloading of information in the form of assignments, message board posts, and other textual objects. The eLearning Suite is less successful at fostering conversation and collaboration. Consequently, these technical features shape the way writing is taught online.

Such limitations call into question the possibilities for student-centered pedagogy in online education. While CMS allow great flexibility in terms of when and from where students participate in class activities (e.g., a student can respond to comment at 2:00 a.m. from her cell phone), the technical features allow for far less flexibility. This is particularly true when instructors and students focus their use exclusively on the default settings of their CMS software. In the following pages, I suggest ways that student and instructors might explore these defaults and work with and against them in an effort to promote agency.

There are broad implications of this approach, but I narrow my focus to assignment design and sequencing. My discussion takes cues from the rich history of scholarship in composition studies focused on the role that assignment design and sequencing might play in teaching writing (see Bartholomae, 1982; Bishop, 2001; Sommer & Saltz, 2004). Because comments are recorded in an online environment, researchers have the unique opportunity to carefully study the text of not only student writing but also class discussions and less formal comments. I draw heavily on these comments in order to suggest a way that assignments might be used to investigate technology and disciplinarity. For instructors, such an investigation takes place in the composition and revision of course documents. For students, the investigation occurs in responding to these course documents. In the following I detail a sequence of assignments and the student responses elicited. I have used pseudonyms to protect student identities and, in an effort to represent comments truthfully, I refrained from editing the content of the student prose.

Investigating Technology and Disciplinarity

In an effort to help students begin engaging with the CMS technology, I composed a sequence of assignments that suggested students use technologies outside of the Desire2Learn tool-set to conduct a small group discussion. I asked students to:

> Use different means to communicate. For example, your group might collectively create a Wiki[1] or use a chat program like AOL Instant Messenger[2], or you may even want to meet in person over coffee. Although you may not be familiar with some of the software listed here, it might be worth your time to experiment with a different approach to communicating. Regardless of how you interact, **everyone must be able to participate**. In other words, don't meet in person unless everyone can make it; don't create a group blog[3] unless everyone is willing to post [original emphasis].

Each of the footnotes in this assignment leads to URLs for sites that gave technical definitions of the related technology. My expectation was that students would follow these links, use a non-Desire2Learn technology, have productive discussions, and, perhaps, reflect on the material constraints of Desire2Learn. Admittedly, my expectation was ambitious. However, I found support for this ambition in scholarship claiming that "students are often more technologically adept than their instructors" (Vie, 2008, p. 10) and that "extra-curricular composition" has contributed to "the creation of a writing public that, in development and in linkage to technology, parallels the development of a reading public in the 19th century" (Yancey, 2004, p. 298).

By the time the assignment was due, all of the groups decided to post to the message board rather than experiment with "different means of communicating." More disappointing than the lack of experimentation was the lack of discussion that occurred in the more familiar software. On average, each student produced only two comments during the weeklong project. I acknowledge that small group discussions do not always provoke intense conversation, but this small number of comments seemed more troubling than a group of reluctant students.

Re-reading the assignment, I'm struck by how technologies (wikis, blogs, etc.) were treated as if their use was self-evident; the assignment tells students to use the technology without considering any of the social or material conditions that shape these technologies and their use. The assignment mentions AOL's Instant Messenger program but doesn't invite a discussion of the software. Issues that might have been discussed include what operating systems the program runs on (personal computers, mobile phones, web browsers), or the third-party clients that work with AOL Instant Messenger features (Adium, Trillian, Google Talk), or if students even use this program anymore. Instead of inviting these types of discussions, the assignment offers links to websites with broad, non-technical instructions on how to use the software.

I was also struck by the way the assignments presume that challenging the educational and communicative possibilities of the CMS was something students might want to do. This assignment does not offer a reason for engaging in the extra work of moving outside of the eLearning Suite. I had not communicated any of my reasons for why investigating the limitations of technologies might be useful for students.

In the brief discussions prompted by the assignment, there were indications that students did not, in fact, consider experimenting with a different means of communication to be the lofty goal I imagined it to be:

> CAROL

Any ideas on how we want to communicate? I am fine with just using D2L, but can we please start the essay ASAP?

> LEIGH

D2L seems to be the best choice. we have to do all our work on d2l anyways we might as well conduct our group work here.

After reading through the responses, I composed a two-part assignment designed to encourage the kinds of discussions that I thought might help students move toward greater agency. In these assignments I asked students to investigate the "technology" of small group discussion. In the first part of the assignment, students were asked to reflect on their group's interactions using the eLearning Suite. The assignment frames the issue by explaining that:

Now that we are in the fourth week of class, I expect that most of you are beginning to settle into a pattern for interacting in this course. In other words, I expect that most of you have figured out what you need to do to login, to download and read assignments, to post to the discussion boards, and a host of other "technical" tasks.

Before those practices become too comfortable or too natural, I would like you to critically reflect on how you have been engaging in them. I want you to think and write about what you have been doing for class and how it has been useful (or not useful). Specifically, I would like you to examine how you and your colleagues have been participating in class discussions.

This assignment deliberately calls attention to the seemingly innocuous tasks of using a CMS. Practices like logging in, downloading assignments, and posting to discussion boards are standard activities—activities that Lane might suggest are built-in to the design of CMS software. At the same time, the assignment casts these practices as activities that have been mastered by students. In other words, the assignment asserts that using the eLearning Suite is a learned activity, one that warrants critical reflection.

After framing the issue of classroom practice as learned rather than natural, the assignment asks students to consider the interconnectedness of discussion, the CMS interface, and "college research writing" (the nominal topic of the course). Specifically, the assignment suggests that students "spend some time thinking about how useful class discussions have been for complicating, developing, broadening, or challenging your understanding of 'college' or 'academic' research writing." Students posted their responses to the discussion board and, for the most part, took on an unexpectedly focused, critical tone. Here is a representative posting:

SHANNON

This is just a simple observation I have—I don't expect a solution. I noticed not many people, very much including myself, rarely respond to someone commenting on their observation/essay/etc. I personally think it's because people usually comment a day or two later from the initial post and sometimes the original author forgets what the whole point of their post was so student and instructor texts produced in an online first-year they don't feel inclined to actually respond to one-another. There isn't really much you can change about that because this, of course, is an online environment and you can't make everyone sign onto D2L at the same exact time.

This comment might be read as a form of resistance, but I see evidence of Shannon working toward a more complex understanding of material/social features that shape class interaction. She notes that because "this . . . is an online environment you can't make everyone sign in at the same time." Read generously, her comment points to the connection of the technical features of the eLearning Suite (specifically, its asynchronous communication) and the student attitudes that the CMS seems to prompt. I argue that Shannon is thinking past the surface level of the CMS interface (e.g., how to post a comment) and into what it might mean to use the CMS interface (e.g., the implications of posting comments in accordance with Desire2Learn's default settings).

This assignment exploring the interconnectedness of discussion, the CMS interface, and "college research writing" might be read as a kind of transitional assignment, a way to help students begin investigating the course software. If students were following the built-in pedagogy of the eLearning Suite, then this assignment asked them to reflect on the benefits and limitations of that pedagogy. The goal of this assignment was to create a context for an assignment that asked students to push beyond familiar uses. This second assignment asked students to meet again in their small groups, but, before meeting, students were required to read through their classmates' reflections on small group work. As the assignment describes it, the reading of their classmates' reflections was a step toward "re-imagin[ing] our approach to small group work." Students re-read the comments and made 80 posts—roughly four per student—regarding their plans for their next group meeting. This increase in posts suggests that students were more invested in reconsidering the technologies of class interaction in a purposeful way. Students responded well to being asked to investigate how the material/social features of course technology "worked" for small groups and then to tinker with those material/social features.

When it came time to engage in small group work, the students began to exercise an agency with the course technologies that stood in stark relief to our early small group work. One group used the eLearning Suite's message board to schedule a time to meet via an instant messenger program unaffiliated with Desire2Learn. In the CMS, I am able to track nearly everything students do or write. The software allows me to read students' message board posts, find out when students log in, calculate how long they are logged in at a time, check how many messages they have read on the discussion board, track which files they have downloaded, and a host of other analytic functions. When students use an off-site instant messenger program, I have no oversight. I only know that these students communicated because they told me. I cannot say if removing their discussion from my review was their goal, but I am intrigued by their choice to go off-site with their group work—especially considering that earlier in the semester they seemed disinterested in synchronous technologies (I offered to conference with students over the phone, in person, and via instant message. No one took me up on the offer). The synchronous features of instant messaging allowed students to interact in almost real time. This feature stands in stark contrast to the eLearning Suite's asynchronous communication system where comments were often separated by hours and sometimes days.

What was most interesting about this group's work was that they began on the eLearning Suite's message board and then moved to instant messaging. In effect, the group acknowledged Shannon's comment that it is not possible to require everyone to meet on the discussion board at the same time and

then moved past it. These students took in the characteristics of their surround (the CMS does not encourage synchronous communication; everyone
in class is conditioned by asynchronous communication; no one wants to
do too much "extra work") and then acted in responsible ways to that surround. That is, the students acted with an agency that emerges from their
reading of the course requirements, their classmates, their individual desires,
and the parameters of the assignment. I contend that having to work through
an assignment that required them to consider their surround—specifically,
the technological features of the eLearning Suite—prompted this agentive
action. Students only became open to off-site technologies when they took
time to explore the workings of the CMS. Admittedly, students did not pry
open the black boxes surrounding the message board and then hack into
the source code in order to remake the interaction in ways that served their
needs. Such an activity would be intriguing, but ultimately not necessary in
this situation. Instead, students investigated the limits of the default settings
of the CMS and decided that their time could be better used with another
technology. The eLearning suite was not thrown out, but its usefulness was
recast in fairly dramatic ways.

It is worth noting that the decisions this group made resist the conventional wisdom that asynchronous communications appeal to students by allowing them to respond in their own time. This choice suggests that the students
had goals other than (or in addition to) having enough time to formulate a
response. Perhaps they were frustrated by the time it took to compose, revise,
re-read, and post a response to the message board. Perhaps they wanted to
communicate in a space that their instructor could not monitor. Perhaps they
just wanted a more personal interaction. These possibilities speak to the idea
that student agency is not a fixed quality, but an emergent process of meaning making. Given the dynamic characteristics of agency, assignments like
those listed above become important for maintaining a responsive, student-
centered pedagogy.

A second small group from this class engaged in a similarly agentive action without ever leaving the strictures of the discussion board. Like the
first, this group used the message board to schedule a time that all group
members could be online. However, rather than augment their interactions with an additional technology, this group used the asynchronous message board as a way to communicate in near-real time. To orchestrate this

pseudo-synchronous discussion, students all logged in at the same time and began posting messages. On average, replies came within three minutes of the previous post (i.e., Student A posts. Three minutes pass. Student B responds), but several posts merited quicker replies. This approach is not as fast as AOL Instant Messenger; however, it is remarkably faster than the default use of the eLearning Suite's board discussion. Additionally, this pseudo-synchronous approach created a permanent, shared record of the conversation. Students had the option to return to their discussion to re-read what they and their classmates had written. In fact, several students from this group quoted from their discussion in their essays for class, a textual move that nicely linked their essay writing to the goals of the course.

As the first group did, this group seems to have spent some time considering their surround—specifically, the limitations of the message board, the understanding of the course goals, and the parameters of the assignment. This group's choice to use the message boards in an unconventional way reflects the first group's assessment of the limitations of the eLearning Suite, but addresses these limitations quite differently. Given virtually the same conditions, this group developed an innovative manipulation of existing technologies, indicating the range of work possible in FYC courses. While this group did manipulate the software, they remained somewhat removed from the inner workings of the software. They did not, in other words, move completely past the opaque interface to understand the long strings of code that make the message board function. There is an argument to be made for teaching students to engage in the work of manipulating code at the command line level, but there is also a distinct value to bending rather than breaking software. Redesigning the code that controls the message board is beyond the scope of the assignment students were given. Their choice to make modest changes to the software speaks to an awareness of the labor involved in adapting software. It is, in effect, a way of responding to the demands of their surrounding conditions in the responsible ways that Cooper describes in her discussion of agency.

Opening Future Study

In the previous examples, normalized notions of CMS are investigated and modified in order to serve concerns beyond dominant uses. These changes do not dramatically shift the mechanics of these technologies. Students did not reprogram the CMS to include synchronous discussion, nor did they reinvent the conventions of small group meetings. What they did was open these technologies in order to examine the social/material conditions implicated in the default usage. Drawing on their reading of this information as well as their own experience, students made small but meaningful changes to the implementation of these technologies. In doing the work of opening these technologies, students strayed from the opaque surface of the interface and reworked technologies to serve different ends.

I argue that the work these students were encouraged to do with technology should be the work they are encouraged to do with language as well. In an essay exploring language difference, Min-Zhan Lu (2006) contends that English is a "living" language that changes as it is used (p. 607). That is, English is not a set series of rules, but a system that is amenable to change. This change is difficult, however, because institutional structures pressure English users to conform to a certain standard. However, Lu points to an alternative approach, to a "living-English user." As she explains, "Living-English users focus energy on how to tinker with the very standardized usages they are pressured by dominant notions of educational and job opportunities to 'imitate'" (p. 610). I find Lu's use of the word "tinker" striking because (a) it implies that small changes might have meaningful effects on larger standards and (b) it elevates the role of the tinker, the amateur, the *student* in compelling meaningful social change. I see my students' modifications of eLearning Suite as a relative of living-English work. In much the same way, folks who are not dominant users—who are not programmers or system administrators—might have a meaningful impact on how standardized systems work. In other words, the work of the students cited in this chapter echoes the work that they do with language.

This complex relationship between language work and technology work defines (or *should* define) the identity of online FYC courses. Face-to-face FYC courses offer students the time and space to explore the relational, multiple characteristics of writing and reading. Online FYC courses do the same but add technological elements that complicate the experience of exploring writing and reading. I argue that such complications might be used as a way to augment instruction and promote agency.

References

Bartholomae, D. (1982). Writing assignments: Where writing begins. *Fforum*, *4*(1), 35–45. Retrieved from http://comppile.org/archives/fforum/fforum4(1)files/fforum4(1)Bartholomae.pdf

Bishop, W. (2001). Sequenced research writing assignments. In W. Bishop & P. Zemliansky (Eds.), *The subject is research: Processes and practices* (pp. 242–251). Portsmouth, NH: Boynton/Cook.

Cooper, M. (2011). Rhetorical agency as emergent and enacted. *College Composition and Communication, 62*(3), 420–449.

Horner, B. (2000). *Terms of work for composition: A materialist critique.* Albany, NY: State University of New York Press.

Lane, L. (2009). Insidious pedagogy: How course management systems impact teaching. *First Monday, 14*(5). Retrieved from http://firstmonday.org/ojs/index.php/fm/article/view/2530/2303

Lu, M. (2006). Living-English work. *College English, 68*(6), 605–618.

Sommer, N., & Saltz, L. (2004). The novice as expert: Writing the freshman year. *College Composition and Communication, 56*(1), 124–149.

Star, S. (1991). Power, technology, and the phenomenology of conventions: On being allergic to onions. In J. Law (Ed.), *A Sociology of monsters: Essays on power, technology, and domination* (pp. 26–56). New York, NY: Routledge.

Turkle, S. (2011). *Alone together: Why we expect more from technology and less from each other.* New York, NY: Basic Books.

Vie, S. (2008). Digital divide 2.0: "Generation m" and online social networking sites in the composition classroom. *Computers and Composition, 25*(1), 9–23. doi:http://dx.doi.org/10.1016/j.compcom.2007.09.004

Yancey, K. (2004). Made not only in words: Composition in a new key. *College Composition and Communication, 56*(2), 297–328.

PART II

NEGOTIATING
IDENTITY ONLINE

Creating and Reflecting on Professional Identities in Online Business Writing Courses

Patricia Webb Boyd

CONSTRUCTING AND REFLECTING ON PROFESSIONAL identities is not often discussed in Business Writing textbooks. Nor, based on the kind of assignments typically given in Business Writing courses, is it foregrounded in assignments. A hallmark of business writing courses are problem-based assignments that provide a contextual situation in which students are to imagine themselves: *You've been asked by your boss to research social media trends in business and write an informative report. You are the HR manager of a small firm, and you have been tasked with announcing to employees that there will be no raises this year. Your paper sales company has to update its fleet of cars this year, and you are asked to make a recommendation of the type of car the company should invest in and whether the company should lease or buy the cars.* It could be argued that these scenarios do indeed deal with professional identity because students are asked to play a role as a professional in order to complete the writing assignment. However, the identity they are asked to don is typically seen as a mask they put on in order to complete the assignment, not an inherent part of who they see themselves to be. They are students completing an assignment, not professionals engaging in communication practices.

Further, even though problem-based assignments ask them to adopt a certain identity, these assignments do not typically address how to enact the professional identities or how to reflect on the creation of those identities. Students are told to imagine themselves as HR representatives, CEOs, and business managers, but they are not taught how to enact professional identities in various scenarios; instead, even in problem-based learning, the main focus—sometimes the only focus—is still on the communication process (if not genres), not reflecting on what it means to be a professional writer. Yet this sort of reflection not only helps students to learn the material more deeply but also helps them to "persist longer in the face of difficulty" (Eliot

& Turns, 2011, p. 631) in their future professions. Making identity construction an explicit part of the curriculum, then, should be an important goal so we can help our students understand not only what activities they will engage in as professionals, but also how to make sense of those experiences (Ibarra, 2004).

Online class environments can assist with achieving these goals by providing rich spaces for public reflective writing and for trying on professional identities in active and engaged ways. The physical location of face-to-face classes can hinder our efforts to encourage students to actively see themselves as professionals. On-campus classrooms are laid out in ways familiar to students, positioning them clearly as the student and the teacher as the university-authorized expert. Thus, while we may be able to encourage students to theoretically discuss professional identities, the traditional classroom offers few opportunities to practice and test out professional identities to see the kind of response and impact they generate.

With online classes, though, the virtual-ness of the environment can lend itself to students seeing themselves as professionals who are learning, not as students learning about professionals. Online classes are certainly located within the educational system, and students can easily align their experiences of this different environment with their usual expectations. The teacher still assigns and grades the work, sets the course agenda, and decides upon the kind of interactions that will occur—all the things students are used to teachers doing. However, online courses can offer us different possibilities. As Andrews (2002) argues, "online community lacks the physical cues of the face-to-face world. It . . . allows a person to change his or her identity and reduces the face-to-face world influences of norms on individual behaviors" (p. 65). Further, Hoadley and Kilner (2005) show how "technology may be employed to change or distort the social context in which the learner operates to facilitate more or better learning" (p. 36). Because online courses are not located in the physical environment of the university and do not have the cues of a physical classroom, online forums can create a community of professionals who are learning how to successfully negotiate not only professional writing but also professional identities.

To achieve these benefits, though, we must carefully build these online spaces. In this chapter, then, I explore how we can deliberately build online business writing classes to teach students not only the kind of writing they will need in order to be successful in business environments, but also to reflect on the ongoing creation of professional identities, especially during times of transition. Drawing on Petriglieri and Insead's (2010) concept of identity workspaces, I insist that we should make identity production and reflection on that production central parts of our course goals. After laying out the theoretical foundation for my argument, I present and analyze two course assignments that I use in my business writing classes that illustrate how online communities can be important and effective identity workspaces.

Production of Professional Identities: Identity Workspaces Online

It is widely accepted that professional identities are based on "the various meanings attached to oneself by self and others" in professional arenas (Ibarra & Petriglieri, 2010, p. 11). These identities are constructed in relationship to the "social roles and group memberships a person holds (social identities) as well as the personal and character traits they display and others attribute to them, based on their conduct (personal identities)" (Ibarra & Petriglieri, 2010, p. 11). While identity work is important at all times because it helps to sustain "one's sense of personal agency, continuity, and self-esteem" (Petriglieri & Insead, 2010, p. 45), it is particularly important in times of transition—between school and a job, between one position and the next, or between one company and the next. When individuals are required to perform new identities in order to be successful in their new roles, being able to engage in and reflect on identity construction is crucial for an individual's long-term success.

Where do people learn how to successfully create and reflect on the creation of identities? While colleges do not teach students how to engage in identity work, businesses do not seem to be teaching this identity work either. Petriglieri and Insead (2010) argue that for business employees the process of how to successfully do identity work was once taught by corporations, but with the changing climate, employees are no longer learning how to successfully adapt their identities in companies (p. 52). They found that business schools were not teaching these transitional skills either. These schools tend to focus on teaching what to know (i.e., the knowledge and inquiry that is important to the field), not on how to be a professional, insisting that the important practice of "identity work" is not a central part of business school

curriculum. Petriglieri and Insead (2010) contend that if business schools—
and we can extend their argument to other types of departments and units—
were to become identity workspaces and make identity work more explicit,
students could learn the important identity work that will make them successful professionals and, perhaps more importantly, would learn the process
of how professionals become professionals and how they professionalize on
an ongoing basis.

Petriglieri and Insead (2010) argue that for a space to be conducive to identity work—that is, to be an identity workspace—it must provide students with
a "coherent set of reliable social defenses, sentient communities, and vital
rites of passages" (p. 44). *Social defenses* are a set of collective agreements,
familiar habits and practices, and common discourses that provide a sense of
security and, like personal defenses, help individuals and organizations adapt
to change. Because they make the strange familiar, social defenses alleviate
the anxiety associated with new situations. Although social defenses can limit
visions of possibilities for the future, they can also lead individuals to be more
fully invested in their organizations because individuals may draw closer to
them in order to stabilize their identities, thus creating a greater sense of
commitment to the organization. The second aspect of identity workspaces,
sentient communities, is based on a sense of connectedness and belongingness. Sentient communities are fostered not by completing a particular goal-
driven task, but instead by reflecting on the process of completing projects
and receiving support for the affective components of the identity construction associated with those projects. A key part of these communities, then,
is that individuals receive support from others who are in the same position as they navigate the tricky processes of transitioning into new identities
and integrating them into the multi-levels of identities that already exist in
a person's life (Nystrom, 2009). Within these communities, individuals try
out future selves and imagine what it will be like to be in that role, receiving
ongoing feedback and support from their peers. Petriglieri and Insead (2010)
write, "By providing feedback, targets of social comparison, support and en-
couragement, they [sentient communities] facilitate either identity consoli-
dation or identity transitions" (p. 50), both of which are important parts of
professional identity construction. When students feel they belong in these
communities, they are willing to tolerate more anxiety about the unknown
and are open to experimenting more openly with new ideas, thus overcoming

some of the limitations of social defenses while still being able to rely on the safety provided by familiar discourses and practices that social defenses provide. The third aspect of effective identity workspaces is *rites of passage*. As mythic, universal processes, rites of passages emphasize the transition from the familiar to the new. Rites of passage are "spaces in which individuals, with the assistance of elders and peers, can shape and discover who they are—or, better yet, who they are becoming" (Petriglieri & Insead, 2010, p. 48). Instead of just reflecting on or imagining the role of the professional, individuals actually transition into the role of the professional through well-marked, socially accepted tasks and events that serve as evidence of the transition. Rites of passages are enactments of a social system's current mythology (Campbell, 1972), ideologies, and values (Trice & Beyer, 1984). "Through them initiates do not just learn the cultural narratives that sustain the social group they are about to enter; they become part of those narratives" (Petriglieri & Insead, 2010, p. 49). Through rites of passage, individuals become professionals and are recognized as such through their performances. While there is certainly a consolidation/coherence found at this part of the process, this is not the end of the process, since there will always be further adaptations that will be made, future transitions that will need to be made. Thus, it is crucial for individuals to continually reflect on the transitions, even after coherence has been found again. When individuals experience all three of these features—*social defenses, sentient communities,* and *rites of passages*—in their environments, they can effectively negotiate the identity work that helps them actively create and reflect on professional identities (Petriglieri & Insead, 2010). These three features engage students in learning professional activities and in developing social networks (Ibarra, 2004), encouraging students to make sense of their learning rather than only focusing on learning the material.

Online course environments can be identity workspaces like the ones described by Petriglieri and Insead (2010). Online discussion forums can provide students with social defenses that help them "organize their experience coherently in a way that is tolerable and socially legitimized" (Petriglieri & Insead, 2010, p. 47). While online forums provide distance from traditional classrooms, they also contain some familiar ground. Teachers still give the assignments and still grade. Students still respond to familiar kinds of tasks (in some instances) and they engage in similar kinds of critical thinking. Thus, to some extent, the "organizational method" and "work method" (Petriglieri &

Insead, 2010, p. 47), both of which are central parts of social defenses, can be familiar to students in online courses. Yet, online discussion forums can also be places where students try out professional identities and are introduced to new discourses, and they can provide an important challenge to the complete safety provided by social defenses that Petriglieri and Insead (2010) describe. Thus, online forums can have a mix of the safety of social defenses with the possibilities of change that is needed for encouraging students to see themselves as professionals in our classes, rather than just students completing assignments.

Further, online forums can be excellent places to create sentient communities, "professional communities that individuals invest in, relate to, and identify with" (Petriglieri & Insead, 2010, p. 48). Students in business writing courses are not yet full members of the professional communities for which they are writing and exploring identities, yet they can begin imagining themselves as members of the community through writing and communicating with their peers. The online discussion forum can provide them with a liminal space where they can try out these provisional selves (Ibarra, 1999). They can work together in a public space to produce identities and to reflect on the production of and effects of those identities. Because they do so online, they receive useful feedback from many peers and also see multiple people's engagements with identity construction, both of which are important parts of the learning process. As Petriglieri and Insead (2010) point out, "sentient communities provide references for 'social comparisons'" (Festinger, 1954, as cited in Petriglieri & Insead, 2010, pg. 48), which help students put their own practices in context. By being exposed to the multiple ways their peers enact professional moves and by engaging with multiple reflections on why they made these rhetorical moves, students deepen their understanding of not only what professionals produce but also how professionals create their identities through communication.

Online spaces can also help achieve the processes associated with rites of passage. Whereas sentient communities emphasize peers supporting each other affectively, rites of passage focus on students performing professional identities and presenting themselves as fully developed professionals. The three parts of rites of passage are an isolation from the old way of life, an introduction into a liminal, unfamiliar space, and a re-integration into society as a new identity. Online spaces can assist with this process by asking students to construct themselves online as professionals and to engage with their peers as professionals. The lack of physical cues in discussion boards can result in a sort of liminal space where students can experiment with identities. It can temporarily insert individuals into a space where "the normal rules of everyday life are suspended for a concentrated period" (Ibarra & Petriglieri, 2010, p. 15). In the discussion boards, this happens in a community of peers/colleagues. The transition from student to professional is guided by their peers and instructors who are positioned as fellow professionals. Being online is an excellent place for fellow travelers to be consistently available, thus making discussion forums a good place for enacting rites of passage.

In the next section, I outline and analyze two assignments I give students in my online business writing classes. These assignments ask them to write social media documents in which they construct themselves as professionals. I demonstrate how the online environments provide unique opportunities for constructing and reflecting on professional identities. My assignments make the process of identity construction a more central part of our curriculum. They help students not only to become better students but also to persist more successfully in their future careers (Eliot & Turns, 2011, p. 631).

Comparison of Academic Writing/Writers/Identity to Professional Writing/Writers/Identity

Overview of Assignment

This discussion board assignment occurs within the first two weeks of the semester of my upper division business writing courses, which are taken mostly by juniors and seniors from the business college at my university. Students are asked to compare the writing they have done in their other, more traditionally "academic" writing classes (e.g., history or first-year writing courses) to the kind of writing they have done in their business courses, business arenas, or the writing they imagine that professionals in their chosen future professions might do. This assignment not only asks them to compare the kind of writing that is done in terms of generic conventions (e.g., research paper versus business plan), but it also asks them to consider the different audiences writers address and the strategies they must use to most effectively reach those audiences. As the discussion progresses, students begin to discuss the identities associated with the various writing tasks, comparing what it means to write as a student and what it means to write as a business professional.

Social Defenses

This assignment aligns with Petriglieri and Insead's (2010) social defenses because it provides students with a sense of security, encouraging them to participate more actively in the structure of the course because of the familiarity of some of its features. They begin by discussing something they are familiar with—writing they have already done. This type of assignment is particularly useful in a discussion board because making their ideas public allows them to see others' interpretations of the different kinds of writing and the different approaches to writing. Discussion board assignments like these can establish a common language that sets the tone for the class.

The discussion forums provide opportunities for familiar commonalities between the students, but I would add that the discussions could also transcend the conventions associated with the academic "place." This discussion forum assignment reassures students that they have commonalities, and it also provides a chance for them to broaden their experiences by seeing what different interpretations other students have and by asking them to consider the identities associated with the writing genres. While this type of assignment could be done in a face-to-face classroom, completing it online provides a durable record of the conversation and allows students to reflect in more depth on the differences and similarities between the ideas across time since the discussion lasts more than the length of one class period (Rollag, 2010, p. 502).

Sentient Communities

The discussion board assignment allows students to make sense of their previous experiences within a social context, thus providing them not only with access to different opinions but also with the opportunity to receive feedback on their reflections. The discussion board created through the assignment, then, can serve as the sentient communities that Petriglieri and Insead (2010) describe. Students' own perceptions of their previous learning are expanded by their peers' responses to them. Through ongoing interactive engagements with each other's perceptions and experiences, these discussions can create the senses of connectedness and belongingness that are central to sentient communities. Students are also provided with an invaluable opportunity to begin to imagine themselves in new roles by considering what professional writing is and how it requires writers to act in different ways. By discussing online what professional writing is and how it requires different roles and discursive moves, students begin to see multiple approaches to producing professional identities. Finally, by providing descriptions to newcomers to the field about how to become professionals, they are testing out new identities in an environment where they are receiving feedback, thus experimenting with a liminal space that is encouraged in sentient communities where they can imagine themselves as other than what they currently are. Again, these discussions could be had in face-to-face discussions, but online discussions provide a durable record of the initial forays into reflections of identity construction, discussions I have students return to later when they complete portfolio projects at the end of the semester. They are also able to engage with a greater number of peers and are thus exposed to and interact with a greater number of identity possibilities and reflections on those identities.

Personal Brand Assignment

Overview of Assignment

For this assignment, students are asked to create a personal brand statement that they then post in the "Background" section of their LinkedIn page. Before and after creating this statement, they interact with their peers in discussion boards in which they reflect on the process of creating a coherent professional identity for themselves. In the first discussion board, they reflect on the purpose of personal brand statements and experiment with possible ways of presenting themselves; in the second discussion board (held after their personal brand statement has been written), they analyze the effects of their rhetorical choices on creating a particular professional image. In both discussion boards, they receive feedback from multiple peers who, through their ongoing comments and discussion, help them make the transition from "student" to "professional."

For example, in Ryan's first personal branding statement, his "personal mantra," as he called it, was "conquer the grind," which was based on a quote from a high school football coach. Comments from his fellow students suggested that recruiters and future employers would not care about his high school experiences and might, in fact, see a reference to high school (and especially a quote from a coach) as immature. One peer stated that "an inspirational quote from someone else isn't what a personal brand statement is about" (Amanda). After reading the feedback, Ryan revised his personal brand statement to include "I will conquer whatever the day brings to me, no matter what the challenge." In his reflections, he stated, "I kept the 'conquer' part, but took out the quote to sound more professional since students said it was not professional. I really didn't think about how a quote from my coach would be seen as unprofessional." In his description, he transitioned from seeing himself as a student to trying to position himself more professionally, based on the comments from his peers.

Another example comes from Nicole's personal brand statement. Her first one was short: "I am a creative, reliable worker with a passion to lead." Her peers commented that the word "passion" did not seem professional and that her description was too short and generic, writing that it did not give a good sense of how she stood out from others. One student asked, "What do you mean when you say you are 'reliable'? How are you more reliable than others?" In her revisions, Nicole took some of their suggestions, expanding her descriptions and directly addressing their questions about what made her stand out: "I am a strategic, problem-solving person who is dedicated to leading my team to success. I stand out from the rest because I am consistent in my work, and I always strive to be better than the best. I am a creative, reliable worker with a passion to lead." However, she did not change part of her original statement. She reflected: I felt my original statement captured who I am and did sound professional. I would stand behind it and send it out. That's why I didn't change it." Both Ryan's and Nicole's examples show that students used the comments from their peers, their reflections on those comments, and their own work to consider how to professionalize themselves, even though they used the comments in slightly different ways, depending on how they wanted to present themselves.

While the personal brand assignment could be handed in to the teacher or given to one or two peers, presenting it on the LinkedIn page and receiving feedback from multiple peers helps students' transition from students into professionals. Further, the discussion boards encourage them to reflect on the process of creating themselves as professionals and provide them with multiple interpretations of how to create professional identities as well as extensive interactive feedback on their rhetorical moves in their personal brand statements. Reading and reflecting on each other's personal branding statements exposed them to multiple ways of constructing professional selves/identities. The discussion board illustrated students' critical thinking about the way rhetorical moves impacted the professional identity presented. Students' comments on each other's personal branding statements illustrated that they expanded their perspectives on ways to present their own identities in their statements:

> I think your personal brand statement gave a clear picture of who you are. You sound like a hard worker and a strong leader because you emphasize your experience in the military. My own experiences don't compare to yours. I couldn't make myself look like the professional you are. (SARAH)

> The only thing I would say is that you come off a little too strong about being a leader and taking control. You might look at Nancy's statement to see how she talked about leadership values. (RYAN)

> You talk about being a team player well. You don't scream "Leader" or "Follower." You show a clear balance of the two. I think this is so important for a professional. It shows that you take charge but you are also able to take instructions. An important dynamic in a professional workplace. I wish my statement did this better. (SOPHIE)

They position themselves as professionals evaluating the statements and expect the statements to be professional. They acknowledge that there are multiple approaches. These assignments, then, mix features of rites of passage (creating and presenting a professional identity) and sentient communities (reflecting on and receiving feedback on professional identities).

Rites of Passage

This personal branding assignment is a way for students to integrate different spheres of their lives to create a coherent professional identity. This practice is a form of a rite of passage because it helps students transition from the familiar space—that of student—into the new identity—that of a professional. The online space can be created in such a way as to remove it from markers of traditional classrooms as to isolate students from the familiar rules of "student." Asking students to engage with each other as professionals in the discussion boards puts them in the process of rites of passage by isolating them from the known—that is, being students. Then, the discussion boards and the multiple drafts of the personal brand statements provide them with the opportunity to exist in the liminal space that is the second part of the rites of passage. Doing so online means that they have ready access to experts and fellow travelers through their discussion board and through LinkedIn—a hallmark of rites of passage. After experimenting, they then consolidate their experiences into a coherent identity and present it on LinkedIn, thus re-integrating as a new professional who is not just observing or imagining being a professional but is actually acting as a professional. Posting their personal brand statements online helps them become a part of the important move of professional identities into a virtual arena, a rite of passage into the professional Web 2.0 generation (Greenhow et al., 2009).

For example, Grant's original personal branding statement gave specific instances in which he solved complex problems while working with his brother on construction sites. He also told personal stories about school projects he completed that involved using the same kinds of skills and listed academic achievements that were evidence of having those skills. All of these achievements were already listed on his resume. In his original statement, he even chose to include the fact that he played competitive piano and violin. In his reflections on his statement, he wrote that he was trying to overcome the fact that he was so young by emphasizing all he had achieved, but in his final statement, he realized he didn't have to justify his age; he could find the commonality among all of those experiences, draw them together, and use them to present himself as a professional. His second personal branding statement was as follows: "I am strong at solving complex problems, simplifying situations in order to understand how to successfully move forward in them." His revised statement, which he posted on a fledgling LinkedIn page, emphasized outcomes—that is, what he can achieve because he has the skills—rather than just examples of what he did with those skills; thus, it is clear that he condensed those individual experiences into a professional identity.

Further, in Karli's original personal branding statement, she compared herself to brands like Coach and Nike, writing that she thought she should have a catchy phrase like them to make herself *look* professional. She then went on to describe specific work situations she found herself in and what she had done in them, presenting them as one would in a cover letter. However, she did not present herself as a professional, but as a college student who was working at a part-time job. For instance, describing her experience at a part-time retail sales job, she wrote, "I completed all the tasks that my supervisor told me to while I worked my shift." This statement suggests that she completed her job, but did not take any initiative or did not necessarily see herself as a professional in that environment. The more she progressed through the Business Writing class, received feedback from her peers, and wrote documents which encouraged her to position herself as a professional, the more she shifted from seeing herself as just a worker to seeing herself as a professional. Her revised personal brand statement, while still the "catchy" statement she initially thought she should write, positions her as a professional and shows that she has professionalized her image of herself, as a result of interactions with her peers in the online environment (through discussion boards and exposure to LinkedIn samples). She writes: "I am a young professional looking to bring new and innovative business products and strategies into being in order to benefit the company and its customers."

Throughout their own writing, discussions with their peers, reflecting on their work, and revisions of their personal branding statements, students drew on multiple parts of their identities and began to build coherent representations of themselves as professionals. Their condensed statements allowed them to present themselves in more powerful ways that emphasized how their skills produce outcomes that would benefit companies they might be interested in working for, rather than merely presenting a list of experiences they have had. Receiving feedback from their peers and actually posting their work online made students more responsible for their work because they knew their work would be made public to a broader audience than just the teacher.

Sentient Communities

The sentient communities created through the two discussion boards help students better develop as professionals. Throughout these discussion boards that occur later in the semester, students practice being professionals because the forums are set up as conversations between professional colleagues rather than between students. Further, the discussion boards provide individuals with feedback on the effectiveness of their rhetorical moves in both the discussion boards and the personal brand statements. Individuals, thus, reflect on their progress toward joining the community of professionals. The discussion boards are effective identity workspaces for this kind of professionalization because they are removed from the typical classroom environment yet also provide enough familiarity that students feel comfortable enough to experiment and try out new identities. The process of trying out new identities is an affective one, and a key part of sentient communities is for members to share the emotions and feelings about the experiences they are having as they create their identities. The discussion boards encourage individuals to explore the affective domain of identity construction. The personal brand assignment asks students to use pathos to create a professional identity, and then the peer feedback they receive asks students to respond to that pathos. Many of the students included features of pathos in parts of their personal branding statements. The following examples were all the final revisions the students did for the class, so there are no revisions to include, but their peers' comments on the rhetorical effects of the choices would help students as they continued to hone their statements in the future.

In her personal branding statement, Jamie relies more on pathos than she does on logos. She does not present herself as much as a professional as she relies on personality traits, although she does touch on how she acts when working with others, a situation in which she will find herself in many professional settings:

> I am an exceptionally hard worker and am always up for a new challenge. Also, I am enthusiastic by nature, and I take advantage of that when working with others and when trying something new. (JAMIE)

Her peers commented that her post needed to focus more on the outcomes of these personality traits in professional settings in order to show how the type of person she is would benefit the company to which she was applying.

Keegan's personal branding statement created quite a discussion. His statement relies primarily on a pathetic approach, explaining that he depends on his intuition and concern in order to work with customers and businesses to achieve results. Yet, he uses these emotional factors (and even controversial factors, since intuition is not necessarily accepted by some) to convey the outcomes he wants to achieve as a professional, even though he never uses the word "professional." He writes:

> Through my intuition and genuine concern for others, I build long-lasting, fruitful relationships with my team, my business partners, and clients to better myself, them, and the business at hand. I prefer to look for the positives in everything and bring them to the surface. (KEEGAN)

His peers acknowledged that his use of "intuition" and "concern" might be off-putting to some readers, but for the most part they liked it, especially since he then went on to focus on the outcomes of his intuition—to better the situation—which is a goal that business associates could certainly relate to. It took quite a bit of discussion for the class to come to a sort of consensus about the benefits of Keegan's use of intuition and concern, though, because the initial response was somewhat negative, suggesting that his statement was too emotional for a site like LinkedIn or an objective statement on a resume. It was interesting to see how the discussion board posts evolved over time to come to a different conclusion than the group's initial responses to his statement.

Finally, Phil's personal branding statement combines personality traits with his definition of what a professional is. Instead of just stating personality traits, as Jamie did, Phil emphasizes that the personality traits he has are the ones that define what a professional is:

> I consider myself an ambitious professional. I'm sure to treat people with respect and understanding while presenting myself with confident maturity. I don't like to put limits on possibilities and always find a way to get to a return on an investment. (PHIL)

His peers responded positively to his branding statement because of his situating emotional factors (like how he treats people) within a framework of being professional rather than just within being a "good" person. In fact, they labeled his approach much more logos-based than pathos-based, overlooking the pathos that was used because of the ends for which he used the pathos.

Making this kind of peer feedback public aids in building sentient communities along with helping individuals make sense of their rhetorical moves and the effectiveness of their use of pathos in their professional identity construction. It shows them that logos is not the only method of professional identity construction and helps them reflect on the effects of pathos. It also shows that there are multiple ways to effectively incorporate pathos into personal branding statements and multiple interpretations of the effect of those rhetorical moves. Exploring issues like pathos, which inherently connects the professional to the personal, builds a sense of connectedness and belonging among the group, thus encouraging them to be more open to experimenting with and trying out new identities, in effect expanding their repertoire of possibilities (Petriglieri & Insead, 2010). Doing so online is beneficial because individuals can more easily see themselves as professionals rather than students in a nontraditional environment, can have more ongoing interactive engagements with each other, and can have a durable record of their progressive development of identity across time.

Conclusion

Making identity work an explicit part of our curriculum in education can be a useful way to help students learn to professionalize themselves. In my online business writing courses, my assignments ask students to enact professional identities while reflecting on the creation of those identities in order for them to learn not only the material that professionals write but also to learn how professionals create themselves as professionals. This metacognitive reflection provides students with a deeper understanding of their developing identities as professionals (Akyol & Garrison, 2011). Doing this identity work online in identity workspaces like the ones suggested by Petriglieri and Insead (2010) provides students with many benefits, such as giving them time to "formulate and edit their responses" (Rollag, 2010, p. 502) and providing them with "a permanent record of the conversation that can be reviewed by students and faculty" (Rollag, 2010, p. 503). Because they are engaged with multiple perspectives in an online setting, students also "confront alternative perspectives and understandings" (Akyol & Garrison, 2011, p. 185) and renegotiate their perceptions. While some students did not feel that being online encouraged them to feel like professionals—"I don't think being in a classroom versus doing homework online made me feel more professional. It still felt like I had the responsibility of a student to get my homework done, not a professional to get professional work done" (Jayden)—most students felt that the online features of the course encouraged them to explore professionalization in a way that their face-to-face classes did not. Throughout the online class, students give and receive useful feedback about their experimentation with professionalizing themselves, and they are provided with a public arena in which to post their newly developed professional identities. When we use discussion forums and other online spaces to create identity workspaces, we provide students with important arenas to create themselves as professionals and reflect on those roles as professionals, thus teaching them skills they will need now as they transition from students to professionals and in the future when they find themselves transitioning to different roles in their careers.

References

Akyol, Z., & Garrison, D. (2011). Assessing metacognition in an online community. *Internet and Higher Education, 14,* 183–190.

Andrews, D. (2002). Audience-specific online community design. *Communications of the ACM, 45*(4), 64–68.

Campbell, J. (1972). *Myths to live by.* New York, NY: Viking.

Eliot, M., & Turns, J. (2011). Constructing professional portfolios: Sensemaking and professional identity development for engineering undergraduates. *Journal of Engineering Education, 100*(4), 630–654.

Festinger, L. (1954). A theory of social comparison processes. *Human Relations, 7,* 117–140.

Greenhow, C., Robelia, B., & Hughes, J. (2009). Learning, teaching, and scholarship in a digital age. *Educational Researcher, 38*(4), 246–259.

Hoadley, C., & Kilner, P. (2005). Using technology to transform communities of practice into knowledge-building communities. *SIGGROUP Bulletin, 25*(1), 31–40.

Ibarra, H. (2004). *Becoming yourself: Identity, networks, and the dynamics of role transition.* Paper presented at the 2003 Academy of Management Annual Meeting, Seattle, WA.

Ibarra, H. (1999). Provisional selves: Experimenting with image and identity in professional adaptation. *Administrative Science Quarterly, 44*(4), 764–791.

Ibarra, H., & Petriglieri, J. (2010). Identity work and play. *Journal of Organizational Change Management, 23*(1), 10–25.

Nystrom, S. (2009). The dynamics of professional identity formation: Graduates' transitions from higher education to working life. *Vocations and Learning, 2*, 1–18.

Petriglieri, G., & Insead, J. (2010). Identity workspaces: The case of business schools. *Academy of Management Learning & Education, 9*(1), 44–60.

Rollag, K. (2010). Teaching business cases online through discussion boards: Strategies and best practices. *Journal of Management Education, 34*(4), 499–526.

Trice, H. M., & Beyer, J. M. (1984). Studying organizational cultures through rites and ceremonials. *Academy of Management Review, 9*, 653–669.

SIX

Free to Write, Safe to Claim: The Effect of Writing on Dispositional Change for Sociology Students

H. Mark Ellis

IN THE FIELD OF SOCIOLOGY, the challenge for professors is to get students to look at social problems from a more complex, broader perspective than is normally the case. Ideally, at the completion of a course or degree in the social and behavioral sciences, students should be able to demonstrate a change in disposition toward self, others, and their environment. However, teaching students about systems of oppression, social differentiation versus social stratification, power structures, and historical facts and legacies is often met with contempt. Students do not come to our courses as empty containers that we have to pour knowledge into. We have a lot of undoing, redoing, and filling in to do. We have to convince and persuade them to believe and see various truths and other lived realities. They may resist "hearing and seeing" objective data based on their own positions subject to power and privilege. They may not be ready for such messages. They may not like or relate to the message sender, and they may not like the way in which the message is being sent or asked to be explored. In this chapter, I will argue that the online environment may be the best way to deal with the specific challenges that students confront in a sociology class. The chapter will conclude by demonstrating how online classes have the potential for effecting dispositional change in students.

The Pedagogical Goal of Dispositional Change in Sociology

For college students, the totality of the college experience is intended to produce a positive and affirming transformation. Courses of study, residential experiences, campus involvement, and exposure to new people, ideas, skills, and expectations all contribute to what sociologists call "dispositional change." Sociologists have studied such change both from the wider perspective of the college experience and the narrower perspective of specific courses. In sociology courses, for example, students learn analytical concepts that help to deepen their understanding of the world and their place in it. They also learn about the experiences and realities of others, typically people unlike them, with the goal that they might experience some dispositional change to replace unexamined stereotypes. Even if all sociologists do not agree that the manifest goal of teaching sociology is the transformation of student behaviors, ideas, or attitudes, transformation becomes a latent consequence of exposure to new skills, ideas, and people that are intended to provide students with the tools to make well-informed decisions and evaluations of world events. Of course, dispositional change is not limited to sociology. Studies have shown that just being at the university can affect dispositional change. In his longitudinal study on working-class Canadian college students, Lehmann (2014), for example, studied the daily lives of working-class students in a middle-class university, including their encounters and interactions with others. The students reported gaining new knowledge, growing personally, expanding their repertoire of cultural capital, and changing their outlook on life. They developed new attitudes and tastes about a range of issues including food, politics, and their future careers. What we learn is if students remain open-minded, take full advantage of the college experience, and embrace the expectations of intellectual and personal growth in and out of the classroom, dispositional change and positive transformation is possible. Students can become more aware of themselves, others, and the world by the time they complete college.

In their courses, sociologists attempt to effect dispositional change in a more focused and specific way and to measure the success of these courses at achieving this change. In one such course, the Sociology of HIV/AIDS at the University of Alabama, Lichtenstein and DeCoster (2013) demonstrated a reduction in the stigma of HIV/AIDS by the end of the semester. Pre-and post-tests were conducted on student attitudes of people living with HIV/AIDS. Post-tests confirmed that there was a greater tolerance of people living with HIV/AIDS and a greater awareness of HIV stigma and its outcomes.

Though sociologists want students to become better critical thinkers, teaching about racism, sexism, homophobia, classism, ageism, religious and ethnic hatred, social injustice, and systems of oppression is not easy. Even when confronted with "objective" data, a dispositional outcome is hardly guaranteed. Garoutte and Bottitt-Zeher (2011), for example, used budget exercises in introductory level sociology courses to examine if such assignments would have an impact on how students understood social inequality, poverty, and social stratification. While the post-tests did not show dramatic results in change of attitude about structural inequalities, some students did move away from individualist-blame approaches to understanding poverty and considered social systems or system-blame approaches and explanations more by the end of the course. Transformation and dispositional change in attitude at the end of a sociology course thus is not a given. Conceivably, it can take several different courses before students begin to see and understand patterns. Connecting the intellectual dots does not happen overnight. While the real goal of dispositional change is to have students reinterpret social problems in light of social systems and structural problems, some students may suspect that the professor is simply trying to shift the blame for social inequality to all white males. The challenge is to get students to think about why some groups seem to have access and resources to achieve goals in life and others don't. Transformation and dispositional change have to be deliberate goals facilitated by a wide range of pedagogical tools including lecture, reading, writing, discussion, online discussion board writing, journaling, drafting and redrafting of papers, and so on. Even if we can't see an immediate change or dramatic post-test results at the end of a course, we have sown the seeds of social consciousness and hope to see the fruits of our labor at the completion of a degree and or in the actions of awakened, well-informed, and well-educated citizens in the near or distant future. While sociologists have studied dispositional change on college campuses and in face-to-face courses, it has been largely unexamined in online courses.

The Challenge of the Physical Classroom
Versus the Online Classroom

In a face-to-face classroom, a sociology professor frequently confronts a myriad of challenges. The discussion of sensitive social issues and problems, for example, during an in-person class can contribute to personal discomfort and peer pressure. It may threaten the disclosure of personal identities, values, beliefs, and experiences that students or professors may not want to share in public places where they are visibly present. This can disrupt the emotional balance in traditional classroom spaces where participants don't feel safe or comfortable to fully participate and explore the complexity of multi-pronged, difficult social

issues. A person's race, ethnicity, sex, gender, political affiliation, sexual orientation, and the like make the challenge of presenting and discussing sensitive and
controversial topics a challenge for both the students and professor.

Moreover, there is also the issue of "hidden" diversity. Even the most ho-
mogeneous demographic classroom has "hidden" diversity. Diversity can
come in the form of ideological differences, social class, sexual orientation,
sexuality, and so forth. These "invisible" statuses when mapped onto a person's race, sex, gender, and age make presenting and discussing sensitive and
controversial topics a challenge for both the students and the professor. In
order to present and engage in the exploration of these ideas, no party in the
learning environment can be shut down.

At the same time, personalizing or making the course content relevant to
students' lives is essential to the learning environment in a sociology class.
Students must see themselves in the curriculum or the application of what
they are asked to learn in their daily lives or in their future careers. The challenge is to invite personal involvement while still maintaining an environment of respect and safety.

This chapter will argue that writing in an online course environment is a
better medium than speaking face to face for facilitating a change in students'
attitudes around controversial social issues. The online environment allows
the instructor to introduce highly personal issues while still maintaining the
element of safety necessary for constructive engagement. Online writing facilitates this type of exploration without threatening to embarrass students
or shut down participation. The online classroom can be an alternative space
where people's personal experiences and identities can be shared and protected, thus leading to greater exploration of intellectual ideas and to a better
understanding of where people are coming from. As such, the online environment can better facilitate the discussion of controversial material.

Online environments allow the instructor to introduce, shape, monitor,
and direct highly charged personal issues that are of social concern and have
far-reaching societal implications while still maintaining the element of safety
necessary for constructive engagement and participation. Bomberger (2004)
argues that posting private information in online discussion board forums
could contribute to public embarrassment. I, however, would submit that if a
student shares private information in a public way in an online environment
that they have had time to think about disclosure and do not have to face

in-person embarrassment or humiliation where classmates put an immediate face on that student. There are ways for students to post their ideas in online courses without revealing their identities while allowing them to explore sensitive issues that they may not want to disclose or that they are uncomfortable discussing in face-to-face classroom settings. The online classroom can be an alternative space where students' personal experiences, identities, and ideas can be more easily shared and protected, where they are given more time to think through issues than in an in-person class.

However, we have to take into account that online writing can also allow for less inhibition than in face-to-face courses. The question then becomes, what happens to discussion and "presence" when it moves to an online environment? While there is no professor in front of the classroom in an online course, the professor is still present in many ways such as in lecture notes, in responding to chat-room postings, and in posting specific objects of learning available to students such as video clips, web links, and so on. Students and professors are aware of this somewhat invisible and amorphous redefinition of professor and student presence. This presence and its effect on the way that students interact with each other and the instructor must be renegotiated in an online course. The medium for this renegotiation is writing. In online courses writing becomes presence.

In the face-to-face classroom, writing is often used as the gateway to discussion. However, in the online classroom, writing serves multiple purposes. First, it can slow down verbal thinking. Students have the time to think about the question and their responses. An online environment, for example, can give shy students, who are reluctant to speak, a voice and more time to think through complex issues rather than giving a surface-level response. Second, students in an online course can let down their guard when writing and not feel the pressure of being ridiculed or perceived as insensitive. Finally, writing allows students to articulate varying and often opposing points of view as a way to understand their own subject-positions around complex issues.

Writing in academic chat rooms such as discussion boards in the Blackboard course management system, I would argue, engages students in a common dialogue where the exchanges have the potential for positive collective action. These exchanges can achieve a common understanding of issues among participants and allow for thoughtful reflection of opposing viewpoints. On the discussion board, students can re-read, study, examine, and reconsider varying perspectives articulated by their peers who do not always share the same life experiences and value systems. From my observations of discussing "hot-button" topics face to face in a traditional class versus writing in an online course, I have concluded that students are better able to individually and collectively present and discuss issues more comprehensively and openly in online discussion boards and with online group papers to a far greater degree than students in face-to-face courses. This chapter argues that such online discussions are critical to the desired outcome of a shift in attitude and to a better understanding of self and others.

Methods

In order to explore how online writing facilitates dispositional change, I will examine the postings from a sociology course I teach online. I have not named this course. I do not use student names, nor do I describe students in any way that can lead to their identity. For the purpose of this study I have analyzed three students' postings at various points in the semester as they worked their way toward writing a group paper. In the courses that I teach online, students are required to do weekly discussion board activities similar to weekly challenges found on reality television shows such as Top Model, Project Runway, Survivor, Top Chef, and the like. Students are required to post a response to the assignment and to respond to at least one other classmate. They are encouraged to respond to different students each week. Depending on their interest level in a particular topic, students sometimes engage in actual written dialogue with each other. I am not a participant in the weekly discussion board assignments. I, however, provide collective comments after a discussion board assignment is closed. These weekly discussion board assignments help to set the stage for the longer group project by getting students to feel comfortable "talking" with each other.

Online Discussion Board Writing and Its
Role in Dispositional Change

For the longer semester-long group project, I divide each class into two groups. Each group must work together for the semester on a group paper based on a topic that they choose from a list that I provide. Such topics might include

legalization of syringe and needle exchange programs; sex workers as entre-
preneurs; parental responsibility for teenagers' deviant behaviors; condom
dissemination in prisons; and using death row inmates to test drugs. Once
the students select a topic and are put into groups, they are then expected to
contribute to the paper each week. For the rest of the semester, they work on
the paper collaboratively.

The group paper writing process is divided into several stages throughout the semester which include: (a) brainstorming; (b) shaping the research
question; (c) research, analysis, and discussion; (d) drafting and editing; and
(e) reflection and evaluation of final group papers. During the brainstorming phase of the project, students post why they are interested in this area
of research and present possible ideas and research questions. From there,
students enter the "narrowing phase" and begin to think about data and the
research process. At this point students spend time organizing the division of
labor for the group paper.

Once they decide what research they need for the paper, the students go
off on their own and do individual research. Each student must use four to
five scholarly sources to write the individual sections. During the drafting
and editing phase, the group members have to figure out how to present their
individual sections and write in one voice, constructing a single argument. At
the end of the project, students are asked to evaluate what they have learned
by writing a group project together.

Because online courses leave a transcript of students' interactions, they
provide a wealth of material for study—an advantage both for instructors
like me who want to understand how these interchanges affect students' dispositional changes and also for students who might be asked to trace their
own growth. The interactions revealed by these transcripts and the changes
that occur over time for students provide interesting data. Issues of identity
politics and affect emerge in the discussion, and this is where I see the most
transformation in students' disposition.

The Brainstorming Phase: Blame-Based
Response in Initial Student Postings

For the purposes of this chapter, I will analyze one semester-long group paper
discussion board. I will focus my discussion on three different stages during

the drafting of the group paper: brainstorming, research, and evaluation. Using these three stages as guideposts, I will analyze student comments to demonstrate how their disposition changes over time throughout the writing of the group project. For this group project, students chose to write about the issue of legalizing syringe and needle exchange programs for illegal IV drug users to prevent the spread of HIV.

During the initial brainstorming phase of this online group writing process, students candidly express their ideas, interests, and feelings on a topic prior to conducting research. This is the first set of exchanges that they have with one another and myself, the professor in this group paper discussion board. To get started, I ask students to respond to the following question: Why did you choose this topic and what do you find interesting about it? Here is how three students initially responded:

STUDENT #1 (response to my assignment prompt):
What they are basically saying is that by making needles available that will prevent the spread of HIV and other stuff. No new cases and no re-infections. That is ridiculous. . . . How do you think they get the drugs? They hustle or prostitute themselves and snatch purses. They get the drugs any way. A needle alone is not the answer. What's next, the government should supply the drugs? . . . The professor gave a link for the CDC and it's mostly young Black and Latino males that do these drugs. If they are that stupid, oh well. . . . They shouldn't get any of my money to support their habits. We all have a sad story. We shouldn't pay for their stupidness.

STUDENT #2 (response to student #1):
The government would have to regulate the entire process. Do we want that? . . . Did you all understand the needle kit? Is the government keeping Black people high and stressing males wearing condoms to stop Black and Latino males from making Black and Latino babies? Do you think the government really hates Black[s] and Hispanics that much? Maybe in the past, but not now . . . I agree with you that it's a waste of money. Once an addict, always an addict. You can't change Black people and poor ghetto people. . . . You will never solve that problem.

STUDENT #3 (response to student #1):

You know the professor is a participant in this group paper discussion board, right? It's more than just Black and Latino people, it's also those crack ho's. They should be locked up and prevented from having babies. It's female addicts that are wrong. Everyone just sticks into them and all for what, a high? Didn't we talk about sterilization in one of our discussion boards or something? Ho's should not be allowed to have babies and especially nasty ones that shoot drugs. What kind of mother would they be? How could you feel good about yourself bringing a life into the world like that? Your kid would be all jacked up. The drug mothers are the worst. They have too many issues going on.

In this brainstorming stage, students tend to blurt out their feelings and ideas without filtering their comments and speak with candor regardless of who is teaching the course or who their classmates are. For example, while some students in my online courses have taken in-person courses with me before and know me on some levels and know what I look like, others have not. Unless they take the time to look on the department's web page, they might not know that I am an African American male. In addition, many students don't know each other and make assumptions about the person behind a written posting. This is where the issue of (re) constructing and reading presence of self through writing is relevant.

We can also expect students to rant about issues such as race and gender and espouse personal ideologies and utopian ideals about how the world ought to be versus how the world is organized based on empirical evidence. Bomberger (2004) suggests that more conflict can arise in an online course than in a face-to-face course because students are less inhibited to speak. Even when they have had time to think, sometimes their remarks still can still be raw, harsh, and rude. While that definitely is the case, I would argue that students' comments during this phase are most likely their initial beliefs prior to in-depth research of the topic. Their attitude during this phase is "just blurt it out or get it out."

In the example above, student #1 misuses CDC data to make a value judgment that Blacks and Latinos are "stupid" rather than examining the social influences that lead to and maintain drug addiction. To seem impartial, many students will use objective data to support person-blame explanations of systemic problems. As the discussion board exchanges in the group paper continue, I ask students what social conditions may account for drug abuse and failed drug addiction rehabilitation. During the brainstorming phase in the semester, student #1's response is crafted out of anger and resentment that he has to pay to support someone's addiction. The issue of harm reduction and harm prevention is not understood, and his thinking is more emotive than solution-oriented. Needle exchange programs in this context are supposed to prevent new cases of HIV vis-à-vis needle-sharing while managing and monitoring those with HIV to promote better needle-sharing practices among illegal IV drug users. In addition, while this student is aware of how crimes of prostitution and theft relate to purchasing drugs, he is not fully aware of what it means to manage a drug addiction. Last, we see that he is critical of the government and sees potential conflict in promoting such programs. He implies that government prioritization of HIV prevention is more important than preventing drug-related crimes. He doesn't offer an analysis nor does he understand how solving one social problem creates new ones. Writing at this point appears to be more about emoting and expressing personal beliefs and values. As the student demonstrates, thinking, speaking, writing, and emoting are all interconnected processes. In this online context writing becomes thinking, speaking, emoting, and presence.

In response to student #1, student #2 comments on the idea of government conspiracy. When I wrote the assignment for this group, it included ideas and information on government conspiracy, needle exchange kits, and the like. Like student #1, student #2 also questions the role and ability of the government to regulate these proposed needle exchange programs. Student #2 does not seem to buy the theory that the government is involved in a racially motivated conspiracy and suggests that race is no longer a problem or issue for the government. At this point in the semester this student, like student #1, is also using person-blame explanations for this problem when she writes, "once an addict, always an addict." The student goes on to declare that Black, Latino, and poor ghetto people can't be changed rather than asking how social structures might be changed or might be blamed for maintaining the persistence of this problem. In responding to the initial post, student #2 basically agrees with student #1 without questioning any of the implied assumptions of the post.

Student #3 is clearly aware of my presence in this group paper process when he reminds the group that I am a participant. After acknowledging my presence, he nonetheless feels no compulsion to self-censor his comments in light of that fact. Instead, he feels free to blame female drug addicts and cast a gendered judgment on women. When the issue of prostitution is raised as a means to maintain drug addiction, the assumption this student makes is that it is only female drug addicts that prostitute themselves to maintain drug addictions. The student also makes a moral judgment about mothers as prostitutes and drug addicts and goes so far to suggest that females in this context should be sterilized. When we hear the word prostitute, we think "female." When we hear the word prostitution, we think about punishing the prostitute—the female. This student has strong views about regulating the female body. It is clear this student has extreme contempt toward female drug addicts. The student does not comment on the government conspiracy theory of controlling Black and Latino male addicts' reproduction. This choice might suggest that this student prioritizes racialized comments as more offensive to male professors of color than sexist comments.

If I were a female professor for this class, I wonder if this student would have crafted such a response. This student is aware of my presence and avoids under-rotated racialized comments at this point. The student suggests that is it not okay to make comments that might be racially off-putting to an African American male professor, but that it is perfectly fine to blame female drug addicts while never commenting on the moral character of male IV drug users.

These blame-based responses are a necessary part of the process through which students use writing to initiate dispositional change. In this initial brainstorming process, writing takes on some of the qualities of spoken dialogue as students just "blurt" out ideas. However, as the process moves forward, students use writing to reference other sources and facts to support theoretical assertions. They try to streamline their comments and at the same time advance a logical and cogent argument. Once they edit and write in one voice, they understand that what they have been doing, in essence, is writing out a position paper. They have looked at all sides of an issue and have made sense of complex social interconnections.

The Research, Analysis, and Discussion Phase in Online Group Work

After the brainstorming phase, the group must develop an agreed upon research question and trajectory/outline for the paper. The temptation during this stage is for students to divide the work and go off on their own. As they research specific parts of a subject, I require students to make sense of how all the parts fit and to report what they have learned from the literature and from each other. Their exchanges during this phase are more thoughtful and show evidence of critical analysis as they begin to move away from personalized moral judgment. To demonstrate how their thinking transforms during this next stage, I will examine postings of the three students cited above. The following postings are not responses to each other but are summary reflections about what they are learning as they research this topic.

STUDENT #1

I am researching how crimes are connected. No matter the crime, there are underlying causes and root causes. . . . The professor gave the example of the shootings at Columbine High School and asked us to consider a causal chain or flowchart, proximate and distal causes, and micro and macro forces that produced the outcome in Columbine. If I do the same for this case, I have to ask why people even use drugs in the first place? It's not so much that drugs are available, but why do they start using drugs in the first place? When I was looking at the facts from the CDC, I noticed many of these illegal IV drug users are young, poor Black and Latino males. Is this a gender issue, an age issue, a race issue or a poor people issue? . . . I'm finding stuff on gateway drug theory which is about what drugs people first start to use and how some people eventually move from pills, smoking, snorting, drinking and move to needles. I am really interested in this stuff and I read a piece on drug use as a way of escapism. . . . I want to know why these poor young Black and Latino males have a need to escape reality. . . . It's not easy putting this puzzle together.

STUDENT #2

I said I would do research on managing an addiction. Managing an addiction and paying for drugs is hard work. . . . Some users want to break the cycle but are afraid to seek help because they are afraid they will end up in the criminal justice system and go through hell if they can't stay high. That's why these syringe exchange programs won't work. If you have to turn in dirty needles for clean ones, what happens if you get caught with needles that aren't prescribed? The idea of the program is good in terms of managing the spread of HIV infections but it isn't well thought out in terms of breaking addictive cycles.

STUDENT #3

I guess I never thought about the whole prostitution issue when the professor raised it in the assignment. I was like, how is prostitution related to this? I get it. You have to pay to maintain a high. Where do you get the money to do that? What is even more interesting is that since so many of these users are males, I am reading how male users also do prostitution. At first I thought what women is going to go to male drug addict prostitute. . . . Many of these drug users are on the street and don't have one place to sleep. They are dirty and many of these sex acts take place in public places that are nasty. They are meant to be quick man-on-man sex acts. . . . In some cases kids run away from home or something and then they have to prostitute to make it. When they get involved with that they turn to drugs to numb the pain. I was reading how young teen runaways in California will do anything to make it. There is an entire street value of sex out there. What you do and where you do it and for how much. That's easy money and less risky than robbery. . . . If a female user gets pregnant that is even more trouble. I'm interested in female users and how they got into using needles and their street stories. . . . The male stuff is nasty.

During the research, analysis, and discussion phase in an online group paper project, students are engaged in fact finding and in making sense of how issues, ideas, concepts, theories, and lived experiences are interrelated. In the previous responses, we see the students raising more complex questions in a way that was absent from their initial postings. Students come to understand that social problems are not a question of right or wrong. Student #1, for example, is a much more critical thinker at this point as he uses CDC data to question the profile of illegal IV drug users and not blame them. He is examining the role that race, gender, age, and social class might play in one becoming this type of drug user. His inquiry is guided by an interest in what makes these groups of people susceptible to this type of drug use. In his research he has now taken an interest in gateway drug theory and drug use as a means of escaping reality. The question of why young Black and Latino males want to escape reality is a quest for understanding root causes of this problem and how Black and Latino men navigate social systems on a daily basis. What makes life for them so bad or different from other groups that they have a need to escape reality by taking drugs? The post represents a shift in thinking and attitude, from blaming the victim to trying to understand how different groups of people in the same social system experience vastly different realities. When students are asked to find evidence to support an argument, their thinking slows down and their commentary and analysis become more precise, logical, rational, and cogent even if they don't know how to piece these findings together at this point. Their writing becomes a representation of objective reality guided by facts and not emotion.

During this phase, student #2 is now looking at the nuts and bolts of how these syringe exchange programs might work rather than simply asserting that poor Black, Latino, urban illegal IV drug users can't change their ways. This student looks at how these programs are set up to fail these users. I encourage students during this phase to look at drug paraphernalia, possession laws, and mandatory minimum sentencing and what it means to exchange dirty needles for clean ones and get caught as a drug user while doing so. This student is realizing that there are several reasons why drug users won't come forward and participate in these types of needle programs. The student is also grappling with the idea that the true intent of the program is to stop the spread of HIV and not to stop addiction. Students are asked to critique social policies aimed to manage or reduce a social problem and to come up with their own solutions. While this post does not represent an alternate solution, it shows evidence of questioning existing social policies and finding cleavages and contradictions.

Student #3 continues to pursue an interest in prostitution during this research, analysis, and discussion phase of the process. I suggested to this group that they read D. Kelly Weisberg's book, *Children of the Night: A Study of Adolescent Prostitution*. Student #3 read portions of it and was trying to piece together how young people who run away from home turn to the streets and become homeless and how they have to deal with a life of drugs and crimes such as prostitution. This student sees the connection to prostitution in financially maintaining a drug addiction but is more interested in the sex acts, where these acts took place, and the street economy of sexual transactions.

The use of the word "ho" is no longer present in this student's postings, and he realizes that males commit sex acts for money too and do so primarily with other men. The student is not ready or interested in examining male-on-male sex acts to maintain a drug addiction but is interested in how females manage prostitution and maintain a drug addiction. This seemingly homophobic resistance to studying male-on-male sex in this context gives rise to this student's interest in gender sensitivity to female drug addicts. Moreover, this student was open to exploring how runaways, prostitution, and homelessness are all interconnected to managing and preventing HIV infections.

In examining their posts, Students #1, #2, and #3 teach us that objective presence means thinking before you "speak" and in this case before you write. While all three students are still evolving in relation to the subject of the group project, it is clear both from the rhetorical stance and the content of their postings that there is evidence of dispositional change. The "blurts" of the brainstorming phase were an important way for them to enter into a conversation from their own subject positions; however, by the second phase of the process, their writing is more qualified and probing.

The Reflection and Evaluation Phase: The Emergence of Dispositional Change

In the final course discussion board, students explain the grades that they would assign to their own group paper and those of the other groups. I ask students to reflect on a range of issues including what have they learned about society, their topic, the group writing process, and the technology of online learning. Before I report what these three students posted during this final stage, let me summarize the final paper for this group.

The final paper for this group focused on policies to prevent new cases of HIV infection vis-à-vis illegal IV drugs. It was clear to me that the group did extensive research on gateway drug theory and grappled with patterns of addiction. They were able to humanize drug addicts and see them not as "stupid" people or "ho's" with poor decision-making capabilities and corrupt morals. They were able to see how the cyclical characteristics of social systems trap various groups. In this particular case it was clear to me that while the paper was not technically well presented or clearly focused and at times lacked supporting evidence, students did grasp the complexity of social problems. In other words, while the quality of their writing was not as good as I would have liked, the writing process itself did change their attitudes about how they think about people and social problems. Students walked away from this paper knowing what questions need to be addressed and how what seems like a singular social problem impacts on all social institutions. Below are these students' final reflections/evaluations of the group project.

STUDENT #1

I would give this paper a B. We tried to do too much and answer too many questions. It was all interesting and we didn't do a good job editing . . . I got to know some people in class and maybe I will see them in person. I really liked how we each thought and had to contribute to the thinking through of these issues. . . . I never knew about this issue before and I am glad I learned that there are many sides to social problems. . . . I also learned how schools, families, and religion all tie to this problem. . . . The lesson learned is that social problems impact us all.

STUDENT #2

We deserve at least an A-. We put in a lot of work. There is too much writing for this course but it was interesting reading all the posts and how each person in my group thought about these issues. . . . It wasn't just a professor spouting off at us. . . . I also liked when people commented on my work and what they thought I was saying. This forced me to be clear as possible even though I was interested in so many things related to this topic and in criminal justice. . . . I also learned that many crimes are both structural and personal. . . . Our social system keeps many people stuck in poverty and on drugs.

STUDENT #3

I think a B or B+ would be good for us. It was hard editing this paper and putting it together. We did a lot of writing and as we pieced this together, the flow seemed to make sense. It really didn't always read as on paper and seemed more strung together where we were asking our own research question. I think we had way more information that the other group. . . . I don't like group work, but I like hearing how others think. No one could be shy in here we all had to contribute and I liked that. . . . I know that I wouldn't have said half the stuff in here if I were in a regular class or at the library with my group. Online courses require more reading and writing if you want to get heard or make a point. . . . I don't consider myself to be controversial but whenever I speak in class everyone always jumps on me. . . . I like playing devil's advocate. . . . If we had less reading and fewer writing assignments in this course, I would have gotten even more into this group paper.

What we learn in these reflections is that voice is important. Students who may feel shut down or intimidated in in-person classes have an online space where they can be heard through their writing and where they can articulate their voices. While they are aware of the professor's presence through his postings, they also appreciate hearing and learning from their classmates' varying points of view. The fact that discussion boards run on asynchronous time means that students can take time to think about their ideas and how they want to respond. Student #1 demonstrates broader thinking in this phase and sees how social problems impact on all areas of life. Student #2 also sees how social cycles and structures can be underlying causes of the problems that an individual experiences. This student has begun to frame these issues using the language of criminal justice. Like many students, Student #3 reports that there is more reading and writing in online courses, but he liked learning from classmates. This student also felt free to express himself without fear of being shut down. As he comments, "I know that I wouldn't have said half the stuff in here if I were in a regular class or at the library with my group. . . . I don't consider myself to be controversial but whenever I speak in class everyone always jumps on me." Once I remind students of netiquette and a few discussion board ground rules, students still feel free to openly express ideas during the brainstorming phase and in all of the other phases of the group paper writing process as well.

Interestingly, all three students comment on how much they have learned from each other. Student #2 specifically writes: "It wasn't just a professor spouting off at us." In online courses, students have the opportunity to write their way into dispositional change. This is especially important in a sociology class where the course deals with "hot-button" topics. Rather than the instructor dictating what students should be thinking, they come to their conclusions through written dialogue and collaboration. However, this change can only occur if the instructor allows them the space to offer their own initial opinions and the opportunity to work their way to more theoretical and fact-based positions. In this way, the online discussion board highlights student presence in contrast to instructor presence.

In addition to the final discussion board, some students take the time to send me e-mails at the end of the semester. Below are three additional students whose posts were not presented above but add further reflection on the online course experience and on online writing.

STUDENT A

This course was a lot of work. I learned a lot and was glad I worked with other students. I liked hearing how they thought about things. Not everyone thinks alike. Everyone should have to take an online course.

STUDENT B

There was a lot of writing and reading in this course. I never had to write and re-write so much before. It forced me to consider writing in stages. We had to do many drafts and have everyone agree. That is annoying but I think I am a better writer. When do we find out our grades?

STUDENT C

I kept on flip flopping as I was doing the group paper. I didn't know what to think or what my real views were. I had a whole semester to think and rethink and consider things that I never thought about before. Drug addicts have it hard and I think I want to major in Sociology. You just can't blame people for their problems. You really have to look at the whole thing. Are you teaching any more sociology courses? What are some criminal justice types of jobs? Who in the department can advise me?

I usually receive more e-mails after courses end from online students than students who are enrolled in my face-to-face courses. I believe this is the case because I am a group member in the group paper discussion boards throughout the semester as I help to explore ideas with my students. They know I am in there along with them, and they eventually treat me as an equal. As long as we all do the intellectual work together and respect one another's ideas, I believe we all appreciate learning together. I establish a deeper rapport with them because I am not in front of the class at a podium talking at them. I do not think that I would get these e-mails if they did not feel a sense of community and sense of getting to know one another and me. Students will always suck up to professors during that final window of assigning course grades, but I believe some students are truly transformed.

While most of the students liked to hear various points of view from their peers, they were divided about how they felt working in groups. Some liked the group work, but many did not. Their objections centered mainly around how group work affects their personal grades and their personal schedules. On the other hand, many do express that they like to read what others have to say about a given topic. In addition, some mentioned that they feel more confident as writers and as thinkers when leaving the course because they had to write and read so much. Finally, many report that online courses offer the opportunity to think and debate a topic before they have to commit to a final position. The time to think was a decided advantage for students in an online class; they spoke in positive terms about having time to digest and explore material in a different way than in face-to-face classes, where discussion felt rushed, definitive, and final.

When it comes to the success of the final online group paper, their responses and postings suggest a dispositional change in students' beliefs and values. In online courses, I can observe how group and individual writing can evolve throughout the semester. The same is not possible in face-to-face classes because most semester-long group work is done outside of the class in spaces that I am not invited to. I can observe some dispositional change in students in in-person classes by listening to the language they use and in their individual papers. While I could have students in face-to-face classes use online tools to have discussions and write group papers, students have critiqued this pedagogical strategy and report that it is time-consuming and that they did not sign up for an online course.

Finally, in an online course, students do not tend to censor themselves as much as students do in face-to-face classes. Overall, they seem more comfortable expressing their thoughts in this type of environment as the semester progresses and the sense of familiarity increases among participants.

Conclusions: What Have We Learned?

Anonymity, safety, and presence through writing are a part of how dispositional change occurs in online learning environments. It is important for students to feel safe to comment, and anonymity provides this safety. Anonymity might make it more likely for students to rant and to express offensive racial or gender ideas because the presence of the professor is less directive and less authoritarian than in traditional classroom spaces. However, such rants are the linchpin in the process of dispositional change.

Time to reflect is critical in this transformation process as well. In face-to-face classroom discussions, students are asked to participate on the spot and in many cases have not had the time to think through issues carefully. During traditional classroom discussions when we ask a student a question that we have thought about for many years, we expect students to spout out well-crafted responses in seconds. We are disappointed when they provide a one-sentence response. We shouldn't be surprised with short and uninhibited responses in person or online given the fact that we live in a social media and twitter era where brevity and curtness are normative.

Online writing takes on the role of speaking and presence. Writing is dialogue in the group paper discussion board and is not a monologue where students are responding just to the professor. Writing is a way to express thoughts, speech, and emotionality and to exchange ideas among group members. Once students move from the brainstorming phase of group writing, which can include flaming behaviors, social insensitivity, a lack of civility, and other uninhibited utterances, they are tasked to turn those visceral ideas into arguments that they can explore and prove or disprove. Fact-finding, research, analysis, and discussion promote positive exchanges among students where they are expected to make sense of empirical evidence. Students often resist hearing about systems of oppression and social inequality until they are asked to construct and present an argument that may be derived from their own ideological framework. When students discuss objective facts among themselves and have to agree upon a shared central thesis that is supported throughout an entire paper, online writing creates an environment for critical reflection where students can revisit postings of ideas as the paper evolves. The student moves from resistant, emotive, and subjective to critical and objective.

College students should graduate with critical thinking skills, people skills, and technical skills. Those skills should be acquired through traditional face-to-face classroom encounters, taking online courses, working in groups, and service learning. Social sciences and sociology in particular are not in the business of moral engineering with the mission of producing extreme leftists. Behavioral sciences have two primary disciplinary burdens, which include: (a) the descriptive and (b) the explanatory. We must first observe what people do by way of data collection and then we must analyze and explain why they do what they do. Our discussions are framed within theoretical paradigms that in the end will suggest ways to understand observations that we render as questions or problems. We ask students to become strangers in the world in which they live and to understand realities outside of their daily existence while they are in our classes. This type of journeywork requires them to step back and re-think what they know to be true. Reflection through writing and discussion is key in advancing this mission.

Online courses can engage in high stakes learning activities where sensitive and effusive subject matters can be explored with more reflection and thought than in face-to-face courses. When questions are posted in discussion board activities and assignments, students have time to research how they want to answer or speak to potentially volatile social issues. They don't feel put on the spot as they do when called on in class to participate in these types of discussion. The African American professor is not in front of them when they are "speaking" or writing about issues of race. Their classmates are not looking at them. There is no dry mouth. Their shyness seems to dissipate. They usually feel more at ease to bring more of their personality and life experiences to the class when they write online. The boundaries to "speak"/voice/articulate a point of view are removed. They share examples that may be telling of their political affiliations, their religion, their social class, and their beliefs on many social issues.

Some will argue that "ranting" about racism, sexism, heterosexism, and the like is more likely in online learning environments than in face-to-face classes. Students must examine their own ideological positions while directly or indirectly asserting their own identity politics. If they "blurt" ideas out in discussion boards that are racist and sexist, it is a starting point. As instructors we can work sentence by sentence and idea by idea to help them learn how to support and defend their positions. My personal mission is for students to see complexities in what they think are singular simple social issues. I take them on a journey in my courses and I want to bring them to a different place once they leave. They may walk in thinking that all Black people are "stupid" and deserving of their plight because of bad decision-making. When they look at entire social systems, they understand much better the way that social systems are determining factors in people's lives.

I need help in doing this. This is why I have a group paper in my online courses. I am one voice, students are another, and the texts another, and we all try to make sense of it. When students feel that their voices matter and that their experiences and ideas contribute to the learning environment, they engage with the subject material and are more apt to participate freely in the discussion. There is no podium in online courses. There is no professor-centered physical or symbolic space at the front of the class for students to gravitate toward. When they do group work in online courses and the professor is a part of the group, there is a sense of equality and shared responsibility. Students often ask if it is okay to present their opinions and speak from the "I." I tell them that an opinion is an informed argument or a point of view that presents evidence. There are informed and uninformed opinions. In online courses, my role as professor is less intrusive than in face-to-face classes.

Some online courses do not require group work or much interaction among students. In those types of online courses, it is like 20 independent students with one professor. The professor can examine how a student's attitudes can change over the semester based on lecture notes, the readings, films, and so on, but not based on interactions with other students. It is this interaction with other students that can have a profound impact on how they see their own positions in the world and how they see the positions of others. It is great to have students work as a team to craft an argument and collectively support and defend it. In so doing, their beliefs and values are challenged, sometimes re-affirmed, and many times transformed. Social science explanations may not always produce two plus two equals four, but our final explanations and explorations should at least be narrowed from a range of immutable and reasoned empirical realities. Students must examine their own ideological positions while directly or indirectly asserting their own identity politics.

References

Bomberger, A. M. (2004). Ranting about race: Crushed eggshells in computer-mediated communication. *Computers and Composition, 21,* 197–216.

Garoutte, L., & Bobbitt-Zeher, D. (2011). Changing students' perceptions of inequality? Combining traditional methods and a budget exercise to facilitate a sociological perspective. *Teaching Sociology, 39*(3), 227–243.

Lehmann, W. (2014). Habitus transformation and hidden injuries: Successful working-class university students. *Sociology of Education, 87*(1), 1–15.

Lichtenstein, B., & DeCoster, J. (2013). Lessons on stigma: Teaching about HIV/AIDS. *Teaching Sociology, 42*(2), 140–150.

SEVEN

Facework: Negotiating Identity Through Writing in Online Class Discussions

Linda Di Desidero

Introduction

Facilitating the understanding of discipline-based knowledge is one of the primary tasks of the online professor. By creating and managing discussions effectively, the professor can also facilitate students' development of identities—personal identity, academic identity, and professional identity—that both undergird and stimulate knowledge creation. In my experience, processes of identity development and display become powerful aspects of student learning. As students write on the online discussion board, they construct themselves as members of that academic community, they enact identities in the discipline, and they come to view their learning as something that falls increasingly within their own control. This chapter examines aspects of identity negotiation on the discussion board as they relate to learning.

In processes associated with the creation, display, and enactment of identity, one of the most significant resources that people use is known as *face*. *Face* is typically characterized as the public self-image that individuals assert for themselves. In any social situation, we display only certain aspects of our self-image; this may be understood as our face in that particular context. Most readers will be familiar with the concept of *saving face*, or the set of behaviors that allow an individual to retain honor and dignity in a potentially embarrassing situation. While this is a common use of the concept, there is much more to the idea of face than simply avoiding embarrassment. Face is a resource that individuals use to display identity and to respond to the identities of others; it is a consideration in all human interaction.

In communication contexts, individuals employ a set of communication behaviors and strategies designed to enact, enhance, save, or harm face (an individual's own face or the faces of others). These discourse strategies are collectively known as *facework*, and they are used broadly in research to help us understand aspects of interpersonal communication (in disciplines of sociology, anthropology, linguistics, and communication studies). Traditionally, studies of facework analyze real-time face-to-face interactions in which individuals communicate with one another. While people present face and conduct facework through many different channels and signs in interpersonal relationships, in the online classroom the primary medium in which face is presented, established, honored, affirmed, or affronted is writing. This chapter examines the facework strategies that students employ in an online course as they construct a range of personal and academic identities.

In creating their online personal identities through the use of facework strategies, students establish a "presence." In a face-to-face course, facework is less important because the teacher is in charge, and the students are not obliged to participate and interact with everyone in the class. As a consequence, less is at stake individually for a student than it is in an online class. However, in an online class where everyone participates and must interact with each other, the dynamics between and among students necessarily change. Students must establish their own identity in relation to others in the class before they can move onto enacting a more scholarly or professional demeanor. To establish these personal identities, students use facework strategies.

Teachers and scholars may not be aware of the complex identity negotiation that occurs when students interact on the online discussion board. In the online classroom, writing is the student's primary channel through which to interact not only with the professor, but also with each other. Student-to-student interaction is just as important as professor-to-student interaction because students achieve academic success not merely by acquiring knowledge but by forging and negotiating disciplinary identities. In online classes, writing serves as the medium for the process of identity negotiation; this process occurs to a modest extent when students submit writing to the instructor, but it occurs to a greater extent when students interact with each other.

In this chapter, I analyze discussion board interaction in my Senior Seminar in Communication Studies—a capstone, discipline-based writing course—to examine the processes through which such identity construction occurs. Over the course of the semester, students enact and display identity in three distinct stages: personal, academic, and scholar-professional. As students progress through these stages, they employ a range of facework strategies that allow them to establish presence, build alliances, take risks, and claim authority. After displaying initial personal identities, students use the discourse strategies associated with facework to align themselves with others and to initiate relationships with their classmates. On the strength of these relationships, students use different strategies to identify themselves with communities—first as communication studies majors and then as researchers in the discipline. Because this process takes place in writing, online courses afford both students and teachers a unique opportunity to analyze students' rhetorical moves and to understand the relationship between writing, identity construction, and disciplinary knowledge.

Background Assumptions/ Framework: Face and Facework Strategies

Face may be broadly viewed as the way in which we display ourselves to others in a given situation. It is a public self-image, our "sense of favorable social self-worth" (Ting-Toomey & Kurogi, 1998, p. 188); it is the view of ourselves that we present to others and that we and they act upon in specific contexts (See Brown & Levinson, 1987; Domenici & Littlejohn, 2006; Goffman, 1959; Scollon et al., 2012; Ting-Toomey 2004). Face is mutable, fluid, and variable. Because of the consistently tenuous and variable nature of face in human interaction—that is, because face is always "under construction" and may be readily enhanced or diminished—attention and care must constantly be directed toward the manner and meaning of interactions associated with face as a display of identity.

In all forms of interaction, individuals employ specific communication strategies that may be understood as facework. Individuals conduct facework that presents or displays themselves to both specific and generalized others in typically positive ways with respect to the way in which they want to be seen or with respect to the aspect of identity that they wish to display. Individuals also conduct facework that responds to the facework strategies of others, supporting (or threatening) positive views of the self. In given situations, face accrues and evolves as community members enhance concepts of individual and collective face over time.

With the ideas of Erving Goffman (1959, 1967, 1979) and H. P. Grice (1975) as points of departure, scholars such as Brown and Levinson (1987) attempt to delineate the universal principles that undergird exchanges in human interaction and that explain both cooperation and conflict—in other words, the ways in which facework strategies are used to create meaning in discourse. Intercultural and conflict scholars such as Stella Ting-Toomey (2004), Domenici and Littlejohn (2006), and Scollon, Scollon, and Jones (2012) explore the ways in which we can examine and evaluate facework strategies in given situations in order to understand the causes and possible resolutions of conflict. Facework scholars recognize the links between culture, identity, and discourse strategies.

In an online classroom group—typically in response to the professor's discussion prompts—students conduct facework to establish, honor, and affirm the positive values of both individual face as well as group faces (including groups of senior communication studies majors, military members, racial/ethnic/gender group members, etc.). People use facework to enhance their own faces and to protect their faces from potential or anticipated attacks. They also respond to the facework of other individuals with supportive or non-supportive facework strategies. Opportunities to conduct facework in an online classroom are largely established by the ways in which the professor sets up the class discussions: When students are encouraged to talk directly about themselves and about their learning in the discussions, they can readily engage in processes of identity formation using tools and strategies associated with facework.

Specific facework strategies in interaction might include the following (adapted largely from Brown & Levinson, 1987, and Ting-Toomey, 2004):

- Expressing solidarity by actions such as claiming common ground. This honors the face needs of the subject by viewing these needs as desirable or shared; helps to build community
- Expressing respect or regard for the other individual with mode of address or flattery, etc.
- Expressing restraint by hedging or apologizing or using additional forms of politeness that acknowledge the other's need for autonomy
- Avoiding confrontation with off-record or indirect facework, such as using irony, understatement, overstatement, metaphor, rhetorical questions, etc.
- Inviting challenge or provoking confrontation by bald insult or direct threat to an individual

In face-to-face interaction, any of these strategies could be implemented non-verbally, with facial gesture or physical movement, for example. In the online classroom, these strategies are enacted through writing.

Use of such facework strategies is culture-dependent; that is, members of some cultural groups are more likely to employ specific strategies more successfully than others. In fact, critical language theorists (see Fairclough, 2001; Fowler et al., 1979; Gee, 2001, among others) would argue that the array of facework strategies that are available or acceptable in a given situation would depend on an individual speaker's status in the context. In the online classroom, the array of facework strategies available to the professor and to class leaders would be different from the array available to struggling or under-prepared students, for example. Given the gendered behavior expectations of a society or a group (see Maltz & Borker, 1982; Mullany, 2010, and others), we would also expect to see differing arrays of facework strategies available to masculine members and to feminine members. However, because identity display is not physical in the online environment and because it must be established largely through written interaction, we might expect some of these facework expectations to be mitigated or weakened online.

All communication presents potential risks or threats to face. Individuals typically draw on one of two types of culture-driven discourse strategies to address these threats: solidarity strategies and deference strategies. Individuals can express solidarity in conversations by claiming common ground and by expressing agreement with the speaker. Individuals can express deference by hedging or apologizing, by flattering, and by using honorifics (or formal titles of address such as "Dr." or "Professor"). Within all interaction, individuals manage face threat while negotiating identity using solidarity or deference strategies.

In order to accept an examination of facework in written online classroom discourse, we need to be able to view writing as essentially dialogic in nature. The general idea is that writers write for specific readers—who are also constructed through the text and about whom much is known. When this writing occurs in interaction, the relationship between writers and readers evolves over time as each attends to the other's face needs. And when this interaction occurs in a classroom context, it can become a powerful aspect of learning.

Research Goal, Method, Expectations

The research on face and facework has typically been used to describe, explain, and predict aspects of live, face-to-face interaction. Identity development and display, however, is part of all interaction, including online interaction. I investigate the ways in which these concepts are completely relevant to discussion board writing, as discussion board "talk" becomes a kind of speech communication for students in an online class.

This study comprises a qualitative analysis of interaction on the discussion board in an online communication studies classroom. I examine the ways in which students interact, particularly with respect to the facework strategies that they use to enact identity, build connections, and display agency over their learning. I also examine the process of identity development as it relates to learning, occurring in essentially three overlapping themes or phases throughout the semester: Personal Identity, Academic Identity, and Scholar-Professional Identity. In the analysis of the data, I attempt to show how individuals' use of facework is strongly connected to learning as it patterns over time in these identity themes.

The data here represent the discussion postings of students and professor in an online communication class, COMM 495 Senior Seminar in Communication Studies. It is a writing-intensive capstone class, typically the final class that students take before graduation. All students in the class share the group identity of communication studies majors who are or who expect to become professionals in the field. Students in the data sample are adult, non-traditional students ranging in age from 24 to 59, with 30 years being the average age. The class is diverse: One-third of the students in the class are active members of the military stationed around the world; one-third of the students are full-time students; and one-third identify as members of ethnic/racial minorities. The class is conducted fully online in a standard online learning management system. All students are adept in the online classroom environment, as is the professor.

The course requires two lengthy writing projects: (a) a curricular portfolio containing selected works from the student's completed communication studies courses accompanied by a long essay that introduces the pieces and analyzes the insights and value represented by each piece; and (b) a staged professional/academic research project in each student's area of specialization (speech communication, media studies, professional writing, journalism) with a number of sequenced deliverables due throughout the semester (proposal memo, annotated bibliography, progress report, summary report, presentation, first draft, and final draft). Content and analysis for each of these tasks is explored and developed at length in the online classroom's discussion board area.

The class is structured over eight weeks of discussions with several discussion topics in each week. In a typical week, students are asked to post substantial content-based responses to several different discussion prompts by Saturday, and then they are asked to respond to a minimum of two other students in each topic by Monday, thus engaging in online talk about content and process.

The discussion topics might be viewed as occurring in three sequential stages, each of which allows students to display and develop their identities with increasing complexity and depth through their interaction with others.

- *Personal Identity*: In the initial "Meet Your Colleagues" discussion, students have the first opportunity to choose which aspects of themselves to reveal to others and how they will connect with identity displays of other students. Exchanges in this discussion can be involved and lengthy, as these are senior students in the last course of their curriculum. The initial discussion allows students to display personal identities, which might reflect their roles as students, as family members, as writers, as group members (gender, race, ethnicity, military, etc.), and as professionals. Through this initial discussion, students build their personal connections within the online community. In this stage, students rely heavily on deferential facework as they seek to form alliances with each other that will be necessary for classroom collaboration.
- *Academic Identity*: Following this initial discussion, students interact with each other as they present and analyze pieces of their student portfolios. What is revealed in these discussions is personal—as students are talking about their own significant experiences in the discipline—but it is also discipline-based. The portfolio discussions allow students to examine and display the ways in which they have connected with communication studies in their time as students, and to speculate

on the ways in which their studies have contributed to their personal development as they look to move forward professionally. In this stage, students' facework often becomes less deferential and more direct. They move beyond their identification with each other and begin to identify with the academic community. As students feel more secure in their interpersonal connections, they feel free to take greater risks.

- *Scholar-Professional Identity*: The final and longest set of discussions allows students to interact with each other about their research projects. Discussion prompts are designed to facilitate knowledge and learning in student research areas, as students are asked to clarify ideas, share research, analyze data, evaluate significance, and explain findings to each other on the discussion board. This period of the course includes peer review and presentation activities, both of which are conducted on the discussion board. Having begun to build personal and academic relationships with each other, they respond to each other's research with probing questions and new ideas. As students become more confident in their scholar-professional identities, they begin to position themselves in relation to their material and to claim greater authority and agency over their work. They conduct facework in their interactions with each other that helps foster and support this authority.

Over the course of the semester, students engage in processes that allow them to first display personal identities and develop personal connections, which then contribute to the ability to create new knowledge as they build discipline-based identities and, ultimately, scholar-professional identities on the discussion board. These processes can be effectively set up and facilitated by the professor, as my findings indicate.

In the rest of this chapter, I present and analyze data from three students—Samantha, Carol, and Tony—as they conduct facework to enact identity, develop relationships, and cultivate agency and control over their work in the online classroom. This analysis demonstrates how students use different facework strategies in order to achieve success. Samantha and Carol form a close personal alliance as they move through the different phases of identity construction and claim authority over their own academic work. Tony's strategy is to build close relationships with many students as he presents himself modestly as a leader among them.

Samantha and Carol: Forging Identity Through Alliance

From the beginning of the class, students used facework to enact personal identities that eventually led to building alliances. In this first example, Samantha and Carol used collegial and supportive facework to build a strong working relationship with each other. This began as they displayed personal identities, and it continued as they responded to each other with enactments of their academic identities.

Personal Identity

In their first public discussion forum, many students—men and women alike—introduced themselves modestly, making themselves approachable to the whole class. For example, Samantha, a military spouse in her 30s, was one of the brightest and most accomplished students. Her facework strategies, however, allowed her to build her identity modestly—without boasting, for example, which might have created face-threat to others. Samantha introduces herself by writing, "I lived in the same small town in Michigan my entire life. I thought I had life all figured out. Then we moved to Europe . . . I realized that I didn't know too much about anything!"

Samantha's introduction displays a rather complex rhetorical move. She begins by employing deferential facework in describing her small-town background. At the same time, we also learn that she has lived in Europe, which suggests a certain worldly knowledge or sophistication. Her contributions to discussions frequently refer to her past naiveté and her subsequent enlightenment. Presenting herself as an individual who knew less about everything at one point and who had so much to learn displays a sympathetic and likable identity for Samantha early in the course. Such deferential facework allowed her the space to be more critical to her peers later on. Her response thus demonstrates a skillful combination of deferential facework with a nonthreatening claim for authority, two moves which are key to students' later success in the class.

Another important strategy at this early, personal stage of the course concerns community building. This strategy is an important component of Carol's facework. Unlike Samantha, Carol is slow to disclose much personal information in posts addressed to the entire class. While her introduction is twice as long as Samantha's, Carol reveals only one piece of personal information, and rather indirectly at that. She writes, "I completed my A.A. degree in 1979, so you can do the math and know I am no youngster!" In this post, Carol clearly wants her audience to know that she has a degree, but she modestly undercuts her own academic achievement by referring to her age and to the fact that she earned the degree a long time ago.

As she responds directly to the introductions of several students in the class (even though she is required to respond to only two), Carol reveals quite a lot about herself on this more intimate level of communication. She writes to one student:

> Welcome . . . I am a Marylander also. . . . It's been 2–3 courses a semester including summers for the past two years, and I am ready for a break. I have two daughters, both working on . . . degrees. . . . At my age, I'm enjoying the academic journey and don't want to just "push" through classes to get finished, I want to make sure I walk away with something from every class. . . . What are your thoughts?

Carol aligns herself with the other student here—as a Marylander and a part-time adult student—and they begin to construct themselves as working parents whose children also attend college. She lets others know that she's a committed student pursuing a degree when she talks about how many courses she has taken over the past two years, including summers. But she also admits how tiring that can be when she writes, "I am ready for a break." This last comment lets her audience know that even though she's clearly worked hard, she's not superhuman and thus needs "a break." Her facework shows that Carol can effectively balance the information that she puts out to her audience. At the same time, she's eager to portray herself as a serious student who "want[s] to walk away with something from every class." Aware that she's talking to an audience, Carol ends this post with the question, "What are your thoughts?" Ending with a question demonstrates that she's not just interested in presenting herself, but in listening to what others have to say—a strategy that helps to build alliances with others in the class.

In addition to using facework to signal identity, students used it to build (sometimes selective) personal connections with others on the discussion board. For example, in her response in this first discussion thread, Carol honors Samantha's face, admiring her travel experiences and commending her parenting:

> Samantha—I am really envious! I've never been outside of the United States. . . . It must be challenging to do your own school work as well as homeschooling your three children . . . you must juggle your priorities very well! . . . You, Sherry and I are all on our last class before we graduate . . . a wonderful thing after all our hard work.

While Carol's response to Samantha underscores their differences on the one hand, she nonetheless finds their one shared commonality to focus on—that they are taking their last class together—and she personalizes this commonality by remarking on their mutual attention to "hard work" to accomplish the goal of graduating. Through her facework, Carol builds an alliance with Samantha despite their differences. Such a strategy is especially important in this senior capstone class as students have only eight weeks to get to know one another. In this distance-learning program—where students will probably never meet each other in person because they hail from all over the world—the urgency to build alliances quickly is more pronounced. In that sense, facework takes on a heightened significance in making connections with others.

In subsequent stages of identity construction, Samantha and Carol continue to support each other in their research discussions, thus solidifying their identities as writers and as scholar/professionals. This relationship evolves throughout the course and reflects the changing nature of their facework. As they comment on each other's research, they use complimentary facework that is deferential, funny, sincere, and interested. Their facework strategies become more direct over time, which seems to help each of them work through their research and gain control over their ideas.

Academic Identity

In the initial stage of the course, students used facework that allowed them to reveal identity and establish online presence while building connections with classmates. Having done this, they now begin to enhance their personal identities by incorporating a more academic face. Here, the focus of their connections shifts toward identifying with the larger community of students and with the field of communication studies. Having begun to forge personal alliances, they now refocus their facework in order to accomplish academic tasks.

The following post by Samantha illustrates this bridge between personal and academic identities. As she begins to display her academic identity, Samantha discloses information about ways in which her academic work helped her personal growth. She writes:

> I am a much different person today than I was when I began my studies. . . . I grew up in a small town. I lived in the same house my entire life. I knew how to live in that atmosphere. It was only when I moved overseas that I realized that there is so much more to communication than I knew. Since that time, I have taken linguistics courses, intercultural courses, gender and communication courses and multiple writing courses geared for different audiences. I have learned that communication is a much more complex thing that [sic] I had once thought.

While she continues to employ the same deferential facework that she initiated earlier in the course, Samantha also begins to identify herself not only personally, as a small-town girl who has grown up and traveled, but also academically, as a student. She thus supplements the old portrait of herself with a new one by rehearsing her extensive academic background in the discipline when she lists all of the courses she has taken.

In the next discussion topic designed to develop and further reveal academic identities, Samantha writes:

> One common thread that I found as I looked over my previous assignments was that of learning about and understanding my audience . . . as a communicator, the message we present can impact an audience for years to come. . . . As communicators, it is our responsibility to reach the entire audience, not just those that fit into stereotypical roles.

Note that Samantha turns her personal insights about her academic identity into a responsibility for the group. She invokes the face of all communication studies majors when she writes of "our responsibility" to understand audience. Samantha thus begins to build the identity of the group and to align herself within it.

Carol responds to Samantha's post with a more direct question about writing. In this response, Carol assumes her modest face by claiming that she does not want her specialized knowledge to make her appear to be conceited:

> I did not have the opportunity to take the intercultural communication course but I will say that several of my business courses brought the importance of cultural differences to the forefront. I feel when I started this degree, I felt a bit tentative about writing for different audiences, but now I feel I do a more than adequate job (I don't want to sound to conceited here . . . lol). How would you compare your writing skill now with when you first started?

Samantha and Carol then have an extended conversation in which they agree about the practical value of a communication studies degree, about their mutual interests in business and communication, about the role of audience in communication, and about the importance of good writing to any job. Samantha aligns herself strongly with Carol as adult students with workplace experience, which give them, in Samantha's words, "so much more to offer the class by way of examples and real-world scenarios." While this is a private conversation, it is public as well in the sense that it is accessible to all students–who read the discussion postings. As such, Samantha and Carol's work in displaying the face of communication studies majors has value for the group.

In the earlier stage of personal identity enactment, students mixed deferential facework with claims of authority. We can still observe this strategy in the academic stage; however, here the type of authority that is claimed shifts to academic work. For Samantha and Carol, this strategy plays out in a discussion of themselves as writers.

Students are asked explicitly to introduce themselves as writers in one of the early prompts as they display aspects of their academic identities. Like Samantha, Carol was one of the strongest writers in the class. Carol's statements about her writing skills are at first modest, and thus nonthreatening. While she is confident about her abilities, she qualifies her confidence by reflecting a sentiment common to other class members: There is always room for improvement. She writes, "Although it wasn't intentional, many of my communication classes have focused on writing. I feel my strength lies in my written communication skills, although I know improving in this area is an ongoing journey." Through her involvement-based facework moves, Carol avoids seeming superior to her colleagues, even though she was clearly confident in her abilities. Thus, she works to become involved as a member of the class.

But Carol also finds a way to indirectly state that she is a good writer: She invokes autonomy-based facework when she displays external evidence of her writing ability. She does not have to directly state that she is a good writer because she can report on the actions of others that testify to that point. She writes, "I work with many faculty who are not originally from this country and they often seek me out to edit and proofread their memos, reports, etc." As modest as she might be about her own writing, university faculty seek her out for her skills. She mitigates the potentially negative impact of this statement again with a comment about the idea of improvement: "I take this responsibility very seriously, so I strive to constantly improve in this area."

Carol's claim to authority based on her writing skills is important here as both students create their respective academic identities. In the next stage of identity negotiation, Samantha and Carol will build on these claims to establish scholar-professional identities that will prove important to their research projects.

Scholar-Professional Identity

In their moves toward creating more scholarly-professional identities, Samantha and Carol continue to build on their earlier interactions. They used facework strategies to construct a strong working relationship that supported them in their research and that solidified their identities as writers and as professionals. This relationship evolved during the semester and is reflected in the changing nature of the facework, which became more direct and less deferential as time went on.

As the two of them discuss Carol's research, Samantha responds to Carol, "This sounds like a great program. . . . Do you find from your research that this is proving to be successful?" In this response, Samantha identifies Carol as a researcher, comments on Carol's research, and asks her a comprehensive question about the value of a particular program, thus casting Carol in the role of expert on this topic. Carol responds by summarizing findings, sharing her personal opinion, and then asking Samantha her opinion:

> Samantha—The article that I came across . . . addresses the issue about technology causing anxiety for its elderly user. . . . Their take on this benefit is that if the patient is happier, more content, they have less [*sic*] health problems. . . . I for one, however, believe that a person's overall outlook can affect their ability to fight disease and affect their overall well-being. Do you believe this?

Not only is Carol taking control of her research information, she is also extending the ideas from this research article by seeking Samantha's opinion about the relationship between attitude and health.

As they each proceed with their research, their facework becomes less obviously deferential—with fewer politeness strategies and obvious expressions of deference—and more direct interest and bald questions about the research itself. Thus, the discussions have helped these two women build a friendship in the classroom that provides both students with interest in each other's work as well as collegial responses, questions, and comments about the quality of the work. Their facework helps them to support each other in strengthening their identities as professionals and as scholars. And these identities, in turn, help them each create new knowledge for themselves.

Interestingly, as Carol became more confident with her research, she also displayed a greater degree of control over her own ideas and material. There were two junctures in Carol's research and writing processes where she directly disagreed with me, the classroom authority. In the first instance, Carol stated her preference for using only very recent sources, ones that were no older than three years. For the sake of discussion, I asked her if there were possibly older sources for certain ideas that should be cited. Her reply was a grudging acquiescence, followed by her insistence, "I feel it's best to use current sources."

In an interesting face move that surprised me, Carol receives support from Samantha, who injects herself into this discussion. Samantha's comment below constitutes direct support for Carol's position in this minor disagreement, though it might be interpreted as a mild face affront to the professor:

Choosing to include only recent research is a wise choice. I am sure you could complete two different papers using research from past and present, especially relating to science. Advancements are made every day. There was a day when cigarettes were considered healthy. Could you imagine doing a research paper based on early opinions of cigarettes.

By this point in the course, Samantha and Carol had solidified their working relationship. Samantha—or any outside reader—might have surmised that Carol had been under face attack from me in this discussion, and so she needed face support from a friend. Samantha's judgment here and the inappropriate analogy to views of cigarette smoking constitute facework to honor Carol and to display their strong relationship, even though Samantha risks creating threat to her own face by a potential negative judgment from the professor.

Another instance that served to build Carol's view of herself as a scholar-professional was when she disagreed with the professor about her paper's organization. On reading her first draft, I had advised her to integrate her primary source material into the text of her document and to not have it as a separate section. Her response to me on the discussion board was to insist on her original vision of the work, though she admits that she had considered my suggestion, thus tossing a deferential nod my way. Carol took a risk in rejecting my advice on the discussion board, a public forum in full view of all students, so her deference was essential in allowing me to save face. She writes: "After mulling it over a bit, I decided that even though it supported the rest of my material, it didn't fit or flow as well as I thought it would . . . so separate sections it is!"

It was striking to me that Carol felt such strong control over her project and her community identity that she could consider my advice and reject it twice. The source of this confidence lay in her ability to present herself as a writer and as a scholar-professional in stronger and more direct ways over time. She was supported in this by her growing alliances with colleagues such as Samantha. The online discussions allowed her the space to conduct the facework necessary for her to reach this point. These types of discussions would likely never occur in a face-to-face class.

Thus, through their online interaction, Carol and Samantha's discussion board writing has helped each of them to build identities as women, as parents, as communication studies majors, as writers and researchers, and as scholar-professionals with mutual respect for each other's work as well as for each other's personal lives. As such, by enacting identity on the discussion board, students demonstrate their ability to change and evolve in a given rhetorical situation. In effect, their interactions with others show that identity is not constant. Instead, through the rhetorical moves in their facework, students are continually defining and reframing the ways in which they present to others. These reframed identities, in turn, contribute to student agency over their learning.

Tony: Constructing an Identity as a Writer and a Leader

Tony's work on the discussion board offers an interesting contrast to that of Samantha and Carol. Initially, his weak writing skills keep him from adopting the same kind of academic identity that was available to them. However, Tony is a clear example of the ways in which identity negotiation and display can evolve over a single semester and can contribute to significant learning and achievement in a university course. Tony's initial participation on the discussion board was rather hesitant. He had taken most of his classes face to face, and he admittedly felt a little inadequate in the online classroom. But as the course progressed, Tony took full advantage of all the ways in which he could develop relationships and manage his identity through online engagement with colleagues. He evolved from a friendly but slightly disgruntled student into one of the strongest and most popular students in the class, clearly one of its leaders.

Personal Identity

In the first two weeks of the class, Tony contributes to class discussions just enough to meet requirements: He posts a contribution to each discussion topic, and he responds to two students in each thread. By the fourth week of the class, he has requested that the professor create a study group (small group discussion board) for the seven students who have selected the executive speech option as their research project. He enthusiastically facilitates the group himself. In weeks six and seven, Tony even completed several extra peer reviews (beyond the two that were required). By the final week of the class, Tony posts an emotional goodbye in which he confesses that he had at first resented the fact that he had been forced to take this senior seminar online, but that he had gained much, much more than he had anticipated from the class and from his colleagues. This final section of the chapter examines the ways in which Tony used the discussion board to enact and manage his personal, academic, and scholar-professional identities, as well as the ways in which Tony's facework contributed to his learning.

In the Meet Your Colleagues discussion, Tony writes a long (560-word) and somewhat formal letter to the class to initially display aspects of his personal identity. Tony works as a Marine Corps trainer/instructor, and he discloses his enthusiasm for teaching and learning, reflecting a value for discussion-based learning in his own classroom. He talks about his family, his recent deployments, and his impending retirement from service. Tony is deferential in his facework from the beginning, always making it clear that he is interested in people other than himself, and that being helpful is an important aspect of his identity.

Dr. DiDesidero and fellow Communication Majors,

First, I am very excited to finally get to this course. I am very open to this community, and I want to know what you all think and what your experiences have been in this field. . . . Also, to better express myself to those that are willing to learn, and to try and get those not willing to be willing. Everyone wants to learn something.

I have been an instructor, I call us teachers, in the Marine Corps for about 11 years . . . Be gone to the days when someone stands in front of you and drones on about the material, and they do not stimulate the classes learning. I find it is as simple as saying, "What do you think?" this will strike the minds of everyone in the room and the process of learning from each other can begin.

I will retire from the Marine Corps. . . . Honestly, I am tired of getting shot at, blown up, and being placed in harms [sic] way . . .

My wife, of 19 years, and my children are my inspiration. I would not have driven so far without their support . . .

I hope I can be of great service to you all and this course. Again, I am happy to be here and be alive. Please call me Tony, and call me anytime.

Sincerely,
Tony

In response to my welcome message to Tony, he writes:

Thank you very much. Teaching is my passion. I would not say great, but I do love the crowd; when we stimulate each other. I look forward to learning from you and from the class. Okinawa is beautiful, but I really love the culture and the people. I wish this class was face-to-face though.

This post demonstrates Tony's deferential facework when he states he "look[s] forward to learning from [the professor]," but at the same time, he regrets that the class is offered only online, as it is not his favorite environment. Also on frank display here and in his introduction is Tony's inexpert use of language. Tony's postings are filled with frequent sentence fragments, misspellings, and incorrect punctuation—perhaps forming some basis for his preference for face-to-face classes. Though he was not one of the stronger writers in the class, Tony was nonetheless able to use his writing to gain the support of his classmates. While a face-to-face class may not offer many opportunities for self-disclosure, the online environment allowed Tony to honestly reveal much of himself to his colleagues as he admits, "Honestly, I am tired of getting shot at, blown up, and being placed in harms [sic] way . . ." He was one of the least inhibited and became one of the most enthusiastic students in the seminar. His unpolished writing skills did not prevent Tony from conducting facework that was collegial, engaging, deferential, and supportive of his colleagues.

In the early conferences, Tony talks about his experiences in the discipline, about his role in the military, and about his future dreams of becoming a teacher. As he responds to other students, he is forthcoming and discloses personal information readily—particularly weakness. As with Carol and Samantha, this proves to be an engaging facework strategy. Tony also conducts frequent facework to honor the face of other students. He typically closes his posts by thanking the writer, by wishing the writer good luck, or by expressing admiration in some way. In the post below, Tony is forthcoming about his own shortcomings as he compliments Samantha on her interest in speech pathology:

What a great career choice. I had a stuttering problem when I was young. . . . I pretty much taught myself out of the problem. . . . I commend you for putting your efforts toward such a noble cause. Thanks for sharing.

Tony's initial posts are long, thoughtful, and complimentary. He easily discloses personal information, and he is responsive to achievements or problems of his colleagues, thus honoring face. His facework is sincere, supportive, deferential, and very personal—so it becomes easy to see how he gained a prominent role on the discussion board as the class progressed.

Academic Identity

As Tony begins to display his academic identity, he explores the effects of his course of study on his life, thus personalizing the academic.

> I am a completely different person than when I started my degree 3 years ago. Communication is what I think about and breathe everyday. You cannot get away from it, unless you live in a whole [*sic*] somewhere. My teaching skills are better and I feel my students learn more and better from me. I can correspond effectively, I know my relationships have improved because I can feel it. Thanks to all who have touched my studies over the past few years, both the scholarly and those aspiring, like me to be better than what I am now someday.

Here we see Tony extending his comments about the importance of the communications field and its impact on him personally and on his teaching. In doing so, Tony is building community with the other students in the class, all of whom are communication studies majors.

In creating and enacting his academic identity, Tony adroitly uses his personal facework to full effect. Of particular interest is his dialogue with Carol, with whom he discusses writing ability. Here Tony, whose authority is not based on his skills as a writer, is able to honor Carol's strengths without damaging his own academic persona. In the thread below, Tony aligns himself with Carol's writing identity, as he is forthcoming about his own shortcomings. While Carol's comment about grammar and spelling will likely strike a chord with Tony, he conducts facework to finesse any issues. He is clearly one of the spelling and grammar offenders to which she refers, but he handles what may be viewed as a face affront with grace, saving his face and hers in his final response.

TONY TO CAROL:

You know I love to write, but my grammar and spelling are atrocious! Those of us with the passion to put it on paper definitely need to have an expert proof our work. Just typing this I probably used spell check several [sic]. I wish you luck in your endeavors. I do appreciate it.

CAROL TO TONY:

I feel that I am strong in spelling and grammar and confess that I amazed at the number of errors I see in classroom postings. . . . It's a pet peeve of mine . . . [we] should strive to set an example. Do you agree?

TONY TO CAROL:

I sure do agree 100% with you. . . . I am glad there are people like you to look over the ones that love to write, but they have trouble when it gets to the paper. Thanks for the response.

As with his personal identity, Tony's academic identity is developed and enacted with sincere and earnest facework. He is seriously committed to the discipline, and he is openly committed to the communication studies students in this class. By the middle of the semester, he has begun to respond to almost every student in almost every discussion thread. His facework here consistently achieves solidarity with each student and clearly expresses both respect and admiration for each student's contribution. Tony plays a central role in helping to establish group-face and group identity through his postings.

Scholar-Professional Identity

By the midterm, Tony has assumed a leadership role in the classroom. This leadership identity becomes a large part of Tony's scholar-professional facework. In the excerpt below from Tony's first posting to his study group (a group that he had asked me to set up in the classroom), the reader notes that he positions himself as an academic leader and also as a colleague, friend, and peer.

TONY TO SMALL GROUP:

Classmates, I just wanted to see the general consensus on some questions I have, and I wish to learn about how you all are going about this project. I have learned so much already from everyone. . . . Again, it is a pleasure to be working with such a great group. Being Communication Studies majors, it is refreshing to see and feel the compassion this class has for the topics. good luck everyone. Sincerely, Tony

Tony enacts his identity as a small-group leader ("I just wanted to see the general consensus . . ."), but he honors and builds both the small-group face as he does this ("I have learned so much already from everyone") and he honors the large-group face of all communication studies majors.

It is also clear from these examples that Tony's informal use of language structure is on display. He writes in sentence fragments, neglects capital letters, and misspells words. While that might seem rather careless to some readers, no one responded to his grammatical errors or lack of capitalization; that is, students did not seem to view this as a face affront. In fact, I suspect that his language is one of the things that others found endearing about Tony.

Tony's language skills also did not deter serious students from seeking Tony's advice on their projects. Students were required to complete peer review analyses in memo format for two other students. Tony completed peer reviews for all six students in the study group, and he volunteered to complete a peer review for two additional students whose reviewers had not met their obligations. Several students came to acknowledge Tony's role as a leader and a mentor. Kris writes: "Tony, I definitely think you found your calling. . . . You reviewed my paper when you didn't have to. Thank you for going the extra mile to help me." Tony's interactions with his classmates illustrate the different kinds of legitimate academic identities available to students. Whereas Carol claims strong writing skills as one basis for her academic authority, Tony rests his authority on his ability to present himself as a group organizer and a leader in support of other students. In this capacity, his writing is effective, even as it violates formal rules and conventions.

In Tony's presentation of his own research project, the reader notes that his language aligns more closely with his scholar-professional identity. While hints of informality are evident in grammar, mechanics, and word choice, these are not as distracting here as in his earlier posts. Also evident is a sense of the organization, motivation, audience, and strategy for the serious argument in his project.

I wrote a speech for Dr. Jim Sears, a board-certified Pediatrician in private practice. . . . This forum had 500 colleagues in the audience, and the speech was given after lunch. I would also like to mention that in the audience there are also journalists from influential health magazines. . . . My approach was twofold. I wanted to take a pro stance [on the question: Should pregnant women eat fish?], but I also wanted to identify that there is a problem with Mercury pollution in our world's water supplies. So, my second approach was to stress education on this fact. I addressed some of the con-side of views and rounded out the speech with a call to arms, as physicians reminding us of our code of ethics and what we are here to do for our patients.

Thus, we can see that while Tony may not be as strong a writer as other students, his control of written language conventions is greater than it seemed to be earlier in the class. This indicates that some of the "careless" errors in the earlier posts reflect his choice to focus on other aspects of writing that he considered more crucial to the identity he was constructing and presenting to the class.

Tony's final goodbye message to the class also reflects the extent to which his personal connections expressed through solidarity facework become a huge part of his scholar-professional identity. Note that his language here is more formal and less colloquial than his earlier postings, including the salutation for this posting. In his message, he continues to be friendly and deferential to his colleagues, and he directly confesses his change of attitude about learning in an online community:

Dr. DiDesidero and Fellow Students, First, May I say what an engaging and intellectual group of people are in this class. At times I truly felt sub par, but that was at no fault to anyone here. . . . I would like to commend the students because I have learned more from you during this class than any other . . .

Looking back to my earlier threads, I noticed I was leery in my comments. . . . I was not sure how my capstone class would be online. I still complained to [the university] for not offering this class face-to-face. I was wrong. The structure and human interaction was positively there with this class. I enjoyed the communication, I laughed, learned, listened, provided advise [*sic*], and believe it or not, even shed a tear once.

Good luck to everyone here, and I thank you once more for an incredible learning experience that brought it full circle for me. Good luck and God Speed . . .

Sincerely, Tony X. XXX

In sheer numbers of postings, Tony comes to outperform other students—even though he had started out slowly by just meeting the minimum requirements for discussion board work. Throughout the eight weeks, Tony has 174 discussion board postings with an average length of 200 words each. The next strongest participant was Carol, who had 139 discussion board postings with an average length of 150 words each.

Tony's facework in the discussions makes it evident that students who are not strong writers can nevertheless create strong relationships and achieve success in an environment that is itself driven by writing as the primary channel of communication and identity display. Tony began the course feeling resentful that he could not take it as a face-to-face class on his military base. With his admittedly weaker writing skills on display, it is easy to see one reason why Tony might have preferred working in a face-to-face environment: A face-to-face communication channel allows a student such as Tony to easily display identity by using the resources of his interpersonal strengths, which seem to be based on his desire to connect with people, to help others, and to view learning as a shared enterprise. Tony acknowledged his own surprise at finding that he could accomplish this in the online environment through one of his weaker modes of communication—writing. The facework strategies that Tony would employ in a face-to-face class were able to serve him in the online environment as well, perhaps even more effectively, as Tony managed to achieve not only leadership but credibility as a student writer in this environment as well.

Conclusion

This chapter constitutes an initial analysis of the ways in which communication studies students use facework strategies in the online classroom as a means of presenting themselves to each other and to the professor as students, colleagues, writers, and potential professionals. Their choice of strategy is limited by their own constructed identities in the context of the classroom, and by their own expectations of how students conventionally relate to one another and to the professor. This analysis of the data also exemplifies the idea that it is the social practice of writing that allows students to shape their own identities, and that these identities are not rigid clusters of constant features, but instead "variable processes themselves that are enacted in social contexts" (De Fina, Schiffrin, and Bamberg, 2006, p. 2). It is the discourse practice that frames and defines the ways in which individuals present themselves to others, or the ways in which they "perform" identity. In the online classroom, opportunities to perform and display identity must be created by the professor.

This research suggests that writing in the online classroom is a powerful tool as well as a powerful medium not only for facilitating personal growth, but also for facilitating learning. As an identity resource, face is a powerful and complex instrument. When the professor invites students to interact on the discussion board of an online classroom, she is affording students opportunities to enact, display, and develop identities. Through these identity displays and the facework strategies that build community, students come to view their learning—expressed in many forms of writing—as something over which they have increasing agency and control.

On the discussion board, professors can facilitate student learning through identity enactment in the classroom context over time. Initial discussions allow students to signal personal identities as they build relationships with one another in their facework. Subsequent discussions create opportunities for students to enact academic identities within a particular discipline—a discipline that contains clearly defined knowledge, a set of unique values, and an array of acceptable research questions, all of which students can claim as they develop identities as participants in that specific academic community. And finally, the professor can facilitate for students the development of mature identities as scholar-professionals who can take genuine control over their learning and their academic decision making in the online classroom as they become discipline-based researchers and writers who interact with one another.

The application of facework and theories of language in social interaction to contexts such as online education provide strong insights into the processes of teaching and learning themselves, as well as insights into the particular suitability of the online environment for such undertakings. Effectively designed discussion boards allow students multiple opportunities to develop and display identity as they learn content, conduct research, and create new knowledge. When students use facework to build relationships and display expertise in an online classroom community, they are developing stronger identities as individuals, as community members, and as scholars in the discipline. It is the strength of this identity development that contributes to learning.

Author's note: This paper is supported by a 2012 University of Maryland University College Faculty Research Grant.

Appendix 7.1. Sequence of Discussion Board Questions to Support Identity Processes

Class Week	Discussion Topics	Identity Development (Course Deliverables)
Week 1	**Meet Your Colleagues** **Explore/Share Ideas for Personal Essay** **Explore Course Resources** Sample question topics: 1) How did you come to study this discipline? 2) Describe a significant piece of coursework that you accomplished in your curriculum; 3) Where will your major take you? Investigate a career field related to your major; 4) Brainstorm about research interests	Personal Identity Academic Identity
Week 2	**Research Project Models, Ideas, Tools, Approaches** Sample Question Topics: 1) Brainstorm about research interests and potential resources; 2) Who are you as a researcher and writer? 3) What is the value of research and writing in this discipline? 4) Draft your Research Proposal; 5) Review/discuss model projects	*Academic Identity* (Personal Essay)
Week 3	**Specific Topic Ideas, Audience Analysis, Approaches to Information Gathering** Sample Question Topics: 1) Re-Draft your Research Proposal; 2) Analyze your Audience (why should they care?); 3) Describe scope: What questions will your research answer? 4) Review/discuss model projects	*Academic Identity* *Scholar-Professional Identity* (Research Proposal Memo)
Week 4	**Primary Research Tools; Summary Reports on Background/Secondary Research** Sample Question topics: 1) What information will you look for where? Draft an Annotated Bibliography; 2) Summarize info from a primary source, analyze usefulness; 3) Summarize info from a secondary source, analyze usefulness	*Scholar-Professional Identity* (Annotated Bibliography)

continued on next page

Appendix 7.1—*continued*

Week 5	**Audience and Scope Revisited; Summary Reports on Primary Research**	*Scholar-Professional Identity*
	Sample Question Topics: 1) Progress Report Memo on Research Project; 2) Primary Resource Summary and Analysis; 3) Discuss your potential organizational scheme, persuasive strategies, drafting processes	(Progress Report Memo)
Week 6	**Organization; Professional Expectations; Ethical Considerations**	*Scholar-Professional Identity*
	Sample Question Topics: 1) What professional and ethical considerations/decisions inform your work on this project? Analyze issues. How do you handle them? 2) Review rhetorical considerations	(Draft for Peer Review)
Week 7	**Peer Review; Preparing Presentations** Sample Question Topics: 1) Peer review discussions of Peer Review Memos; 2) Presentation discussion posted (all facilitated by students)	*Scholar-Professional Identity* (Peer Review Memo to 2 Peers; Presentation)
Week 8	**Students Facilitate Research Presentation Discussions Coming Full Circle**	*Scholar-Professional Identity*
	Sample Question Topics: 1) Presentation Facilitation; 2) Insights about Identity and Scholarship	(Final Draft of Project Paper)

Appendix 7.2: Sample Discussion Board Rubric

Grade	Features of Discussion Posts/ Responses
A (90–100)	A grade of "A" means that ALL discussion posts have the following features: • Effectively address the topic/question with substance, evidence, and facts at hand • Cite readings or sources or refer to experts (when relevant) • Attempt to reach a genuine insight or new perspective on a topic • Engage opposing points of view • Display courtesy and understanding in responses to others, even when the writer disagrees • Re-title the posting when appropriate (so that readers can more easily follow the discussion) In addition, students who earn grades of A for Participation may post often in the Open Forum, participate frequently in small group exercises, take a leadership role in some discussions, and show consistent support for students across the class.
B (80–89)	A grade of "B" means that ALMOST ALL discussion posts and responses (85% of the discussions) have the features listed above. In addition, students who earn grades of B for Participation may post in the Open Forum, participate frequently in small group exercises, take leadership roles in some discussions, and show support for students across the class.
C (70–79)	A grade of "C" means that MOST discussion posts and responses (75% of the discussions) have the features listed above. In addition, students who earn grades of C for Participation may post in the Open Forum, participate satisfactorily in small group exercises, and show consistent support for students across the class.
D (60–69)	A grade of "D" means that the student's participation in SEVERAL discussions does NOT have the features listed above. In addition, students who earn grades of D for Participation may have any of the following features in their discussion responses: • Simply repeats the question • Contains opinion with no evidence or factual support • Has been written by someone who has not done the readings • Displays a negative attitude toward others • Lacks adequate participation in small groups • Does not respond to discussion at all

continued on next page

Appendix 7.2—*continued*

Grade	Features of Discussion Posts/ Responses
F (0–59)	A grade of "F" means that the student's participation in HALF of the discussions does NOT have the features listed in "A" above. In addition, students who earn grades of F for Participation may have discussion responses with any of the features listed for grades of D.

References

Brown, P., & Levinson, S. (1987). *Politeness: Some universals in language usage.* Cambridge, UK: Cambridge University Press.

Cook, K. C. (2005). An argument for pedagogy-driven online education. In K. C. Cook & K. Grant-Davie (Eds.), *Online education: Global questions, local answers* (pp. 49–66), Amityville, NY: Baywood Publishing.

De Fina, A., Schiffrin, D, & Bamberg, M. (2006). *Discourse and identity.* Cambridge, UK: Cambridge University Press.

Domenici, K., & Littlejohn, S. W. (2006). *Facework: Bridging theory and practice.* Thousand Oaks, CA: Sage Publications.

Fairclough, N. (2001). *Language and power.* Harlow, UK: Pearson Limited.

Fowler, R., Hodge, B., Kress, G., & Trew, T. (1979). *Language and control.* London, UK: Routledge Kegan Paul.

Fowler, R., & Kress, G. (1979). Critical linguistics. In R. Fowler et al. (Eds.), *Language and control* (pp. 185–213). London, UK: Routledge Kegan Paul.

Gee, J. P. (2001). Identity as an analytic lens for research in education. *Review of Research in Education, 25*(1), 99–125.

Goffman, E. (1959). *The presentation of self in everyday life.* New York, NY: Anchor/Doubleday.

Goffman. E. (1967). *Interaction ritual: Essays on face-to-face behavior.* New York, NY: Anchor/Doubleday.

Goffman, E. (1979). *Gender advertisements.* Cambridge, MA: Harvard University Press.

Grice, H. P. (1975). Logic and conversation. In P. Cole & J. L. Morgan (Eds.), *Syntax and semantics, vol. 3: Speech acts* (pp. 41–58). New York, NY: Academic Press.

Maltz, D. N., & Borker, R. A. (1982). A cultural approach to male–female miscommunication. In J. J. Gumperz (Ed.), *Language and social identity* (pp. 196–216). Cambridge, UK: Cambridge University Press.

Mullany, L. (2010). Gender and interpersonal pragmatics. In M. Locher & S. Graham (Eds.), *Interpersonal pragmatics* (pp. 225–249). Berlin, Germany: de Gruyter Mouton.

Scollon, R., Scollon, S., & Jones, R. (2012). *Intercultural communication: A discourse approach.* West Sussex, UK: Wiley-Blackwell.

Ting-Toomey, S. (2004). The matrix of face: An updated face-negotiation theory. In W. Gudykunst (Ed.), *Theorizing about intercultural communication* (pp. 71–92). Thousand Oaks, CA: Sage.

Ting-Toomey, S., & Kurogi, A. (1998). Facework competence in intercultural conflict: An updated face-negotiation theory. *Journal of Intercultural Relations, 22,* 187–225.

PART III

∾ LEARNING ACADEMIC
DISCOURSE ONLINE

EIGHT

The Reading–Writing Connection: Engaging the Literary Text Online

Phoebe Jackson

I N THEIR BOOK, COMPUTERS IN *the Composition Classroom*, editors Michelle Sidler, Richard Morris, and Elizabeth Smith (2008) make an important observation about the introduction of technology into the classroom, stating it "does not simply add a computer tool—it changes the writing, learning, and teaching environment" (p. 6). Their observation certainly holds true with online instruction. A distinguishing feature of the online teaching environment is the opportunity to have a truly de-centered classroom, allowing the instructor to step to the side to relinquish a prominent position. When the role of the professor is de-emphasized in this way, students must of necessity become more active participants in their own learning.

In a traditional literature class, the text mediated by the professor is typically given priority. Reading therefore becomes the central focus for student participation, and writing becomes secondary—a way of interpreting the reading. I will argue that in the online classroom the relationship between reading and writing is open to change. Unlike the traditional literature classroom, reading and writing online can exist on an equal footing. Writing, then, need no longer play second fiddle to the study of literature but can be more wholly integrated with it.

In an online class, students have a different relationship to reading and writing about literature. In the traditional literature classroom, reading and writing can appear to be disconnected and discrete activities, with reading typically taking precedence over writing. Students, and sometimes teachers, treat writing as a process to be engaged in only after the student has figured out what the text means. However, in an online environment, writing and reading can be on par with each other, allowing for a student's continuous engagement and dialogue with the literary text, with textual criticism, and with other students' texts.

Because of this continuous engagement with reading and writing, students come to better understand the recursive nature of both activities and how each is a process. Such a dialogic relationship, I allow, can help to broaden the practice of literary study. Students come to realize the constructed and contingent nature of literary interpretation rather than seeing the text as limited to a single definitive interpretation. As a result, students learn to see themselves not as passive recipients of literary interpretations but as active participants. Moreover, reading and writing about literature online allows students to reflect on their own reading process, because there is a record that documents the stages of this process. Rather than focus exclusively on the interpretation of a literary text, which can typically be the focus of students in a traditional classroom, they come to see that the interpretation *is* the process and that it changes and evolves.

The Reading–Writing Connection

In the traditional literature classroom, it is difficult for students to understand how they can participate in the meaning-making of a literary text. Instead, students tend to be passive consumers of text. In part this situation is due to the way that literature is taught. As Peter Elbow (2002) argues, literature professors tend to see the literary text "as a product," and their students as consumers of a product who should leave class "with some summarizable knowledge about that text" (p. 535). If a teacher views the text as a "product," that orientation speaks volumes about what might take place in the classroom. Such a class would typically be less student-centered and would rely on the professor to dispense knowledge. In a class where the text and reading are privileged activities, students by default are encouraged to be "static, passive readers who react to and who are acted on by texts" (Schroeder, 1999, p. 301). They are not generating different readings, which would allow them to be active participants in class or "to enter into meaning-making dialogue" (Schroeder, 1999, p. 301). Instead, the professor's interpretation and the text as aesthetic artifact are privileged. As Elbow (1996) concludes, reading in that type of classroom thus promotes passivity because it "locate[s] authority away from the student and keep[s] it entirely in the teacher or institution or great figure" (p. 283).

Unlike the pedagogy practiced in many literature courses, scholars in composition studies and literary theory have long accepted the premise of the reading and writing connection. In an early article entitled "On the Possibility of a Unified Theory of Composition and Literature," Patricia Bizzell (1986) explains succinctly how the two are related: "The writer does not put previously conceived ideas 'into' words; she generates ideas through the process of writing. And the reader does not simply take ideas out of the words; rather, he generates his own version of the text through the process of reading" (p. 176). This insight can have important ramifications for the teaching of literature.

In a classroom where reading and writing are on equal par, a different type of learning experience is realized. In his article, "The War Between Reading and Writing," Elbow (1996) argues that when writing plays a more central role in the literature classroom "even reading will benefit" (p. 270). Though he concedes in another article that "it's still difficult . . . to see how readers actively create and negotiate meanings in texts" (Elbow, 1995, p.196), Elbow (1996) nonetheless argues that when more emphasis is placed on writing in the literature classroom, then students can in turn learn "to see reading as 'a process' of cognitive and social construction" (p. 281). This shift in emphasis to privilege writing in the literature classroom allows the student to see both reading and writing as active processes that are continually open to rethinking. Moreover, according to Christopher Schroeder (1999), such a shift also helps students to see themselves as "active meaning-makers engaged in a dynamic, continuous dialogue with themselves, with texts, with other readers in the classroom, and with the world at large" (p. 306).

This essay will argue that the online experience can affect the paradigm shift that Elbow and other scholars advocate. Because online courses require students to engage with each other through writing, students can see how meaning and interpretation can proliferate to produce numerous possible readings of a given text. Equally important, the online experience allows students to create a permanent record of their writing, thus giving them the opportunity to see how meaning is constantly created and re-created through the process of reading, writing, and reflection. Such a shift in learning moves the student away from viewing interpretation as the conclusion at which they arrive. Rather they come to see that interpretation is a changing and recursive process that requires their interaction with a text and with each other. Online classes make this interaction visible and help students build their own changing reactions into their interpretations.

Teaching in the online classroom, moreover, has the ability to change the imbalance of the reading–writing experience of the traditional classroom, where reading is typically privileged. In their article "Computer-Mediated Communication and the Confluence of Composition and Literature," Fischer, Reiss, and Young (2006) argue that the distinction between reading and writing in the online classroom is less significant than it would be in the traditional classroom. In electronic platforms like blogs and discussion boards, the distinction between the practices of reading and writing tends to blur. As Fischer, Reiss, and Young observe, "Instead of using writing in support of the study of literature or literature in support of learning how to write critically, online communication supports a fluid purpose that includes these approaches but focuses more on the middle ground of written conversation about literature and the production of literature as well as the consumption of literature" (p. 164). Thus, Elbow's earlier call for parity between reading and writing can be more easily realized in the online classroom because the distinction between them is less pronounced. As a result, students more clearly see their role as active meaning-makers with a wider audience in the online classroom than they do in a traditional face-to-face classroom.

Also important to a student's involvement with reading and writing is the role of the professor in the online classroom. Since the early 1990s when computers began to appear in classrooms, teacher/scholars recognized their potential to de-throne professors and their authority in the writing classroom. In the 20th anniversary issue of the journal *Computers and Composition*, Kristine Blair and Elizabeth Monske (2003) summarized 15 years of research on the scholarship of writing and computers with a focus on online learning. In their summary they noted "that almost any networked activity will be a means to decenter the traditional classroom space and to disrupt the position of teacher as the figure of mastery" (pp. 441–453); as a result, Blair and Monske conclude, "authority is moved away from the teacher in electronic space" (pp. 441–453). In their book *Role Play: Distance Learning and the Teaching of Writing* Jonathan Alexander and Marcia Dickson (2006) argue that such a move necessitates "a reconsideration of the instructor's role as facilitator" (p. 9). Instructors have the opportunity in such an environment to reimagine themselves as participants in learning rather than as sole disseminators of knowledge.

Unlike the traditional classroom where the professor is typically the purveyor of "grand narrative truths" about literature, the online class changes the dynamic between the student and professor. In an online course, the instructor works alongside students in a more collaborative manner as partners in learning. Because the position of the teacher's role has changed, new opportunities for learning become available. Students come to rely on each other to help contribute to their thinking and learning through an ongoing discussion of literary interpretation using electronic platforms like group discussion, discussion boards, and blogs. By participating in these "new communities" of peers, as Fischer, Reiss, and Young (2006) observe, students change their relationship to the study of literature. "The new communities . . . make students feel more welcome in literary studies and invite them to become insiders rather than emphasizing their amateur status" (p. 167). Thus, doing literary studies online can open new doors for students, allowing them to see themselves as active participants in creating meaning and generating ideas in a community of readers and writers engaged in the same practice with each other.

Teaching Literature Online

In this essay, I will analyze one student's discussion board posts about Kate Chopin's *The Awakening*. Through the mutual processes of reading and writing, the student has entered a "conversation" with other writers to participate in an ongoing discussion of the novel. My analysis of this student's online posts illustrates how she generated ideas about the novel that changed over time through a continuous loop of reading, writing, and reflecting. In so doing, she has learned a basic tenet of literary studies—that interpretation is a continuing and dynamic process.

Having taught this course, Methods of Literary Analysis—the portal class for the English major—both face to face and online, I have come to realize that the online class affords certain teaching opportunities not readily replicated in a traditional classroom. Specifically, in the face-to-face classroom, discussion can seem a bit scattershot with people joining into the conversation, not necessarily in the most thoughtful manner. Since students toss out spontaneous ideas, trying to pull together the conversation in a coherent manner can be challenging. Moreover, it is difficult to know what individual students have gleaned, if anything, from such freewheeling discussions. However, in the online environment, through the process of reading and writing on discussion board, one can observe each student actively engaged in thinking through issues that surface in a continuous loop of reflection. Unlike the experience in a traditional literature classroom, students in an online environment have the space and opportunity to read, write, and reflect. This is made possible, in part, because students can go back to the discussion board to reread their responses and also the responses of other students. Unlike the classroom discussion, the online discussion board retains a permanent record. Moreover, in an online discussion everyone must participate so that students have the obvious advantage of a much wider audience and their varied responses to a text, thus enabling them to better understand the contingent nature of literary interpretation. Finally, through the process of reading and writing online, students find themselves in constant negotiation with other viewpoints, enabling them to understand a critical premise about literary studies—that a single text yields multiple interpretations. While that idea can be articulated and discussed in a traditional classroom, in the online classroom students must actually enact this concept through their reading and writing, allowing them to experience at first hand the dialogic aspect of literary interpretation. Ideally, as a result, they can better see themselves as active participants in an academic community rather than as passive observers of one.

Reading and Writing About Edna Pontellier

My analysis of one student's responses illustrates how she came into conflict with and negotiated different viewpoints from her peers and literary critics. At the same time, her posts document her own reading process that evolves and changes over time through her interaction with the text. This particular assignment took place toward the end of the semester. Beforehand, the students had read some literary theory, so they were somewhat familiar with theoretical terms and approaches. For the last four weeks of the semester, they were assigned to read Kate Chopin's *The Awakening*, along with a biographical and historical article and four critical articles that introduced them to a range of theoretical approaches to reading the novel. Students wrote 250–300 word postings twice a week in response to the readings.

For my part, I kept my presence online to a minimum by not replying to the students individually but by drafting a general commentary that summarized what I had read from their responses. In my commentary, I would copy and paste student responses, grouping them into particular themes I saw emerging from their writing. When doing so, I would frequently ask questions about these responses to encourage them to think further about the conclusions they had drawn. In my commentary, I never offered any specific interpretation of the novel. Finally, I did not grade their individual posts, much to the chagrin of many, because I wanted them to sort through their own thoughts without the intervention of grades.

For the first two assignments, the students read Chopin's novel, *The Awakening*, and posted responses to my general questions. On average, this student wrote about 325 words per post, choosing to start each one with a subject heading, which in effect acted as a mini-thesis. I have shortened the student's posts to focus specifically on her main ideas.

For the first posting on the novel, I asked the students to characterize the main character, Edna Pontellier. This student began her post with the title, "Edna."

Edna Pontellier seems as though she is comfortable in the middle class but she doesn't appreciate what she has in finances or affection. Her husband, Leonce is a good guy but she neglects him as well as neglecting her three children. . . . However, he does feel that that a woman's place is in the home and Edna does not agree with that . . . Edna herself feels there is more to life than just being a mother and a wife. . . . If women feel they must conform now, it must have been even more so during Edna's time. . . . In general, she is not very happy with her life, doesn't appreciate what she has and is not content with being a traditional mother and wife.

Here the student focuses on Edna Pontellier's economic position, which she identifies as "middle class." Though she has only read half of the novel, she is quick to judge Edna's character. She argues that Edna "doesn't appreciate what she has in finances or affection." Interestingly, her comment about finances suggests the way present-day economics finds its way into a reading of the novel. The student goes on to cast Edna's husband, Leonce, as "a good guy," while she criticizes Edna for "neglect[ing] him as well as neglecting her three children." For the student, Edna is clearly the problem, as she "doesn't appreciate what she has." Nonetheless, she can recognize Edna's unhappiness with her marriage and with motherhood, stating: "There is more to life than just being a mother and a wife." However, the student doesn't seem to see these circumstances as a powerful reason for Edna to be unhappy. While she acknowledges that women have to conform, the student doesn't engage with the issue of gender inequality that exists for Edna, although we had already covered feminist criticism in the course. Instead, she concludes Edna "doesn't appreciate what she has and is not content with being a traditional mother and wife." The level of interpretation at this point could be characterized as more personal opinion with some analysis.

In her next posting for the week, the student starts her response with the title, "Selfish to the End." For this prompt, I asked students to discuss one idea that demonstrates a change in Edna by the end of the novel:

> I seem to disagree with several of those comments that have been posted already. Some of the posts seemed to take Edna's side and that she deserved to have her own life, etc., etc. I, obviously, took the opposite side completely. . . . I feel she remains selfish and unappreciative of what she has in life. . . . If she wanted to make decisions solely about herself and only taking herself into account, that's one thing. But getting married and having three children by twenty-eight was a choice as well. . . . At the very end, right before she is under the waves, she says, "Good-by – because I love you" (Chopin 139). She realizes once it is too late that her life is worth living. I don't feel that every completed suicide is a selfish act, but in her case, I think that is the perfect word.

With the first sentence in this post, the student makes it perfectly clear that she has taken into consideration her peer audience and what they have to say about Edna. She is forthright in explaining that her opinion differs as they "take Edna's side," and she does not. Moreover, even though my writing prompt/question implicitly suggests that I see a change in Edna, the student has not been influenced by my question. To her credit, she remains committed to her initial position and gives specific reasons for doing so. In this sense, one can see the importance of the online audience with whom our student writer has chosen to disagree. By reading what the other students have written, the student has had to defend her thinking, placing her in dialogue with others in the class. In that respect, her writing has a specific sense of purpose—to explain why she sees Edna as selfish.

For the student, Edna continues to be the problem. In fact, the student sees Edna's behavior in this second part of the novel as only affirming her initial judgment of Edna's character: "I feel she remains selfish." In her earlier response, the student suggested that women have to conform to societal expectations, but in this posting, she argues that Edna has a responsibility for her actions, implying that there are no societal constraints placed upon women. Instead, she sees Edna as making a "choice" about her marriage and having children. The issue of choice is a point that some students focus on with regard to Edna as they judge her behavior from a 21st century perspective. They do not understand that the choices available to them are not ones readily available to women in Edna's time.

For her next post, the student gave her response the following title: "Giving Edna Another Chance," signaling a change of heart for the student. This assignment asked students to read Nancy Walker's (2000) introduction to *The Awakening* entitled "Biographical and Historical Contexts." Along with their reading, I posted the following writing prompt: "Choose one idea from the introduction and explain how it helps you to understand Chopin's novel." She wrote:

On page four of the introduction, there is an explanation of what women were expected to do and how they were expected to act in society. . . . Walker goes on to explain how Kate O'Flaherty created the character Edna to represent a woman who did more with her life than raise children and keep a clean house. I feel this made me understand the novel better because I took a different look at Edna. I think that maybe I didn't get [sic] Edna a chance. . . . I still feel that she has a somewhat easy, cushioned life with financial security and a loving family. However, after reading the introduction I realize that she is missing a feeling of fulfillment and satisfaction in her personal life. She wishes to accomplish something and feels smothered by her husband and society's standards.

In light of Nancy Walker's essay, which foregrounds the novel historically and biographically, the student has begun to reconsider her initial thoughts about Edna. In her response, she includes some of Walker's ideas to help her reconstruct her profile of Edna as a character. In doing so, she admits that she has been too quick to judge Edna. Thus, she is beginning to see Edna in a new light as someone who "wishes to accomplish something and feels smothered by her husband and society's standards." Moreover, as a result of Walker's introductory essay, the student begins to empathize with Edna, saying, "I realize that she is missing a feeling of fulfillment and satisfaction in her personal life." Interestingly, though she still reads Edna as a person with "a somewhat easy, cushioned life," the student also seems to realize that self-fulfillment and financial security might be separate issues for Edna.

With the next post, students began to read the first of four critical articles that analyze *The Awakening* from different theoretical perspectives. For these reading assignments, I did not expect students to fully understand the ideas under discussion in these difficult theoretical essays. However, since the course is portal one for the major, I did want them to see how literary critics analyze a novel from a variety of theoretical approaches. At best, I wanted them to tackle at least one idea from each article that they found compelling or that helped them to understand the novel so that they had to engage in some way with the article.

Students were assigned to read Elaine Showalter's (2000) "Tradition and the Female Talent: *The Awakening* as a Solitary Book"—a feminist approach to the novel. I used the following writing prompt to begin the discussion board conversation: "Choose one idea from Showalter's article to discuss in your response. Why did you pick the idea you did? How is it important to your understanding of the novel?" The title of her post, "Understanding Edna and Chopin," suggests the student's continued rethinking of Edna's character.

> When I first began reading *The Awakening*, I didn't give Edna Pontellier much of a chance. As I read further, I changed my mind and the piece by Elaine Showalter helped me understand Edna further and begin to feel some sympathy. Showalter made me realize that Edna Pontellier and the author, Kate Chopin . . . both defy the traditional lifestyle women led in this time period. . . . After becoming infatuated with [Robert Lebrun] she sets up a household with her husband's money where she can live independently. Although I do not approve of her decision, I can understand how and why she came to make it. . . . I feel I understand the novel more and Edna's feelings more because I realize what Chopin went through and that she made Edna gutsy and malcontent for a reason.

In this posting, the student's remarks demonstrate how reading different critical perspectives about the novel challenged her initial thoughts about Edna, requiring her to rethink her position. Thus, she readily admits that she "didn't give Edna Pontellier much of a chance." By reading Showalter's article, the student has come "to feel more sympathy" for Edna. Repeating some of the information she has obtained from Showalter's article, the student seems to have a better understanding of the historical circumstances that women like Chopin and her character faced in the 19th century. Thus, she is able to use some of Showalter's ideas to rethink and re-characterize some of her thoughts about Edna. Nonetheless, the student still maintains her opinion about Edna's decision to live alone, which she "do[es] not approve of." But she somewhat mediates her position, by stating, "I can understand how and why she came to make it." The student also recognizes that Chopin and her character are working against societal expectations. She concludes that by seeing Edna's character through Chopin's life, she understands why Chopin "made Edna gutsy and malcontent"—in other words, that there are reasons for Edna's behavior.

The assignment for the next class was to read Elizabeth LeBlanc's (2000) "The Metaphorical Lesbian: Edna Pontellier in *The Awakening*"—an example of gender criticism. For this discussion board post, I specifically asked students to address the idea of the "metaphorical lesbian" or the "lesbian continuum," terms used in the article. I followed that question with asking students to explain how either concept helps them to better understand the text. The student begins her response with the title, "Metaphorical Lesbian."

I also found this piece difficult to understand as well as sort of offensive. I believe if Edna were living in today's society, she wouldn't get a second glance or be considered a lesbian in any way. Edna feels she doesn't fit in anywhere because the other women find fulfillment and contentment in simply being a wife and mother. Edna wants her own "space" and is not a "mother-woman" like Adele. . . . Edna even says on page 256 she would "give up her life and her money for her children. But she will never give her self". . . . I think she means she is not willing to give up the person she wishes she was, a person who is not "restrained" by marriage and motherhood. . . . I felt [the article] gave off this vibe that just because a woman wishes to be independent and not have sex makes her a lesbian.

This piece helped me understand the novel more because it makes it obvious Edna's struggles with feeling independent, not restrained, and coming across as something she is not.

The student begins the post by stating that, "I also found this piece difficult to understand." From this initial statement, it is clear that she has read what other students have written since she uses the word "also." As such, we can see the importance of her peer group as an audience. It lets her know that she is part of a community of readers and writers, who are all trying to grapple with complex ideas, and that she is hardly alone in this process. Reading and thus learning that others in the class have been struggling with the same article, I would argue, allows students to express their ideas and opinions without the worry that they are wrong.

It is clear, however, that the student has not understood LeBlanc's premise of the "metaphorical lesbian." Instead, the student just focuses on the word lesbian and gets stuck there. However, she continues with the theme that she began to pursue and to think about in an earlier post: the idea "Edna wants her own 'space' and is not a 'mother-woman' like Adele." She then supports her argument by choosing an important quote from the novel that helps to explain Edna's attitude about her life: "she would 'give up her life and her money for her children. But she will never give her *self*.'" Afterward the student takes the next important step in her analysis to interpret this quote: "I think she means she is not willing to give up the person she wishes she was, a person who is not 'restrained' by marriage and motherhood."

The student's ability to pursue a line of thinking with supporting evidence and quotes demonstrates her awareness of her peer group audience. In her article "Reading (and Writing) Online," Kathleen Fitzpatrick (2012) discusses the advantage that accrues for students who have such an audience in mind, stating that "practicing over and over the art of staking out a position, presenting evidence, engaging with counterarguments can undoubtedly help produce better writers and clearer thinkers in any venue" (p. 46).

Though she disagrees that Edna is a lesbian, basically misinterpreting LeBlanc's article, the student admits that the essay has helped her "to understand the novel more because it makes it obvious Edna's struggles with feeling independent, not restrained, and coming across as something she is not." In this response, the student again notes Edna's desire for an independent life, but this time she does not pass judgment on it—another step toward re-creating her profile of Edna.

For the next post, the assignment was to read Margit Stange's (2000) article, "Personal Property: Exchange Value and the Female Self in *The Awakening*," written from a new historicist perspective. The student used the following title to begin her posting: Edna=Property.

> In the beginning of her piece, Stange discusses the relationship between Edna and Leonce Pontellier. Stange focuses on how Edna is treated like property. She mentions a remark made by Leonce, "You are burnt beyond recognition" (Stange, 274). The quote goes on to explain that Leonce is looking over his sunburned wife in the way someone would look over his or her property that had been damaged, he examines Edna like an object. . . . More and more, the critiques we have been reading about the novel help me to understand and identify more with Edna. As I've said before, I feel that Edna has a good life with a good family and financial security. But this piece in particular shows that her life isn't as peachy as I had assumed . . . she puts up with more inappropriate treatment that I realized in the first reading.

In this posting, the student has clearly understood the basic premise of Margit Stange's article that "Edna is treated like property." Reading Stange's article helps the student, in her words, to better "understand how Edna feels and why she does what she does." The student then reflects on the articles she has read so far. Reading them has informed her thinking about Edna and resulted in her changing interpretation of the character, and more important she's begun to "identify more with Edna." Interestingly, though formerly the twin issues of "a good family and financial security" usually found their ways into the student's posts, she has begun to see that both issues are a bit more complicated than she had initially observed; she writes, "[Edna's] life isn't as peachy as I had assumed." Moreover, the student now sees Leonce from a totally different perspective. She characterizes Leonce's behavior toward his wife as somewhat problematic—something she had not previously considered in her reading and writing.

For the last class reading assignment, students read Cynthia Griffin Wolff's (2000), "Un-Utterable Longing: The Discourse of Feminine Sexuality in Kate

Chopin's *The Awakening*." In this article, Wolff combines a number of theoretical approaches in her analysis of Chopin's novel, including psychoanalytic, deconstruction, and feminist. For their writing prompt, I asked the following questions: a) In your opinion, what is gained for the reader from "combining theoretical perspectives" as Wolff does in her article? Be specific. b) Choose one new idea presented in Wolff's article to explain how it helped you to understand the novel. Interestingly, the student used the subject heading "The Typical Female Life" to begin her post. Her subject heading suggests that she has come a long way from her initial readings of Edna, whom she previously depicted as having some distinct character flaws.

> As I read *The Awakening*, my opinions about the characters (especially the female characters) changed repeatedly from resentment to understanding and more. Originally, I felt that Edna Pontellier was unappreciative of what she had. Part of me still feels this way, but after reading Wolff's article I understand more what both Edna Pontellier and Kate Chopin were up against in their time. At first I viewed Edna Pontellier as ungrateful. . . . If I were to put myself in Edna Pontellier's place I'm sure I would feel as suffocated as she did. . . . I also have come to feel that what Edna Pontellier did took guts even though I don't agree with what she did. I think she should not have abandoned her children and husband but she should have the right to enjoy more freedom than she had. I understand the female characters much more since reading Wolff's article.

In this final post, the student begins with the phrase, "as I read *The Awakening*," by which we can presume she means the articles about *The Awakening*. Her reading and writing have made her reconsider her initial position about Edna. She explains it as a process of moving "from resentment to understanding and more." In making that point, the student can see that her interpretation has been open to change and that more importantly, reading what other critics and students have to say has helped her to think through her initial thoughts about Edna as a character. When she uses the word "originally," she demonstrates that she is clearly conscious that her interpretation has changed somewhat.

Though she's still partially committed to her original premise ("that Edna was unappreciative"), the student admits to having a better grasp of the social and historical context for women and its significance for both Edna and Kate Chopin. The student has also recast her profile of Edna. Though she still views Edna as "unappreciative," she now realizes that there are more complications in Edna's life than she had previously presumed. With this post, the student demonstrates that she has been able to move from seeing Edna as "ungrateful" to suggesting that she would feel "suffocated" as well if she were in Edna's place. Though the student disagrees with Edna's decision to abandon her family, she has tempered her overall characterization of Edna to arrive at a more complicated view of her. Through her engagement with the novel, her peer audience, and literary critics, the student has written her way to a slightly more nuanced view of Chopin's heroine, as a person, who has "guts" and who deserves some "freedom." Equally important is the final sentence of her post where she concludes that she "understand[s] the female characters much more" because of her reading. Through the process of reading and writing, the student has learned the importance of contextualizing her ideas and of considering the circumstances that inform a woman's life. Moreover, she has been able to arrive at a larger realization about the position of women in the 19th century—that Edna's life is "typical" for women.

When I began to teach Methods of Literary Criticism online, I did not require students to reply to each other's posts. I was concerned that I was overloading them with a lot of reading and writing online already, and I erroneously thought that they might view it as busy work. I have since rethought that aspect of the class. I now require students to reply to peer posts. Doing so has allowed the thread of the twice-weekly discussion to extend itself so that students get to comment on posts and also get immediate feedback on their responses.

Though the student discussed in this essay did not have the advantage of other students replying directly to her posts, she clearly read their posts to learn their opinions about the novel and the assigned articles. Their posts, in effect, became documents contributing to the larger discussion about the novel. Of interest to me is the student's ability to work through these multiple readings and interpretations of text to create and then re-create her own ideas. Though I hesitate to say that this class experience could not be replicated in a face-to-face environment, I do think, as I have argued, that the unique features of the online environment are an important contributing factor enabling students to read, write, and think about the literary text in a different manner than might be possible in the traditional classroom. The dynamics of the literature class online are subject to change because the position of the instructor is off sides. Moreover, the student has a different relationship with her online audience of peers and other writers with whom she has more of an active engagement than typical in a traditional classroom. Finally, the online environment gives the student the space and opportunity to write, to reflect, and to generate new ideas, creating a permanent record of her thinking to reconsider.

In conclusion, through reading this student's posts on the discussion board, we can observe step-by-step how her reading and writing have worked in tandem, allowing her to rethink the profile of Edna, the main character in Chopin's novel. Informed by the critical articles she read and by her peer audience, this student moved from seeing Edna solely as a woman of entitlement to an understanding that Edna is entitled to her own independence. Though the student is not conversant in literary theoretical language, she nonetheless has been engaged with some of the ideas proffered by the authors of the articles and at times by her peers. In turn, this engagement has helped her to create a new understanding of Edna's behavior. Invited through the articles to see the text as it is informed by historical and cultural circumstances, the student has actively written and created a more nuanced portrait of Edna that complicates her initial interpretation of the novel. By doing so, the student has enacted the premise that meaning in literature can yield multiple perspectives and interpretations. Most important, this student's online posts demonstrate the potential and capability of all students to engage in the process of active meaning-making in their writing and reading about literary texts.

References

Alexander, J., & Dickson, M. (2006). *Role play: Distance learning and the teaching of writing*. Cresskill, NJ: Hampton.

Bizzell, P. (1986). On the possibility of a unified theory of composition and literature. *Rhetoric Review, 4,* 174–180.

Blair, K. L., & Monske, E.A. (2003). Cui bono? Revisiting the promises and perils of online learning. *Computers and Composition, 20*(4), 441–453. Retrieved from http://dx.doi.org/10.1016/j.compcon.2003.08.016

Elbow, P. (1995). Breathing life into the text. In A. Young and T. Fulwiler (Eds.), *When writing teachers teach literature* (pp. 193–205). Portsmouth, NH: Boynton/Cook Heinemann.

Elbow, P. (1996). The war between reading and writing—and how to end it. In J. Slevin & A. Young (Eds.), *Critical theory and the teaching of literature: Politics, curriculum, pedagogy* (pp. 270-291). Urbana, IL: National Council of Teachers of English.

Elbow, P. (2002). The cultures of literature and composition: What could each learn from the other? *College English, 64*(5), 533–546.

Fischer, K., Reiss, D., & Young, A. (2006). Computer-mediated communication and the confluence of composition and literature. In L. Bergmann & E. Baker (Eds.), *Composition and/or literature: The end(s) of education* (pp. 143–170). Urbana, IL: National Council of Teachers of English.

Fitzpatrick, K. (2012). Reading (and writing) online, rather than on the decline. *Profession 2012*, 41–52.

LeBlanc, E. (2000). The metaphorical lesbian: Edna Pointellier in *The Awakening*. In N. A. Walker (Ed.), *The awakening* (pp. 237–256). Boston, MA: Bedford/St. Martin's.

Schroeder, C. (1999). Blurring boundaries: Rhetoric in literature and other classrooms. In A. Robertson & B. Smith (Eds.), *Teaching in the 21st century: Adapting writing pedagogies to the college curriculum* (pp. 297–311). New York, NY: Falmer Press.

Showalter, E. (2000). Tradition and the female talent: *The Awakening* as a solitary book. In N. A. Walker (Ed.), *The awakening* (pp. 202–222). Boston, MA: Bedford/St. Martin's.

Sidler, M., Morris, R., & Smith, E. (2008). Reflecting on technology and literacy in the composition classroom. In *Computers in the composition classroom: A critical sourcebook* (pp. 1–19). Boston, MA: Bedford/St. Martin's.

Stange, M. (2000). Personal property: Exchange value and the female self in *The Awakening*. In N. A. Walker (Ed.), *The awakening* (pp. 274–290). Boston, MA: Bedford/St. Martin's.

Walker, N. A. (2000). Introduction: Biographical and historical contexts. In N. A. Walker (Ed.), *The awakening* (pp. 3–21). Boston, MA: Bedford/St. Martin's.

Wolff, C. (2000). Un-utterable longing: The discourse of feminine sexuality in Kate Chopin's *The Awakening*. In N. A. Walker (Ed.), *The awakening* (pp. 376–395). Boston, MA: Bedford/St. Martin's.

NINE

Getting Down to Earth: Scientific Inquiry and Online Writing for Non-Science Students

Kristine Larsen

Introduction

FOR MANY LIBERAL ARTS STUDENTS, the dreaded general education science requirement can be the bane of their existence. Universities have historically (mis-)served these students with massive auditorium-sized courses in which the students can remain anonymous and passive, and the professor and his or her PowerPoint presentations or dusty lecture notes are considered the irrefutable source of all knowledge. Exams are frequently multiple-choice and more often than not graded electronically or by graduate assistants. The students enrolled in these courses are neither engaged with the faculty member nor the material, and often the only interactions they have with each other involve desperate requests for lecture notes for missed classes. Students thus leave these courses with minimal gains in content knowledge and no amelioration in either their misconceptions about or distaste for science. These courses are typically considered a rite of passage to be suffered through in the desperate journey of checking off the boxes on their graduation requirement sheets, rather than an important opportunity to acquire knowledge or hone vital skills such as effective written communication and critical thinking.

As such, many non-science majors take these required courses with the misunderstanding that scientific thinking is primarily a matter of accumulating facts. They erroneously view science writing as the discourse of certainty rather than as the discourse of skepticism. Moreover, because they see themselves on the outside of this discourse community, they believe they must conform to it by regurgitating information in the most unquestioning and unreflective manner.

This chapter will argue that online science courses provide a unique opportunity for non-science majors to engage in scientific discourse. Unlike face-to-face classrooms, online courses provide "safe spaces" where students can use personal writing to interact with each other, thus establishing a sense of community. In this virtual community, students participate more freely. For non-science students, this type of interaction allows them to ask questions, to consider other points of view, and to change their thinking based on scientific evidence. In so doing, it comes closer to actualizing a more authentic scientific inquiry than non-majors are usually able to achieve in a traditional face-to-face course. The online learning environment can aid in shifting a student's understanding of scientific discourse from one of merely absorbing information to one of critical thinking, reflection, and questioning. The key to such a shift is the role that writing plays in online classes.

Scientific Literacy: The Problem of Scientific Misconceptions

For this author, an epiphany occurred when handing back an exam in an astronomy course a number of years ago. A student had made a serious error in calculating the distance to the moon, and when asked why he didn't think it was strange that he had gotten an answer of 7 km, he replied without hesitation "but that's what my calculator told me." What is most disturbing about this incident is not the student's wrong answer but his reflexive acceptance of it ("that's what my calculator told me") and his disinclination to question that certainty. This student, and many like him, views science as a matter of arriving at answers rather than a matter of asking questions. What is more, the status quo of many science courses reinforces this bias by rewarding students who can memorize facts and spit them back on an exam, or who can (either through skill or luck) happen upon the right answer by punching buttons on their calculators. This unquestioning acceptance of "correct" answers is a major obstacle to students becoming scientifically literate citizens who can critically debate important issues such as global warming, nuclear power, and genetic engineering.

Clearly what we seek is deep learning versus superficial memorization or robotic "plug and chug" with no understanding of either the process or the results (as demonstrated so vividly in the example of the 7 km distance to the moon). As Partridge and Greenstein argue, Astro 101 and similar courses should "aim for student learning and attitudes that last—not just until the final exam but for the rest of our students' lives" (2004, p. 62).

Among the stated goals developed by the American Astronomical Society workshop attendees for Astro 101 are that students who leave our classrooms should be

- More confident of their own critical faculties;
- Inspired about science in general and astronomy in particular; and
- Interested in and better equipped to follow scientific arguments in the media (Partridge and Greenstein, 2004, p. 48).

This last goal is especially urgent for all citizens in an increasingly technological society, because "without a basic understanding of how science works, the public is vulnerable to anti-science propaganda, which engenders distrust of science when it comes to social issues, consumer choices, and policy decisions" (Thanukos, Scotchmoor, Caldwell, & Lindberg, 2010, p. 1764). A prime example of this is, of course, climate change and global warming. Survey data compiled by the National Science Board (2010) over several decades has clearly demonstrated that most Americans cannot pass a test composed of basic science knowledge and process questions. Clearly, achieving a basic level of science literacy must be a central goal of any science course for non-science majors, who may confront scientific issues at the ballot box (for example, nuclear power, global warming, and genetic engineering). Standing in the way of science literacy is the prevalence of scientific misconceptions that many non-science students hold.

These misconceptions are problematic because they have been shown to interfere with the learning of correct concepts and factual knowledge (Nussbaum & Novick, 1982). Research has also demonstrated that not only are misconceptions (such as the idea that seasons are caused by the earth's distance from the sun) deep-rooted and difficult to dislodge, but that they are all-too-often held by those who may pass them on to the next generation of learners, namely pre-service and in-service teachers. For example, in their cross-level survey, Bisard, Aron, Francek, and Nelson (1994, p. 42) found that "students enrolled in a general elementary teacher preparation class score similarly to the middle school students they may teach one day" and called this a "cause for concern." Trundle, Atwood, and Christopher (2002, p. 634) summarized the situation:

Because educators are charged with developing a scientifically literate society, a potentially serious problem is presented by pre-service and in-service teachers who themselves hold alternative conceptions about concepts included in the textbooks they use or that are targeted by the national science education standards.

Thus, to cite one statistic as an example, introductory level astronomy courses are offered at the majority of universities and colleges, and have an estimated annual American enrollment of 250,000 students (Partridge & Greenstein 2004, 46). An important part of the audience served by both introductory earth science and astronomy courses is pre-service teachers; therefore, any improvements to the learning taking place in such courses not only directly benefits the students taking those courses, but also has the important indirect benefit of affecting the education of primary and secondary school students who will eventually be served by these future teachers.

Various methods have been employed to try to overcome scientific misconceptions with varying degrees of success, including hands-on activities, sketching out misconceptions, and modeling (Callison & Wright, 1993; Trundle, Atwood, & Christopher, 2002). An outgrowth of the research on student misconceptions in science is the call for educators to make a "special effort to break the 'misconception cycle'" by not only being aware of the existence of such misconceptions, but also by actually utilizing them in the teaching of science (Bisard et al., 1994, p. 42). For example, Comins (2001) and Trumper (2001) have called on educators to identify misconceptions held by students and use them in class discussions in order to help dispel these erroneous ideas and help replace them with a true understanding of the scientific concepts.

While confronting misconceptions head-on may seem like a sound pedagogical strategy, such a call ignores the conditions that have allowed these misconceptions to become so deeply embedded in the first place. The fact is that students' uncertainty about their own scientific abilities, coupled with their dislike of science classes in general, ill equips them to engage in the very sort of dialogue that is likely to dispel these misconceptions. What students require is a safe classroom space for such a dialogue to take place.

One aspect of the online classroom lends itself perfectly to such a project: the fact that such a dialogue must take place in writing. As Rivard explains in his article, "A Review of Writing to Learn in Science," the use of writing can "enhance science learning when . . . the instructional environment sustains a view of scientific literacy that embraces deep conceptual understanding rather than encyclopedic knowledge" (1994, p. 978).

Thus, by engaging students in a written science-based dialogue between themselves and the faculty member as well as between students and their peers, they can more authentically replicate the way science is actually done. This means moving away from writing assignments that search for a singular standardized right answer, such as lab reports and end-of-semester term papers. The answer cannot be gotten from a calculator, memorized for an exam, or even regurgitated back verbatim from class notes. Certainty is thrown out the window. Students demonstrate a more authentic understanding of the scientific process (as well as basic scientific facts and evidence) through their writing when the topic has no set answer.

In online courses, where writing replaces speaking, students are more likely to participate in discussions than their face-to-face counterparts. One can argue that this is true because they have no choice if a graded discussion board is part of the course requirements. However, because of the relative anonymity of the online learning environment, students often feel that there is not the same opportunity for embarrassment if they do not have the right answer at the tip of their tongue. This is because they are not called out to answer questions in front of the entire group with no time to think about what they want to say. In fact, in an online discussion board, students are more likely to offer a hesitant thought or tentative explanation (often prefaced by "I'm not sure, but . . ." or "I might be wrong, but . . .") than in face-to-face class discussions. In the traditional classroom it is often only the "certain" answers that are offered (including wrong or incomplete answers offered with rock-solid belief in their veracity).

In addition, because of the disembodied nature of the discussion board, students also feel less likely to be thought of as stupid if their answer turns out to not be on target. In fact, as will be shown, science-phobic students can bond with similar students in an online environment and more easily negotiate their path toward science literacy within a comfortable and supportive learning community. The next section of this essay focuses on how such writing can help to establish a sense of community online for non-science majors, allowing them to have a voice and to engage in a scientific dialogue. Students,

I will argue, leave the online course rethinking many of their ideas about scientific inquiry, with a new open-mindedness, and with a better sense of the importance of science in their everyday lives. This new awareness about scientific inquiry, no doubt, will help them to become better informed citizens, who might possibly question scientific misconceptions rather than accept them.

For the sake of this article, two specific types of courses geared toward non-science majors will be discussed—introductory surveys in earth science and introductory astronomy, referred to by astronomy educators as "Astro 101." Traditional face-to-face sections of both courses typically fill quickly at the author's home institution, the former (called ESCI 110 Introduction to the Earth) because it is the first course listed on the registration roll for the department (and hence, in the students' minds, it must be the easiest course), and the latter (ESCI 117 Introduction to the Solar System) because of its relatively low designator number and because astronomy is generally considered an interesting subject by many students. Not surprisingly, students enrolling in ESCI 117 often come to the course with serious misconceptions as to what the study of astronomy actually entails, confusing it with astrology, learning the constellations, or merely ogling pretty pictures taken by the Hubble Space Telescope with little thought to the physical principles underlying the importance of those images.

Fostering Scientific Inquiry Through Writing: The Role of Personal Voice and Student Community in the Online Classroom

Since the students in these introductory courses are not science majors, they typically come to the course with bad experiences from previous science courses in high school or college. To establish a supportive, nurturing online writing environment from the first moment of the course, I begin with an introductory discussion board post in which students write a brief personal introduction to explain why they are taking the course. In their article, "Online Learning: Social Interaction and the Creation of a Sense of Community," McInnerney and Roberts (2004) discuss the importance of a "warm-up" or "forming stage" on the discussion board, which can help students to "become comfortable with their sense of 'self' and also to develop their own online personality" (p. 77). Using this type of personal introductory post actually runs counter to what occurs in a face-to-face class, where "objectivity" is the privileged discourse. However, in an online class through writing, students have the opportunity to respond to each other in a more personal way, setting the stage for a completely different class dynamic, where the student's voice is given prominence. Inevitably this introductory thread explodes, as students find new classmates with the same non-science major, or in a similar job, or they re-establish a relationship with a classmate they had met in a previous course. Most importantly, students discover that their classmates are taking the course for the same reason they are (to satisfy a general education requirement and/or certification requirement for education majors) and often that they share the same apprehensions about taking a science course.

The online discussion board thus allows students to talk in a more personal manner, anonymously without the fear of exposure, while at the same time helping to build a stronger sense of community than is possible in a face-to-face class. Unlike in the traditional classroom, personal writing in the online class plays a vital role in establishing a community where all feel comfortable expressing themselves. This type of writing can lead to some surprising personal revelations. One particularly poignant example occurred in a summer class in which one student shared that he had missed the previous semester due to a serious neurological condition. A classmate immediately offered that he had been living with a similar condition for a number of years and offered emotional support and personal experience on dealing with such a life-changing diagnosis. This student's condition would have gone undetected (or unappreciated) in the traditional classroom. However, for this online course, it was a seminal learning experience that opened up the lines of communication and helped to define the learning community as one where honesty and mutual support would be highly valued.

The safe space of the discussion board has the opportunity to carry over into more academic writing. This "we're in the same boat together" philosophy quickly changes throughout the course to a "we're all learning together" mantra, as students spontaneously and without prompts from the teacher share links to interesting content online, or review television documentaries related to the course material in a special discussion thread dedicated to such informal sharing. "Did you see this last night" or "Have you heard about" become recurring phrases throughout the discussion threads. Note here that the informal, personal voice is still prevalent, but now that voice begins to extend itself to the academic work of a science course. By writing to each other to share "personal" knowledge about science content, students begin to have a stake in talking about science topics. This is not the parroting of textbook terminology but the genuine sharing of items of scientific interest. Working together through their written correspondence in this non-major science class helps to establish a completely different tenor than one normally finds in the same course face-to-face. Besides establishing the basis of an online sense of community, students are thrust into a wholly different learning experience than they had expected. This informal sharing of their writing shows them that they each have a voice in the course and that they do have some "expertise" to contribute to the discussion. The writing process online thus builds confidence, which is certainly important in a subject where students' reticence in a face-to-face course tends to make them all too passive. But even more important, their sense of their own expertise, which begins with establishing a personal voice through writing, puts them on course to begin to ask questions rather than to blindly accept answers—a process that was clearly visible in my own online classes. Moreover, through this method of writing, they come to learn that there is no one right answer, which helps to dispel the erroneous simplification of science as a single, well-trodden road toward a monolithic point of view.

For example, in one discussion thread, the students were asked to consider the old saying "look with your eyes, not with your hands" and to explain how this expression applies to astronomers, and whether or not this limits our understanding of the universe. From their discussion board postings, it was clear that students had very different interpretations of this question. For example, one wrote,

> This applies to astronomy because everything we see is out of our reach. Except for astronauts, there are very few of us who get to experience and touch space. The only thing we all have in common is that we are on planet Earth. This hinders the study of astronomy because there is only so much we can learn about other planets from images. Yes, we put rovers on Mars to [take] pictures and hey it's a start! But it's nowhere near as close as we want to be, Astronomers want to be able to go to these planets and get SOLID research.

A classmate countered, "I disagree that if we were able to touch things in deep space it would allow more discoveries. I believe this is because Astronomy is most basically Theoretical Physics and since the laws of Physics are uniform throughout the Universe and we can do experiments here on Earth and send satellites to sample heavenly bodies that pass by, it seems like we have all we need."

In this written exchange, the reader can see that students have an investment in the course material. The obvious advantage of the online environment is the time and space for students to write out their thoughts—to participate in a scientific discussion. Moreover, the back-and-forth nature of the discussion board allows students not only to articulate their ideas but also to test them and to reconsider them, modeling true scientific inquiry. Science-based debate is taking place here in a respectful environment where one student's viewpoint invites an opposing perspective. Such a dynamic would be difficult to replicate in a face-to-face class where factors such as limited time, anxiety about public speaking, and the deference to the teacher-as-authority would work against them.

Writing on a discussion board post also more visibly illustrates to students the necessity to support their individual positions. In one example, students argued for or against the reclassification of Pluto from a planet to the new category of dwarf planet. With this discussion, students who support the reclassification nearly always begin by referencing the official (albeit controversial) International Astronomical Union (IAU) definition of a planet, and then dissecting the three parts of the definition to demonstrate how Pluto fails the third criterion (it is not able to clear its orbit of other objects). As the students above demonstrate, having an audience encourages writers to marshal evidence in support of their claims. To do so, they reference arguments made by outside sources, thus demonstrating their understanding of the importance of backing up claims with scientific information. In this example, students who argued on the other side of reclassification also collected information from outside sources and, significantly, pointed out scientific flaws in the very definition that was used to reclassify Pluto in the first place.

A key point that comes up in many posts is the self-correcting nature of science (a central focus in science). One student noted, "Keeping it a planet just because it's been considered one for a long time isn't true to science. As astronomers learn more and more about space and its bodies large and small, they need to react appropriately and use all of the knowledge they gain. Sometimes, that will mean correcting themselves and reclassifying an object in space, and that's ok." A classmate saw through the scientific language in the IAU definition and realized that it boiled down to scientists coming up with a poorly crafted definition meant to exclude Pluto largely due to its size: "I think it should not have been re-categorized as a dwarf planet due to its size. However, any new 'possible' planets that are found that may be bigger should not be considered a planet. A scale should be created for measuring what qualifies an object in space to be officially made a planet. Does size, does orbiting rate, does chemical composition, and so on make a new object a suitable applicant to become the next planet?"

As these examples demonstrate, when given the latitude to argue a position, as offered by the unique experience of the online environment, students prove themselves quite adept at arguing their individual positions and posing counterexamples to support their conclusions. In writing their responses, they are clearly cognizant of their online audience and frequently will reference each other, illustrating their ability to build on what has already been written. For example, when asked if they thought that astronomers would find evidence of life elsewhere in the universe during their lifetime, one student praised another's work, noting that he liked "the way you put how we don't have technology 'sophisticated' enough to find intelligent life." Another built off this comment as well, but directed the poster to consider how much technology had changed in the past decade and what that could mean for future technological advances. In a final thread, in which students considered the change in their perspective about our home planet, one student took a minority viewpoint: "With all due respect I do not think our world is that fragile, as I actually stated in an earlier discussion as a reply to another student's post. . . . I don't think the earth is fragile because of exactly the things we have learned—all that this planet has endured before us and will endure after us." As this latter student's response suggests, unlike the experience of the face-to-face classroom where passivity dominates, these students show their ability to engage in rigorous debate about science topics by implicitly critiquing each other and at other times by offering advice to extend the thinking of difficult topics. In this type of online discussion, these non-science students speak from within the scientific discourse community rather than standing outside of it, which is what they tend to do in traditional face-to-face science courses.

Their success in these dialogues is an outgrowth of how writing has effectively replaced speaking as the mode of student participation.

Moreover, because the discussion board offers a permanent record of student writing, the online environment lets us see how students change their ideas when reading what others have written, in effect learning from each other. Due to the asynchronous nature of the discussion board, students can ponder what they have read and wrestle with it before returning to the community with a follow-up post in the conversation. By examining the available facts, weighing the relative preponderance of the evidence on different sides of the issue, and coming to a reasoned conclusion (which may be diametrically opposed to one's initial point of view), students engage in an authentic scientific dialogue, and find that often in the process of scientific investigation there can be only tentative, preliminary conclusions.

Of paramount importance in the online classroom is the ability to discuss without rancor such controversial issues as literalist interpretations of the Judeo-Christian Bible and scientific theories (most specifically evolution, the Big Bang, and the ancient age of the Earth). Such discussions are customarily avoided in science classes, and even if the faculty member or a fellow student brings up the topic, many students often appear hesitant to raise their hands in front of dozens (or hundreds) of classmates and voice an opinion or personal concern. This code of silence prevents students who are struggling with apparent contradictions between what they are learning in class and their (or their families') personal belief systems from asking questions. As a result, they may leave the class convinced that science is "anti-religion" or revert to the safety of the default position that science is just something you learn in class then promptly forget.

In contrast, in an online classroom, students can effectively and thoughtfully discuss these topics. In one class, for example, this topic was initially broached when a student offered, "The most challenging theory for me is the big bang because in church we are taught one thing ever since we are little, but then there's a theory that makes more sense to me than the religious one." A classmate quickly added, "I'm so glad I'm not the only one that has this problem. I believe in my religion but at the same time there is a lot of evidence that makes everything so confusing, but I do believe there has to be some truth in both religion and evolution." A third student shared details about her own religious upbringing and her appreciation for the explanations she finally received in science classes. However, she explained that, "As time went by and I got older, I realized that there is no one OR the other, they are connected. Connected as one fills in the blanks for the other. We, meaning humans, need rules, directions, faith in our lives, as much as we need experiments, discoveries, and theories."

In a reply to her post, a student wrote, "I agree! After being told in a college biology class that there really was no possible way for a God to have created this and literally having to answer 'False' to a question regarding whether it was scientifically possible for there to be a higher power I began to wonder how we're so sure that a higher power didn't create the Big Bang." This student's post describes from her experience how easily this topic can devolve into staking out rigid positions in a face-to-face class, effectively shutting down discussion for some students. In this face-to-face course, the student also felt put into a position where she was forced to choose between science and faith rather than consider the natural differences between these two ways of looking at the world.

But in an online environment where there is a sense of community, the tenor of the conversation can be quite different from that of a face-to-face discussion. In the online environment, students can read and take their time to comment and to think through what others have written or to think through their own positions. For example, in this class, after a number of other students shared their personal battles between how they had been taught both science and religion, a classmate noted that he had "found [the student's] pull between religion and science extremely fascinating. I am not a religious person, however I feel like there is definitely something way more powerful and unknown in existence, and that humans are only a small speck in the vast universe." This particular thread continued to be populated with replies and personal observations well past the official due date, demonstrating not only that a respectful discourse about science and religion *is* possible in the science classroom, but that it adds rather than detracts from the learning of science. The asynchronous, anonymous nature of the online learning community in effect allows students to share their most personal connections to and struggles with the material in their own time and in their own way. Moreover, such discussions can take on a life of their own with no single student monopolizing the conversation (and hence class time), as sometimes happens in face-to-face classes. If a student does post an inordinate number of comments, since there is far less of a time constraint placed on the discussion, everyone has sufficient time to have their say.

Because they have established a particular community, where all feel comfortable writing about their thoughts and ideas through the shared experience of the discussion board, these non-science students are quite frank about expressing their opinions. When asked to reflect and comment upon what they had learned throughout the course, students had rather telling comments to make. In her initial post, one student shared "I used to think there were multiple stars in our solar system. For example the constellations, I thought the Big Dipper and Orion were in our solar system. I don't remember being taught otherwise, so it makes sense why I would believe that." A classmate built off her post, and a discussion about the general state of science education ensued. "I think you bring up an enormous point here when you say, 'I don't remember being taught otherwise, so it makes sense why I would believe that,'" she began. "We're about to graduate from college, which means we have about 16 years of formal education under our belts, and I think it's unfortunate that so many of us know so little about our universe. . . . I used to think the terms universe, galaxy and solar system were synonymous! I'm disappointed in our education systems that have failed to teach us such differences, or maybe highlight their importance, so as adults we could have a more appropriate view of reality." In-class lectures on the problem of science literacy and misconceptions rarely instigate this level of passion. Here the students were able to articulate in a highly effective manner their own previous misconceptions about science and the connection of those misconceptions to the state of science education in general.

It should be noted that despite the supportive atmosphere of the discussion group learning community, students will sometimes have questions and concerns that they are not willing to share with such a broad audience. In this respect, the online environment gives the professor an opportunity to engage one-on-one with a student. For some students communicating directly with the faculty member can be empowering, enabling them to ask lingering questions. Professors can also provide sources of additional information, such as trusted websites, to the students, thus encouraging them to continue exploring aspects of the course they have expressed interest in. Students will also (without intending to do so) make evident any lingering misconceptions they still have, giving the faculty member a valuable opportunity to correct these misconceptions without calling out the student in front of others. Since the students are engaging in a private and personal conversation with the instructor, there is no fear of appearing "stupid" in front of the entire class, or worrying that they are monopolizing class time or taking the class too far off topic. Science is a process of asking questions, making discoveries, and refining our questions. Students become scientists when they partake in this process by asking questions of their peers, of their faculty member, and, perhaps most important of all, of themselves.

Conclusion

In order to create a scientifically literate society, we need to effectively model the true scientific endeavor to a wider audience and have that audience try their individual hands at being "scientific." The kind of writing that students produce in online discussion boards comes closer to authentic scientific writing than most writing that is produced in face-to-face classes because it forces students to engage in the process of scientific thinking, and it makes that process visible to them. Their writing is less concerned with the "right" answer; rather, they learn to write "scientifically" by asking questions, acknowledging alternative points of view, and, importantly, demonstrating an understanding that one's own point of view is expected to change in the face of newly gathered scientific evidence. One can only be certain in the moment, based on current understanding. This can be a difficult lesson to learn, but it more accurately reflects the scientific endeavor. Moreover, the nature of online discussion underscores how science is a collaborative endeavor, something that most students do not fully appreciate at first, but which they come to understand quickly in the give and take of the online discussion.

In writing about science in a personal and highly reflective way, students realize that not only is science all around us, but also it can and should be understood by the average citizen. Students find a voice through their written words in a safe and supportive atmosphere—a virtual learning community in which those students who are more likely to remain passive in face-to-face classrooms (where more loquacious students can monopolize the conversation) can enjoy a level playing field.

Students often specifically comment on the learning that takes place in both their own writing and by reading others' comments. For example, one student offered, "I learned a lot from this course and enjoyed reading other people's thoughts and experiences as well." Another student agreed, "I also liked to read what other students had to say about the material in the discussions. I liked seeing many different perspectives on the subject matter." A classmate added, "I was also pleased with the comments from fellow classmates on their attitudes towards taking personal responsibilities in their own lives to make a difference in conserving the natural resources that we do have."

Writing in online science courses allows students to ask questions, to express their opinions, and to demonstrate their mastery of science without the pressure of having to "perform" live in a classroom. The thinking that goes into a response can be deliberate, reflective, and can draw upon multiple sources of information, including the students' previous words as well as those of their classmates. One student initially posted to their class "Science is not my favorite topic, that is why I am completing this course in my senior year." At the end of the course three weeks later, she noted, "I drive on the highways and took the mountains and rock formation after the road was built for granted. Some of the rock formation is at right angles. Now I have a better idea why they look that way and the number of years it took to get that way." A classmate agreed, noting "Science has never been my cup of tea, but during this course I have become more knowledgeable about the topic of the Earth. Everyone should have basic knowledge about the Earth. It shapes our minds to be better people." We should take these students' words to heart when considering the central role that writing plays in online science courses and the effect that the structure of online science courses can have on the writing that occurs in such courses.

References

Bisard, W. J., Aron, R. H., Francek, M. A., & Nelson, B. D. (1994). Assessing selected physical science and earth science misconceptions of middle school through university preservice teachers: Breaking the science "misconception cycle." *Journal of College Science Teaching, 24*, 38–42.

Callison, P. L., & Wright, E. L. (1993, April). *The effect of teaching strategies using models on preservice elementary teachers' conceptions about earth-sun-moon relationships.* Paper presented at the Annual Meeting of the National Association for Research in Science Teaching, Atlanta, GA. Retrieved from http://www.eric.ed.gov/ERICWebPortal/detail?accno=ED360171

Comins, N. (2001). *Heavenly errors: Misconceptions about the real nature of the universe.* New York, NY: Columbia University Press.

McInnerney, J. M., & Roberts, T. S. (2004) Online learning: Social interaction and the creation of a sense of community. *Educational Technology and Society, 7*(3), 73–81.

National Science Board. (2010). *Science and engineering indicators 2010.* Arlington, VA: National Science Foundation. Retrieved from http://www.nsf.gov/statistics/seind10/

Nussbaum, J., & Novick, S. (1982). Alternate frameworks, conceptual conflict and accommodation: Toward a principled teaching strategy. *Instructional Science, 11*, 183–200.

Partridge, B., & Greenstein, G. (2004). Goals for "Astro 101": Report on workshops for department leaders. *Astronomy Education Review, 2*(2), 46–89.

Rivard, L. P. (1994). A review of writing to learn in science: Implications for practice and research. *Journal of Research in Science Teaching, 31*(9), 969–983.

Thanukos, A., Scotchmoor, J. G., Caldwell, R., & Lindberg, D. R. (2010). Science 101: Building the foundations for real understanding. *Science, 330*, 1764–1765.

Trumper, R. (2001). A cross-college age study of science and nonscience students' conceptions of basic astronomical concepts in preservice training for high-school teachers. *Journal of Science Education and Technology, 10*(2), 189–195.

Trundle, K. C., Atwood, R. K., & Christopher, J. E. (2002). Preservice elementary teachers' conceptions of moon phases before and after instruction. *Journal of Research in Science Teaching, 39*(7), 633–658.

TEN

Teaching for Transfer Online: Insights From an Adapted Curricular Model

Liane Robertson

A S THE AVAILABILITY OF ONLINE writing courses increases, it provides an opportunity to consider writing pedagogy, not only about how writing courses are tailored for online delivery but also about how teaching writing in general—regardless of delivery method—occurs in today's academic environment. How students adapt to learning and enacting writing in online courses has applications in the face-to-face teaching of writing at various levels and for all types of writing courses. Through instructing online—through the experience of observing and interacting with students in an online writing course—we gain valuable information about how they understand writing and how we might use those insights in the teaching of writing across methods of delivery.

This chapter reports on a study in which the effect of a course designed explicitly for students' transfer of writing knowledge, using a particular model of writing instruction known as *Teaching for Transfer* (TFT) (Robertson & Taczak, 2017; Yancey, Robertson, & Taczak, 2014), was adapted for an online course in technical writing. Nine subjects ranging from sophomore to senior level were recruited from this upper-division writing course, which took place over a 16-week semester and was taught exclusively online. Through interviews and analysis of writing samples, this study explores how subjects from the TFT-designed online technical writing course offer insights for writing instruction that promotes successful transfer: students in online environments may have more agency, which can allow for greater uptake of the conceptual framework that anchors the TFT curricular model and which is essential for their successful transfer of writing knowledge and practices to new situations.

The Teaching for Transfer curricular model reported in *Writing Across Contexts: Transfer, Composition, and Sites of Writing* (2014) has been successful in teaching students to transfer knowledge and practice about writing into new contexts, but previously has only been studied in traditional classroom delivery. This curricular model—which is defined by its three specific, interlocking components: (a) rhetorical concepts or key terms about writing, (b) systematic, reiterative reflection at key course intervals, and (c) students' development of their own theory of writing—proved effective for some students and not for others in the online environment, just as results for its face-to-face version have shown previously (Yancey, Robertson, & Taczak, 2014). However, students' experiences with the Teaching for Transfer model in the online environment can provide insights into how students might learn to transfer effectively across writing contexts for all means of course delivery: (a) increased student agency contributes to transfer, and (b) a student's commitment to reflection—the specific type of reflection featured in the TFT model—affords the conceptual framework needed to understand how to transfer.

Adapting Writing Content to Online Courses

There are both real and perceived challenges about the restrictions of online courses particular to the teaching of writing. The smaller class sizes and focus on process found in writing courses, as well as the voluminous level and commitment to instructor feedback customary in teaching writing, may seem impractical for online instruction. And because writing is sometimes a considerably personal endeavor, teachers of writing can feel at odds with a course design that features only onscreen interaction. But the online environment also provides an opportunity to understand how our students perceive our instructions or assignments, and to engage students in communication they may not feel comfortable with in a face-to-face classroom (Ko & Rossen, 2010).

Educational institutions recognize the logistical and financial need to acclimate to the current educational landscape, including moving from a campus-based model only toward a more consumer-based model, which might include courses in face-to-face, online, or hybrid formats. While not necessarily a popular shift, the flexibility of online instruction benefits students in terms of convenience, and institutions are finding they must adapt to this model to remain viable in the 21st-century educational landscape. But the new model brings with it a shift in expectations for faculty and students both:

an expectation of increased technological literacy, a shift toward 24/7 teaching and learning, and more flexibility in course structure. This shift often requires more of students, especially those who are new to online courses.

> Suddenly thrust into a world in which independent or collaborative learning is heavily stressed, students accustomed to traditional classroom procedures—taking notes during a lecture, answering the occasional question, attending discussion sections—must make unexpected and often jolting adjustments to their study habits. (Ko & Rossen, 2010, p. 287)

For students, though, this "jolting adjustment" might be beneficial, especially in a writing course with content that students may perceive as familiar or already mastered, which, as research on prior knowledge[1] indicates (Driscoll & Wells, 2012; Reiff & Bawarshi, 2011; Robertson, Taczak, & Yancey, 2012), is a potential barrier to their learning. Online courses have the potential for helping students to re-envision their writing or their approach to a writing situation when that online environment asks them to learn in new ways.

For teachers of writing, this requires adapting our content, our expertise, and our practices to online models of writing instruction for which we develop—not merely retrofit—writing course content that capitalizes on the opportunities offered in an online format while adjusting for the differences in the learning experience this format creates for students. We can't just move face-to-face course content to an online format without considering the different ways learners interpret, respond to, and make use of content online. However, we don't want to compromise writing as content when we move online. With its aim of enabling students to transfer writing knowledge across contexts, the Teaching for Transfer model, maintaining the focus on its particular content—writing concepts, reflection, and a theory of writing—must be adaptable to online delivery.

The Teaching for Transfer Curricular Model

The Teaching for Transfer (TFT) curricular design[2] outlined below is based on research in writing transfer specifically related to the content of writing courses and how students learn to successfully transport knowledge and practice as they move to new writing situations. Transfer is understood by researchers in Writing Studies as a writer's ability to repurpose knowledge about writing for new situations. But transfer is much more complex than that statement represents, and there is some contention among those in our field around the issue of whether writing instruction deliberately aimed at transfer as its goal is efficacious (Robertson & Taczak, forthcoming). Research has demonstrated that we can teach for transfer,[3] but success isn't the outcome for every student and there is no significantly generalizable research currently; as transfer research has increased exponentially in the past few years, generalizability is one of its researchers' main objectives. The question of whether or how transfer can be successful in an online context remains under exploration.

With its three interlocking components, the TFT model is based on the notion that students can transfer knowledge about writing, and practices learned in a writing classroom, to new contexts in which they'll write across college and beyond, when that instruction is explicitly geared to transfer as its goal. Previous research on this particular model (Yancey, Robertson, & Taczak, 2014) supports the idea that explicit instruction with transfer as its deliberate goal can result in students' ability to transfer successfully (see, for example, Bransford, Pellegrino, & Donovan, 2000; Carter, 1990; Perkins & Salomon, 1992; Sommers & Saltz, 2004). Findings from the previous TFT research included evidence that transfer does occur under certain conditions and in certain contexts; the Teaching for Transfer model helped students develop a conceptual framework of knowledge and practice about writing that they were able to repurpose for other contexts of writing in college. The reasons for this success were found to be related to the set of key terms or concepts about writing featured in the TFT course, the use of reflection extensively and reiteratively, and the "Theory of Writing" assignment students developed throughout the semester.

At the heart of the Teaching for Transfer curricular design is a set of key terms or concepts about writing, around which the use of extensive and reiterative reflection is built, including students' development of a theory of writing. This three-pronged approach to understanding writing knowledge and practicing writing in various contexts helps students to access the knowledge they create in the course as well as the prior knowledge they bring to the course and to develop a conceptual framework they can use and re-use for every writing situation in which they find themselves.

The first major component of the TFT design—key terms, or concepts about writing—provides a foundation for thinking about and understanding writing through course readings, writing activities, and four major assignments. Eight key terms emerged from the research as critical for students to understand about writing, and those concepts are introduced, modeled, and reiterated within multiple assignments throughout the course; they include rhetorical situation/exigence, audience, genre, reflection, knowledge, context, discourse community, and purpose. The second component of the course—reflection—focuses on three types of reflective practice: reflective theory, reflective activities, and reflective assignments. Reflection is used in explicit and intentional ways to help students make sense of what they are learning about writing, through everyday reflection writing and through the reiterative, semester-long assignment in which they create a theory of writing. The Theory of Writing assignment, in which students discuss the concepts learned in the course and how they were enacting those concepts in their writing, helped them access their knowledge, make sense of that knowledge as they recognized it and used it in new assignments, and understand how to draw upon that knowledge in future writing contexts. This third and final component asks students to think about their approach to each writing situation; students use this conceptual framework they develop as part of the course, and incorporate other writing experiences, to inform their theory of writing (Yancey, Robertson & Taczak, 2014; Robertson & Taczak, 2017).

For students in the TFT course, one of the reasons they find success in learning about writing is that transfer is an explicit goal, discussed in the classroom and reiterated on the syllabus, assignments, and writing prompts regularly. Students in the course are able to discern appropriate knowledge they might apply to another context from what is not appropriate in a new context, not only because they become familiar with writing concepts and practices but also because they understand the learning objective is to transfer, so they are able to capitalize on opportunities to transfer when those opportunities are presented. The previous research which looked at the TFT course indicated that students who study other types of content in first-year composition courses, and who are not asked to conduct reiterative and substantive reflection as they do in the TFT course, might experience transfer, but that transfer is often serendipitous and context-specific (Yancey, Robertson, & Taczak, 2014). Students have difficulty replicating its success in another context without a conceptual framework of understanding about the writing they're doing (Beaufort, 2007).

One of the reasons students don't successfully transfer across contexts is that the prior knowledge they bring with them to each writing course may act as a barrier to developing new knowledge (Robertson, Taczak, & Yancey, 2012). Prior knowledge has a significant impact on how students understand writing contextually, and therefore on their ability to discern which knowledge is appropriate to transfer to each new context in which they write (Bransford, Pellegrino, & Donovan, 2000). The TFT's conceptual framework helps students move past their entrenched prior knowledge (Robertson, Taczak, & Yancey, 2012; Yancey, Robertson & Taczak, 2014).

Prior Knowledge and Transfer in Teaching Online

As research on prior knowledge conducted by Scherff and Piazza (2005), Applebee and Langer (2009, 2011), and others suggests, students transition from high school to college writing bringing with them some knowledge, often about writing process or literary analysis, but not the inquiry-based writing they'll need to do in college. Additional research indicates students equate school writing with test writing and other forms of evaluation—that writing is a means to an end, to do well on standardized tests, and seen as the price of entry for college (Yancey, Robertson, & Taczak, 2014).

The knowledge students bring from their high school writing, and the testing culture they experience before college, are important to our understanding of the ways prior knowledge influences new learning, and thus growth in their writing. We know from the research on transfer, particularly the National Research Council volume, *How People Learn*, that "all new learning involves transfer based on previous learning" (Bransford, Pellegrino, & Donovan, 2000), so the knowledge, experience, and dispositions students bring into a context shape how they interpret that context (Driscoll, 2011; Driscoll & Wells, 2012). While there are occasions in which prior knowledge can be beneficial to writing in a new situation, there are also occasions in which students draw upon knowledge that worked previously for a specific situation but which they can mistakenly assume is appropriate in any new context. Prior knowledge can thus create a barrier to new learning because of its assumed applicability across contexts (Yancey, Robertson, & Taczak,

2014), and when that assumption is tightly held, it can block a writer's ability to be open to thinking in new ways about writing. Potentially compounding this blockage is the similarity of some college writing content to that of a student's high school experience, reinforcing the misconception that writing works the same way in every situation.

Students make use of prior knowledge and practice in different ways,[4] in part based on how they self-identify as writers. Some, based on successful past performance as indicated by grades, test scores, and other markers which frame a student's self-perception, identify strongly as writers; others, based on less successful experiences, might self-identify as novice writers (Robertson, Taczak, & Yancey, 2012; Yancey, Robertson, & Taczak, 2014). Those who identify strongly as writers can harbor resistance to learning or exploring different ways of writing, demonstrating what Reiff and Bawarshi (2011) have called "Boundary Guarding" behavior, and what Wardle (2012) describes as a "Problem Solving" disposition. Those who do not self-identify as strong writers, and who may have experienced markers that reinforce that perception, are called "Boundary Crossers" in Reiff and Bawarshi's terminology, or "Problem-Explorers" in Wardle's, and are often more open to new ways of thinking about their approach to a writing assignment because they are not as invested in that self-identification as the stronger writers often are.

The Teaching for Transfer curriculum's fostering of a conceptual framework helps students to recognize opportunities for transfer and to move past existing barriers created by prior knowledge. It asks students to work at considering writing as subject matter and to think about writing conceptually. As we know from the research on prior knowledge discussed previously, asking students to think differently about writing—especially as something they think they already understand—can lead to new learning. Developing a conceptual framework about writing, as the Teaching for Transfer course fosters, requires them to explore *what* writing is, on a cognitive level, as well as *how* writing is done (Yancey, Robertson, & Taczak, 2014).

Students' uses of prior knowledge in responding to new writing situations and creating their own new concepts of writing vary, but research indicates that if students understand there is an absence of knowledge they might need for writing in college, they might be motivated to take up new knowledge in more helpful ways, to see setbacks as opportunities, and to be able to create a conceptual framework of knowledge and practice in writing that they can continue to revise and make effective as they move through different writing situations (Yancey, Robertson, & Taczak, 2014). An online course can accelerate such exploration.

TFT Online: Transfer, Prior Knowledge, and Student Agency

Online classrooms can provide an environment that forces students to wrest control of their fate as writers in ways that a face-to-face classroom may not. In this IRB-approved study[5] of the TFT course model's adaptation for online instruction, findings indicated students were receptive to thinking about writing in new ways and to taking increased ownership of their own learning about writing.

In the online environment students are in a state of perpetual performance, without the ability to hide among their classmates. For example, a student who doesn't understand a concept in a face-to-face classroom can abstain from participating in class discussion or provide a response based on the context of others' responses; in the online environment that student is unable to hide the fact that he or she is not grasping course material. The student has to develop a response, not just verbally but in writing, where there is a permanence and commitment to a class discussion posted on the course site. Even consulting the discussions that others have posted on the course site requires abstraction of that information in order for a student to be able to develop a response from it. Students in this study reported that consulting classmates' postings provided an opportunity to reflect on what they themselves thought about a particular concept or about what to write in an assignment, and that this was helpful because of the pressure to perform for each class discussion, something they wouldn't worry about in a face-to-face classroom, as indicated in this subject's[6] interview:

> MARK: The thing is, these online classes are like you're meeting in the professor's office or something . . . you have to answer every question, every time. There's no one else to take the pressure off. You can sit in a [face-to-face] classroom and give off this vibe that you know what everyone's talking about but you can't do that online. You have to really come up with something to say, and it can't just be half-assed thinking because you have to write it out and put it up [on the course

site]. You have to really think about the thing and what you're going to say about it so you don't look like an idiot and so you pass the assignment. That's, like, every class you have to say something smart so you have to work harder I think. It made me work harder, at least, to make sure I was following what was taught.

INTERVIEWER: How did you make sure you were following what was taught?

MARK: I just did the reading for each class, which I don't normally always do, and I guess I made time for thinking about what to write, which is another thing I wouldn't always do. But this class made you think about that . . . about what you needed to write, because it was actually about writing. So you had to break it down. I am a personal trainer, so I know how to break things down into parts for my clients and this was like that. You had to do that for every one of the assignments . . . break it into audience, purpose, context and that stuff. You had to think about why you were writing something, like what the goal of it was and that told you what you needed to do.

INTERVIEWER: So do you always break it down, whenever you write something?

MARK: Yeah, I guess I do. I pretty much think about why I'm writing and the audience for it before I write anything. It saves time. You don't have to go back and fix as much if you know what you're doing before you start. I do that in my other classes too now, when I have to write something, so I know where I'm going with it before I waste any time writing something that doesn't fit the need.

INTERVIEWER: And do you do this for just online classes or any classes?

MARK: No all my classes. And even my work. I guess I learned to do it in the online class because, like I said, we couldn't get away with not knowing that stuff. But I think it was good because I always think of those words, you know, that [instructor] taught us about how to think of writing something . . . you know, audience and rhetorical situation and stuff. I have them all in my phone and I check them when I write something.

Mark evidences in this interview that he has abstracted the concepts from the course and indicates that he has reflected on his approach to new writing situations and continues to do so when he is required to write. His storage of the key concepts from the course in his phone as a checklist provide him with a framework of writing knowledge he can call up onscreen when in a new writing situation. Interestingly, Mark also indicates that the online format of this course forced him to approach his writing assignments with greater responsibility for their outcome, and that he was aware of or perceived the greater evaluation of posting an individual discussion to the course site.

Further, Mark transfers his conceptual knowledge about writing between contexts, including other classes, and brings prior knowledge from his work as a personal trainer to bear in understanding his conceptual framework for writing.[7]

As Mark demonstrates, online courses can create a sense of heightened agency as students take ownership of their learning and progress in the course, and as they are forced to think for themselves. In an online environment, students may not be as quick or likely to ask the instructor for clarification as they do in a face-to-face classroom, given the interface required to access the instructor. Or they might imagine, as Mark did, that what they are posting to the site is a form of conversation with the instructor. In fact all but one of the study participants indicated they would first read instructions, look at assignment descriptions, and sometimes access a discussion forum to get information before asking the instructor. Even when the instructor was ultimately contacted to provide clarification, students most likely had to write an e-mail or post to a discussion forum, and this act of composing the question to the instructor forced them to think about the writing assignment or situation in a way they may not have in a face-to-face course.

This thought process and resulting question engages the student in developing knowledge, sometimes based on prior knowledge or assumption, which provides an insight into how course content is conceptualized, so that the instructor might respond in a more targeted, helpful way to this student. By the time of the instructor's response, the student has engaged in thinking about a writing task, involving conceptualization, reflection, and sometimes multiple iterations of thinking about the writing task in responding to what the instructor writes back, as this example illustrates:

SAMANTHA: How should this essay be? I know our discussion board was to write about what we would do but I just wrote down my main ideas in that discussion I didn't really organize them. Were we suppose [*sic*] to? I am thinking of having three main areas to discuss. Genre, audience, and rhetorical situation. I will use the examples we read to support my ideas but does this sound like the way I should structure it? I know you said we should do more than a five-paragraph essay. I just want to organize it into three main areas to keep it straight and then use whichever readings as my supporting evidence for those areas, with one paragraph for each reading I discuss in each area. Is that okay? If I use 3 readings for each idea is that enough evidence?

INSTRUCTOR: It sounds like you're thinking of organizing your assignment around the three concepts you will discuss, and that you will use at least three pieces of supporting evidence for each concept, is that right? What will your audience expect? What does the genre of "article" suggest?

SAMANTHA: I guess I did kind of organize it if I have 3 areas to discuss. I think I will keep the three areas and then break out each one into the way it is used in one reading, and then the next and the next. That way I can explain to my audience with different examples what is important about each thing.

Samantha practices the development of a conceptual framework in this example by first thinking about the assignment requirements, then reflecting on her discussion forum in which she wrote about her intended approach to the assignment. Later in the course, in a written reflection exercise about a multi-genre assignment, she demonstrates a more sophisticated conceptual framework:

My topic of childhood obesity is very broad, so I have to choose which of my audiences I want to create my web site for. In the audience analysis exercise I decided that my primary audience was parents, with a secondary audience of educators, and also the administration people in schools who decide what students eat and drink at school . . . since this is a web site I have to make the information quick and easy to get, since these users are hunting for specific information like tips or menus or guidelines. My site will be organized around ideas for feeding kids at school, like the tips and guidelines for healthy school lunches. It will also have a page of links to resources that the audiences can click on if they want more information. And it will have a section on teaching healthy eating with lesson plans and articles and fun exercises like name the vegetable and shopping lists for kids to make, and in this genre the information should be easily accessible, where they can pick and choose what is helpful for them, and then if they want to do their own research they can start with the resources. The users for this web site will probably be putting together last minute lessons or meals so it should have things they can download and print or that they can show on a screen in their classroom. It should be the place to go for information on teaching kids nutrition and on providing good nutrition choices in schools.

In this example, Samantha's reflection is an act of invention and demonstrates her understanding of several of the concepts in the course (audience, genre, context, discourse community, rhetorical situation) as she considers how to tailor her website to audiences she has identified for it. It may be easier for Samantha to imagine her audience for this online course assignment than it would be in a face-to-face course for two reasons: (a) she is removed from the context of a traditional classroom, which reinforces that the writing in class is merely academic or forced, without a "real" (or at least imagined as real) audience, and (b) she has greater ownership of her assignment since she chose a topic, decided on and analyzed audiences for that topic, and developed the content for the genre in which she would be writing.

Further, Samantha is forced to think about her assignment as something she is responsible for shepherding through the course, relying on her own approach to understanding and developing the assignment and taking responsibility for reporting to her instructor on its progress and rationalizing her rhetorical choices as she does so, as demonstrated in this exchange:

INSTRUCTOR: How are you progressing with your assignment? Do you
    know which three genres you'll develop and what information you'll
    use from the technical report?

SAMANTHA: I decided on the key points from my research that were going to be important for someone to know, and then I thought about the research sources I found and who the audience was for those. I already have the audience for it [assignment] but thinking about some of the research I did helped me think of more audiences too, even if I didn't end up using them. It just helped me know that my audience was a good choice, too. Next I picked my genres to use and that was easier when I had the audience. I have the web site, the article for the parenting magazine, and the nutrition brochure, so those are my three.

INSTRUCTOR: What makes you sure about those choices? How did you decide on them?

SAMANTHA: I looked back at my research and also at some [research] I didn't end up using, and I also just found some interesting things online. I decided to look for facts about my audience instead of just my topic, and I found statistics about teachers and schools related to this stuff that helped me see what would work. It helped me because the statistics show my audience is a big factor in the issue and what goes on to help kids learn more about healthy eating. So I knew I was talking to the right audience. And then I just know from seeing all the research on this topic that those three genres are something that teachers and schools would use or look at for information.

INSTRUCTOR: Okay, and where do you go from here to complete your project?

SAMANTHA: I'm almost done with it actually. I looked at some samples of brochures that I [searched for online] and I looked at [web] sites for education programs that I had from my research and I started to form my information for these genres. It's so different to write in a brochure because you have so much to say and you can't just stuff it all in there or it won't look right. And the web site is different too. You have as much room as you want to say whatever but no one will read that much. I'm trying to decide what to cut out. I'll probably finish it this weekend when I have time to think about it and use the reflection again to make sure I'm doing all of it how I want.

Samantha is able to transfer the knowledge she began to develop earlier in the semester when she reflected on how to organize a writing assignment, to the later assignment of the web site for which she confidently discusses the key concepts she needs to address in the assignment. She has created a conceptual framework from which she can transfer knowledge about writing to a new situation: she knows she needs to consider audience, to identify the genre and its conventions, and in the case of this technical writing assignment, the context of use for users of her web site. Her written reflection reveals she has learned to think about writing and to reframe her thinking for each new situation.

Since this learning happens in an online environment, where interaction with the instructor is limited to writing and thus forces students to conceptualize prior to communicating, they may have a greater sense of ownership for their work. They *manage* their work using the tools available to them on the course site rather than *react* to instructions for doing work using what they are told by an instructor, as is often the case in a traditional classroom setting. In Samantha's case, she developed the ability to conceive of a piece of writing for a context she had never written previously (a website), without trepidation, because she had a conceptual framework from which to develop her approach to creating the website content.

Not every student is able to develop a conceptual framework, however, as was the case in the original study on the TFT model (see Yancey, Robertson, & Taczak, 2014), and as illustrated in the study of TFT online in the case of Meredith. Not as engaged in the course as Mark and Samantha, Meredith struggled to develop agency as she took a more passive role in her learning, relying on the instructor to tell her what to do, often at the last minute, and demonstrating little understanding of the concepts from the course, in direct contrast to Samantha:

> INSTRUCTOR: How are you progressing with your assignment? Do you know which three genres you'll develop and what information you'll use from the technical report?

> MEREDITH: Can we do any genres or do you want specific ones?

> INSTRUCTOR: Have you read through the assignment instructions? There are a lot of details there but part of this assignment is that it's up to you to decide which genres would be appropriate to your audience.

The point is that you identify the audiences who might be interested in the information you researched for your technical report and then strategize which genres you would develop for those audiences about the information you want to communicate.

MEREDITH: You're the audience, right? What other audiences am I supposed to have?

Meredith not only isn't grasping the point of the assignment, but also is not engaged in thinking about the assignment. This interaction between Meredith and the instructor followed a week in which she failed to complete two class discussions that prompted students to reflect back on their previously completed technical report and to identify potential audiences for the information they had found in their research, beyond the report's audience. Meredith, instead of taking ownership of her learning by catching up on the discussions or looking at what her classmates' discussions might reveal, asks the instructor to tell her what to do, even after the instructor prods her to think for herself. A few weeks later, in a reflection about her work on this assignment after its completion, Meredith does not indicate the development of a conceptual framework she can transfer:

In my report on the environmental impact of Hurricane Sandy I wanted people to know about how bad it was, not just for people's homes but for things like the beach erosion and water contamination. My audience was anyone who cared about the Jersey Shore vacation areas and other areas that got hit, and the mayors of towns and the governor. My genres reached them because they were written in a way that would make the information important to know and easy to understand. My web site reaches the public and so anyone can get this information if they have a computer, so my audience is really everyone. The users of this web site will want to know this information so they can know how the hurricane hurt the area's environment. They will use this information to understand the impact of it and to make sure it doesn't happen again.

Meredith further indicates in a class discussion that she has not abstracted the key rhetorical concepts from the course in working on this assignment:

The concepts are research and factual writing. I had to make sure this writing was based off of the research I got and that I had lots of facts to show the audience what was the result of the hurricane after so it had to be accurate. They had to believe what I was informing them just like our proposal [here she refers to an earlier assignment] had to do. Another concept is genre or informative writing and that is the genre in this assignment so people could get information they needed to know about what happened.

Meredith's reflection illustrates that she has some understanding that audience is important, but she is unable to articulate the relationship between audience and genre, and she does not recall the key terms from the course, let alone think to store them in her phone for future use as Mark did. Meredith's failure to transfer, though, is in part due to her lack of agency. She missed a few of the class discussions that would have helped her develop the framework, but she also isn't willing to take responsibility for her own learning, as her questions to the instructor demonstrate. She does not display a conceptual framework of writing knowledge other than her knowledge about how to incorporate research, prior experience she brought to the course. In her first written post to the course site on the first day of class, she forecasts this by indicating her reasons for taking the class: "I took the online class to make it easier for me to work and go to school. I already have 3 classes and it's an elective for me and writing is something I do okay in, so it should be easy for me to get through."[8]

The Role of Reflection

In the TFT curricular model the role of reflection is critical, much more significant to the content of the course than just as a practice or part of the writing process. The type of reflection advocated in this model is specific in that it encourages students to practice self-assessment which can promote transfer (Taczak & Robertson, 2016). TFT students engage in reflection before, during, and after the process of writing, as a means of determining why they are making certain rhetorical choices as they prepare and continue to write, rather than only after the writing is completed (Taczak, 2015). Students theorize about reflection (and use reflective practice to do so) as well as practice reflection about what they're doing in specific writing assignments and why, and also in the reiterative reflective assignment in which they create a theory of writing. All of this reflection aims toward the development of a conceptual framework of knowledge, captured in the final iteration of the theory of writing assignment, that students can return to, revise, and adapt to various contexts. Students in the course understand that they are creating their own theory of writing, and they understand that theory as "a systematic narrative of lived experience and observed phenomena that both accounts for (makes sense of) past experience and makes predictions about future experience" (Downs & Robertson, 2015, 110–111). This reflection, culminating in their theory of writing, enables students' development of a conceptual framework from which they transfer writing knowledge to new contexts (Taczak & Robertson, 2016; Yancey, Robertson, & Taczak, 2014).

In online courses, reflection can facilitate practice at writing, generate ideas about an assignment, provide a narrative about the process of an assignment, and get students to understand what they did in their writing, just as it can in face-to-face courses, the same way a small group discussion or class discussion can get students thinking about a reading assignment, or an approach to a writing exercise. But reflection can also engage students in thinking about what they think, which aims at a higher level of reflection, or at metacognition, identified as necessary for transfer to occur (Beaufort, 2007; Beaufort 2016; Perkins & Salomon, 1992; Taczak, 2015).

Reflection in the online TFT course is integral because it provides the vehicle for thinking about writing conceptually; more than a delivery method of information between instructor and student, reflection provides an opportunity for students to consider how they have approached past writing situations and how they might approach a current or future writing situation—some reach a level of metacognition that will lead to transfer (Taczak & Robertson, 2016). And because students are engaging in reflective writing, not only for the course assignments but also about their rhetorical choices, they can begin to see writing as not just performance but process—unforced process as these student reflection examples suggest:

> I noticed how my theory of writing is developing when I looked back at the previous reflections I did on Blackboard. I have a better idea now of what I think about writing and what my theory will be, and it makes me

think about how I'm doing my writing, not just in this class but all my classes. (MEGHAN)

I never thought about how much thinking I do for a writing assignment. Not about the topic but about the way I'm going to write it and what is going to make it good. I was never a good writer before this because I didn't think about writing I just did it. (JUAN)

Something that I thought about today is that I have changed how I do assignments. I don't just think about the topic and start writing, I think about the audience and the purpose of it. I think for like hours before I even write anything. I try and come up with a plan first where before I would just write some stuff and hope it was what you [instructor] wanted. Now I think about the things we have learned like audience and rhetric [sic] situation and build thoughts about what I have to write before I just go do it which actually saves time because I know what I'm doing better when I think about it before. (TASHA)

In these examples, students use reflection to *look forward* to conceptualize what they might bring to a writing situation and others that will come up, and they are able to *look backward* to understand the choices they've made about writing in the past. They also *look inward* at themselves and their current writing situation, and *look outward* at how they are situated as writers in a writing context (Taczak & Robertson, 2016). Meghan looks backward at her previous writing, and Juan looks inward at himself and his writing, while Tasha looks backward, forward, inward, and outward in "360-degree reflection" (Taczak & Robertson, 2016, 46).

The limitations of instructor access—or rather the affordance of student agency created by the online course environment—can also facilitate stronger reflection by encouraging students to think for themselves in ways that might be discouraged in face-to-face classrooms where easy access to the instructor results in questions for which students can find answers. Meredith, as illustrated above, is an exception, but these study participants indicated that while they would contact the instructor for help when needed, they were more likely to try to locate the answer or determine a course of action by thinking on their own with help from course reflections that allowed them to explore through prompted, deliberate abstraction of concepts and key information.

Students in face-to-face classrooms often confer with peers, which can be a positive collaboration that is not necessarily mimicked in online courses, despite the digital tools available. In this study, participants reported they collaborated with peers when instructed to comment on something a classmate posted to the course site or in consulting the instructor's "Question Board" on the site when they were looking for answers. While online courses can provide more collaboration than students in this study indicated, they reported that the reflection writing in the TFT online course offered enough time and space for finding solutions or developing an approach to a writing assignment, as Meghan understands:

> I like doing these assignments because I can do them when it makes sense for me to think, like in the middle of the night, when I am not busy and can think in a proper way about my writing. (MEGHAN)

The individual reflection, prompted by reiterative and sequenced assignments as required in the TFT course, and reportedly completed when students have time to consider their writing, helped the online study participants take responsibility for understanding their own thought processes when writing—to understand how they conceptualize writing, and to be able to transfer using the conceptual framework developed.

Just as the participants from the original study on the face-to-face TFT course indicated, once transfer was understood as the goal and reflection as the tool to determine conceptually what they might want to transfer, subjects in the online study indicated that they began to anticipate opportunities for transfer and to expect to transfer from one situation to the next. In other words, they were motivated to transfer by a greater understanding of transfer, as Landon tells us:

> In this assignment I felt like a switch came on for me. I realized that the genres had different expectations from different audiences and that I was thinking about the audience, purpose, genre, discourse community, context, and exigence when I made them. Even before that, when I thought about making them, I was thinking of those key things from the class. And then it hit me! I was doing transfer! I was thinking about what I learned in the first assignment we did about the rhetorical situation

and all that and then I was thinking about the genres for this assignment and bam! I took it from day 1 to this assignment now, and then I even started thinking ahead to our last assignment that is coming up. I totally know what to do for that. (LANDON)

Conclusion

Extensive reflection as practiced in the TFT model online allows students to work toward metacognition, which is essential for new learning (Bransford, Pellegrino, & Schwartz, 2000; Sommers, 2011). And when students have a greater sense of agency for their writing (Yancey, 1998), they develop a stronger conceptual framework about writing—a framework that will promote transfer to new contexts. Students can be encouraged to achieve these outcomes in any course, but working in online classrooms affords specific possibilities.

In an online writing course, just as in face-to-face courses, content about writing like that featured in the TFT course allows students to develop the conceptual framework needed to formulate a successful approach to their future writing contexts. Writing concepts can be adapted for any course. The concept of "exigence," for example, is one that a student in first-year writing can begin to understand, or that a technical writing student can perhaps develop more fully as a concept around which to build a technical report, or that a graduate student can master as a concept for which a researched response might be developed. Content about writing privileges writing as more than merely an activity, but as a conceptual process involving both theory and practice. The online course environment, as a space that encourages student agency, can provide students the opportunity to abstract meaning through reflection about writing that can lead to the development of a conceptual framework for transfer.

When goals for writing are explicit, including the ultimate goal of transfer, and students are able to conceptualize the writing they're engaged in according to these goals, they have greater agency. When students in the TFT course understand the goal of the course is to transfer, they eventually begin to actively seek opportunities for transfer, both within and outside of the course (Yancey, Robertson, & Taczak, 2014). They understand the sequence of assignments and what those assignments are designed to do to make them better writers, rather than viewing assignments as something the instructor concocted to merely evaluate their writing for a grade. This is heightened in an online course when students take responsibility and develop agency, as Mark did by connecting what he was learning about writing to the work he did as a personal trainer and by abstracting the concepts from the course and planning to use them again and again. Subjects in this study indicated that—for some students at least—the online environment might be more efficacious to transfer when writers use the kind of reflection featured in the TFT course to understand their thinking; and when they become agents of their own learning (Nowacek, 2011), students can envision where their knowledge about writing can be used in another context and they can seize that opportunity to transfer.

The research reported in this chapter regarding the online adaptation of the TFT model was supported by a grant from the Research Center of the College of Humanities and Social Sciences at William Paterson University of New Jersey.

References

Adler-Kassner, L., & Wardle, E. (Eds). (2015). *Naming what we know: Threshold concepts in writing studies*. Logan, UT: Utah State University Press.

Applebee, A., & Langer, J. (2009). What's happening in the teaching of writing? *English Journal, 98*(5), 18–28.

Applebee, A., & Langer, J. (2011). A snapshot of writing instruction in middle schools and high schools. *English Journal, 100*(6), 14–27.

Beaufort, A. (2007). *College writing and beyond: A new framework for university writing instruction*. Logan, UT: Utah State University Press.

Beaufort, A. (2016). Reflection: The metacognitive move towards transfer of learning. In K.B. Yancey (Ed.). *A rhetoric of reflection* (pp. 23–41). Logan, UT: Utah State University Press.

Bransford, J., Pellegrino, J., & Donovan, S. (2000). How experts differ from novices. In *How people learn: Brain, mind, experience, and school: Expanded edition* (pp. 31–50). Washington, DC: National Academies Press.

Carter, M. (1990). The idea of expertise: An exploration of cognitive and social dimensions of writing. *College Composition and Communication, 41*(3), 265–286.

Downs, D., & Robertson, L. (2015). Threshold concepts in first-year com-
position. In L. Adler-Kassner & E. Wardle (Eds.), *Naming what we know: Threshold concepts of writing studies* (pp. 105–121). Logan, UT: Utah State University Press.

Downs, D., & Wardle, E. (2007). Teaching about writing, righting misconceptions: (Re)envisioning "first-year composition" as "introduction to writing studies." *College Composition and Communication, 58*(4), 552–584.

Driscoll, D. L. (2011, December 21). Connected, disconnected, or uncertain: Student attitudes about future writing contexts and perceptions of transfer from first year writing to the disciplines. *Across the Disciplines, 8*(2). Retrieved from http://wac.colostate.edu/atd/articles/driscoll2011/index.cfm

Driscoll, D. L., & Wells, J. H. M. (Fall 2012). Beyond knowledge and skills: Writing transfer and the role of student dispositions. *Composition Forum, 26*, 1–15.

Ko, S., & Rossen, S. (2010). *Teaching online: A practical guide* (3rd ed.). New York, NY: Routledge.

Moore, J. L. (2012). Mapping the questions: The state of writing-related transfer research. *Composition Forum, 26.* Retrieved from http://compositionforum.com/issue/26/map-questions-transfer-research.php

Nowacek, R. S. (2011). *Agents of integration: Understanding transfer as a rhetorical act.* Carbondale and Edwardsville, IL: Southern Illinois University Press.

Perkins, D. N., & Salomon, G. (1992). Transfer of learning. *International encyclopedia of education* (2nd ed., pp. 2–13). Oxford, UK: Pergamon Press.

Reiff, M. J., & Bawarshi, A. (2011). Tracing discursive resources: How students use prior genre knowledge to negotiate new writing contexts in first-year composition. *Written Communication, 28*(3), 312–337.

Robertson, L., Taczak, K., & Yancey, K. B. (2012). Notes toward a theory of prior knowledge and its role in college composers' transfer of knowledge and practice. *Composition Forum, 26.* Retrieved from http://composition-forum.com/issue/26/prior-knowledge-transfer-php

Robertson, L., & Taczak, K. (2017). Teaching for transfer. In J. Moore & R. Bass (Eds.), *Understanding writing transfer: Implications for transformative student learning in higher education* (pp. 93–102). Sterling, VA: Stylus.

Robertson, L., & Taczak, K. (forthcoming). Disciplinarity and first-year composition: Shifting to a new paradigm. In R. Malenczyk, S. Miller-Cochran,

E. Wardle & K. Yancey (Eds.), *Composition, rhetoric, and disciplinarity.* Logan, UT: Utah State University Press.

Scherff, L., & Piazza C. (2005). The more things change, the more they stay the same: A survey of high school students' writing experiences. *Research in the Teaching of English, 39*(3), 271–304.

Sommers, J. (2011). Reflection revisited: The class collage. *Journal of Basic Writing, 1*(30), 99–129.

Sommers, N., & Saltz, L. (2004). The novice as expert: Writing the freshman year. *College Composition and Communication, 56,* 124–149.

Taczak, K. (2015). Reflection is critical in the development of writers. In L. Adler-Kassner & E. Wardle (Eds.), *Naming what we know: Threshold concepts in writing studies* (pp. 78–79). Logan, UT: Utah State University Press.

Taczak, K., & Robertson, L. (2016). Reiterative reflection in the twenty-first century writing classroom: An integrated approach to teaching for transfer. In K. B. Yancey (Ed.), *A Rhetoric of Reflection* (pp. 42–63). Logan, UT: Utah State University Press.

Wardle, E. (2007). Understanding "transfer" from FYC: Preliminary results of a longitudinal study. *WPA: Writing Program Administration, 31*(1–2), 65–85.

Wardle, E. (2012). Creative repurposing for expansive learning: Considering "problem-exploring" and "answer-getting" dispositions in individuals and fields. *Composition Forum 26*(1). Retrieved from http://compositionforum.com/issue/26/prior-knowledge-transfer-php

Yancey, K. B. (1998). *Reflection in the writing classroom.* Logan, UT: Utah State University Press.

Yancey, K. B., Robertson, L., & Taczak, K. (2014). *Writing across contexts: Transfer, composition, and sites of writing.* Logan, UT: Utah State University Press.

Notes

1. For more on prior knowledge, see the special issue on transfer in *Composition Forum 26* (2012).

2. The Teaching for Transfer (TFT) curricular model is detailed by Yancey, Robertson, and Taczak in *Writing cross Contexts: Transfer, Composition, and Sites of Writing* (2014), and by Robertson and Taczak in their chapter in *Understanding Writing Transfer: Implications for Transformative Student Learning in Higher Education,* edited by Jessie L. Moore and Randy Bass (2017). The curricular model's three

interlocking components described here are the foundation of its content, but a more contextualized explanation of TFT appears in these publications and research around it is discussed at writingacrosscontexts.blogspot.com.

3. For more on transfer research see Perkins & Salomon (1992), Beaufort (2007), Downs & Wardle (2007), Wardle (2007), Moore (2012), Yancey, Robertson & Taczak (2014), and others.

4. Students draw upon prior knowledge in three different ways (see Robertson, Taczak, & Yancey, 2012; Yancey, Robertson, & Taczak, 2014): (a) *Assemblage*, in which new knowledge is grafted onto existing knowledge ineffectively; (b) *Remix*, in which students integrate what they learn, value, and know about writing with what is new in college writing, and continually conceptualize about writing; and (c) A *critical incident*, or setback in which efforts fail, providing an opportunity to rethink their understanding about writing.

5. This IRB-approved study included 10 participants who were enrolled in an upper-level technical writing course designed using the TFT curricular model.

6. All names used are pseudonyms.

7. Mark's transfer between contexts is similar to that of Rick's reverse transfer between two classes in the previous study of the Teaching for Transfer curricular model reported (see Yancey, Robertson, & Taczak, 2014).

8. Meredith's disposition is not unlike subjects in the original study on the TFT curriculum, which indicated that students' sense of themselves as strong or strong-enough writers and of writing as something already mastered can create resistance to new ways of thinking about writing (Yancey, Robertson, & Taczak, 2014).

ELEVEN

Hybrid Spaces and Writing Places: Ecoliteracy, Ecocomposition, and the Ecological Self

Christopher Justice

SINCE THE 1990S, ECOCOMPOSITION SCHOLARS have examined how places—broadly defined—influence composition and discourse. As Dobrin and Weisser (2002) write, "classroom, political, electronic, ideological, historical, economic, and natural environments" play a critical role in shaping human discourse and textual production (p. 9). Drew's (2001) insights about the writing classroom itself, Reynolds's (2004) examination of the cultural geography of city streets, Hothem's (2009) analysis of suburbia, and Walker's (2010) critique of local land-use conflicts at an Arizona ski resort, to name a few studies of place-based writing pedagogy, demonstrate the impact environments have had on discourse and composition. As Dobrin and Weisser (2002) argue, "place" is the first and most important factor shaping discourse because "environment precedes race, class, gender, and culture" (p. 32). Our first primal experience of reality resides in the dynamics of place, and this phenomenon is enacted repeatedly when we compose. But more scholarship is needed in understanding how exactly place influences composition and discourse. As Dobrin and Weisser (2002) add, "the relationships between the imagined spaces of cyberspace, the discourse used to create those locations, and the discourse used within those places must be further theorized and considered" (p. 174).

Place influences composition and discourse in many ways, but one area that warrants more attention is how place affects student identity, particularly how students perceive themselves as writers through the agency of a composition classroom. Weisser (2001) argues that because "identities are fashioned only through our connections with other humans" (p. 81), we must expand our concepts of identity so they encompass our "ecological selves" (p. 86). Eckersley (1992) defines this "ecological self" as "based on an ecologically informed philosophy of internal relatedness, according to which all organisms are not simply interrelated with their environment but also constituted by those very environmental relationships" (p. 49). Classrooms in general foster these connections and relatedness, but hybrid writing courses in particular exponentially expand the number of places and relationships available for cultivating students' ecological selves. Therefore, hybrid writing courses can help students improve their overall identity as practicing, improving writers.

Cooper (1986) captures this dynamic succinctly: "ecological" is not simply a buzzword for "context," but rather a conceptual framework for examining how writers "interact to form systems: all the characteristics of any individual writer or piece of writing both determine and are determined by the characteristics of all the other writers and writings in the systems." She adds, "the ecological model postulates dynamic interlocking systems which structure the social activity of writing" (p. 368). The unique digital environment constructed within a hybrid writing course creates a provocative *network* or system of systems that maximize students' and instructors' potential for exploring how places influence composition and discourse. This theoretical context sets the stage for evaluating two critical elements of hybrid writing courses: their spatial and intellectual duality.

Given the popularity of online learning and writing-in-the-disciplines (WID) courses in higher education, disciplinary discourses often converge with electronic places to form unique textual ecosystems. Within those systems is a co-constitutive dynamic—where electronic place shapes discourse, and discourse shapes electronic place—that has opened new opportunities for scholarship. How disciplinary discourse affects and is affected by the electronic places and digital classrooms found in hybrid writing courses warrants further attention. Among their many benefits, hybrid writing courses allow students to write publicly for audiences beyond their instructor and peers and add another dimension of "place" by doubling the instructional places where students interact. By examining the unique qualities of each place, students can reflect more deeply about how exactly these places influence their composing processes.

With this introduction in mind, I turn to my work as the University of Baltimore's (UB) writing program administrator. From 2007–2012, I administered an upper-level general education course titled WRIT 300-Advanced Expository Writing. WRIT 300 includes three distinct features: a hybrid delivery system with a WID and advanced curriculum. In this context, a "hybrid" course requires students and their instructor to meet once a week in a traditional, face-to-face setting, while the rest of each week's instruction occurs online. The primary focus of this WID curriculum emphasizes the following elements of each undergraduate major's discourse community: topics, texts, genres, audiences, and prose and documentation styles. Although the course was rolled out in spring 2008, we continually assessed and refined its curriculum; future WID elements to incorporate may include disciplinary discursive conventions at the semantic, syntactic, and orthographic levels; the inclusion of key content such as disciplinary theories and concepts; and the application of discipline-specific compositional and research methodologies. And finally, the advanced composition curriculum refers to an emphasis on student-driven rhetorical choices; the interrelatedness of style, form, and content; and multiple rhetorics including digital and visual.

Students from each undergraduate major enroll in their major's specific section, and each major has a curriculum tailored to its disciplinary needs. UB's undergraduate majors include the following disciplines: applied information technology, business, community studies and civic engagement, corporate communication, criminal justice, English, forensic studies, government and public policy, health systems management, history, human services administration, jurisprudence, psychology, and simulation and digital entertainment. Business students enroll in WRIT 300-Business sections; criminal justice students enroll in WRIT 300-CRJU sections; etc. Throughout our assessment of this course, students' disciplinary knowledge improved, and repeatedly in student evaluations students consistently endorsed this discipline-specific focus for its newness (it doesn't "feel" like your typical writing course) and its relevance and applicability to other courses in their degree program. Since 2008, I have evaluated this course's progress and have led four subsequent modifications. Below I share the lessons I have learned to extend ecocomposition scholarship into one of composition studies' most powerful currents: hybrid/online courses and the ecological literacy they facilitate.

The "Place" of Composition

Composition scholars have been wrestling with the concept of place for decades. As early as 1971, Emig questioned the role place plays in composition: "Under what conditions—physical, psychic—do students start to write?" she asked (p. 2). Berkenkotter (1983) was concerned about compósition studies' tendency to conduct research about the composing process in unnatural settings. She urged scholars to "pay close attention to the setting in which the writer composes" (p. 127) and suggested more research be conducted with individual writers, not groups or classes of writers, arguing, "We need to replicate naturalistic studies of skilled and unskilled writers" (p. 140). She thus implicitly emphasized the role of place further. Arguing for a more "socially collaborative" model of composition, Odell (1984) suggested that composition research focused too much on texts, and instead, should focus more on institutional contexts and how they affect compositional processes.

By the mid-1980s, social constructionist views of writing crystallized into a coherent camp ready to challenge process, expressivist, and cognitive writing theories. The post-process movement in composition studies was launched. As Hawisher and colleagues (1996) note, this turn toward examining the physical and social contexts of writing encouraged scholars to move "beyond the individual writer toward the larger systems of which the writer was a part" (p. 65). Taken to its extreme, Slovic (1999) suggests, "Language without context, without grounding in the world, means next to nothing" (p. 34).

Social constructionist theories inspired significant attention about place. However, criticisms about place's role in composition inevitably surfaced, and one was the role ideology played in defining specific places. Writing classrooms—and academic places in general—were perceived as unique locales antithetical to public spheres. However, Reynolds (2004) challenges this dichotomy that describes academia as unreal: She calls the "real" world "a mythological place that composition specialists are being asked to colonize" due to recent emphases on public writing and writing "beyond" the curriculum. Reynolds states, "To claim that writing classes are mere rehearsal for the 'real world out there' reproduces a binary relationship between the world and the academy that geographers and many postmodern spatial theorists would reject" (p. 44). Though she acknowledges some differences exist, academic and public places are constructed in fundamentally ideological ways. Space matters, and public places are as ideological as academic places.

Others have expressed concerns about how place is positioned in academic discourse. Killingsworth (2006) explains differences between the words "place" and "space," specifically in ecological discourse. He argues that historically the words have been used so cavalierly that they are often treated synonymously. However, "places, which have histories both natural and social" are significantly different than "space, which is an abstraction, an empty signifier. Space is not mapped; it is projected and filled." He urges ecocompositionists to "keep alive and separate the idea of place as more than a metaphorical ghost" when examining "computer environments and virtual realities" (p. 86–89). His point is important because students in hybrid courses often perceive their digital classrooms as extensions of "cyberspace" or as empty spaces that have been filled and "roped off" by instructors, not places that students and instructors can co-construct, or more radically, places that students themselves can influence and construct during a semester.

Bowden (1993) has suggested that "container metaphors" pervade composition classrooms, which are often framed as empty vessels that need to be filled. Since much college writing is too often only shared between students and instructors, students perceive their texts as intimate and private, claiming them as "my papers" and thus positioning themselves in anti-rhetorical ways. Hybrid writing courses shatter this "public–private split," as Reynolds calls it, by creating a definitive public place within the academy where students can deliberately share texts and contribute to class discourse digitally and interpersonally. Furthermore, in hybrid writing courses students can construct meaning about their texts online *and* through face-to-face interaction, a dynamic that engages students with different learning styles and forces them to think critically about relationships between these places.

Hothem (2009) urges scholars to focus on everyday places and make "everyday life a subject of serious inquiry" (p. 37). Nothing could be more paramount to the academy's mission, and in today's digital culture no object may be more pervasive in students' lives than computers. Hothem's notion can be applied to hybrid writing courses by requiring students to examine how computers create electronic environments that function as unique places. As Dobrin (2001) writes, composition is "a study of relationships" (p. 12), so unpacking computers and the electronic places they create as compositions themselves comprised of intricate relationships, similar to the texts we ask students to produce, is an ideal next step, especially when framed within the context of emphasizing metacognition and the writing about writing strategies advocated by Downs and Wardle (2011). Requiring students to interrogate and write about the networks that constitute a hybrid writing class, and particularly the mundane and habitual acts they take for granted when writing online, is a critical step in helping them understand how electronic places influence their own discourse and texts.

Hybrid Spaces and Writing Places

How can the construction of multiple academic places in hybrid writing courses help teachers and students realize different choices and possibilities in their writing?

To answer that question, the literature about hybrid courses should first be framed within the context of online learning, because the former is the latter's progeny. Nicol, Minty, and Sinclair (2003) explain how the values, norms, and communicative acts embedded in online learning have introduced new discourses. Communicating in digital environments prioritizes other modes of communication beyond the written such as visual, auditory, and digital communication, which lead to new discursive practices. Online courses offer instructors opportunities to teach these modes in an integrated manner. Second, Nicol et al. argue that online learning creates linguistic artifacts or archives of written discourse, such as in low-stakes writing exercises that would otherwise not be preserved or publicized. These archives can expand student reflexivity and intrapersonal awareness when students are asked to review them.

To demonstrate this latter point, WRIT 300 instructors were encouraged to ask students to review their and peers' writing samples from previous Discussion Forum posts and to examine their effectiveness in light of current topics. During the semester, many students wrote several thousand words of prose for different types of exercises, which produced a prolific archive of student-generated writing, not textbook-generated writing, which students often perceive as impersonal and without context. For example, when reviewing grammar or punctuation topics, students were able to analyze their own prose and revise it. When covering different compositional strategies, students were able to compare and contrast their own styles with their peers' and determine the strengths and weaknesses of both. And when discussing visual rhetoric and approaches to composing visual arguments, students were asked to identify how different types of visual media (photographs, motion graphics, color, etc.) could enhance their messages. By emphasizing this recursivity and by using such an archive, students were able to chart their progress more accurately and to see themselves as writers who were continually improving their compositional skills.

Brown (2004) writes how online learning allows students to prioritize their learning; choose which learning styles best suit their needs; and determine how best to transfer their learning. Peterson and Caverly (2005) believe online discussion forums allow students and instructors to develop a social presence that facilitates authentic communication, which in turn helps struggling students persist through challenging peer and instructor feedback. The sustained, extensive reading and writing activities help students apply and refine cognitive skills such as synthesis, summarization, and evaluation. And instructors can establish their "teacher presence" by focusing online efforts on "conversation and learning rather than procedural confusion" (p. 38).

Authentic communication between instructors and students, especially in the context of providing feedback on student writing, is critical. In WRIT 300, instructors routinely encouraged students to review all online feedback, not just feedback directed at individual students. For example, given the public nature of the digital classroom, Student A could read my feedback not only on his writing, but also on Student B, C, and D's writing. The more students saw my feedback as consistent, constructive, and evenly distributed, the more they embraced my feedback and viewed revision as a positive experience. Furthermore, the same also happened with peer review. Some students expressed concern or frustration about peer reviewing. However, as the semester progressed, and the hybrid format helped cultivate a culture of textual collaboration, students wanted to engage in more peer reviews. In fact, some students reported they sometimes read my feedback on another student's writing, and then read that student's text to "make sense of" my comments. Another key element in hybrid writing courses that helps facilitate authentic communication is a simple, but often overlooked, one: time. When students write online, they have more time to compose. Of course, not every student will use his or her time wisely, but the intellectual "space" needed to produce quality writing is expanded.

Hybrid writing courses allow instructors to establish a more dynamic "teacher's presence" because they allow students to see instructors as not only teachers, but as writers. Given the volume of writing required in online courses, instructors often respond in writing to student questions, exercises, and related activities, often through exchanges directly with students.

Instructors can therefore use their writing as a model for students and adopt different styles of commenting (formal, conversational, encouraging, critical, technical, or more general). Instructors can also vary *how* they respond to students by mixing anecdotes, data, visual sources, and other types of information and by using different tones and appeals in their responses to motivate students. Instructors can do this in traditional classrooms, but students in the digital portion of a hybrid writing class can see all of an instructor's written responses, something that isn't easily available in a traditional writing classroom. Moreover, instructors can balance their online writer's persona with their face-to-face persona, which helps students see them as instructors, classroom managers, scholars, professionals, practicing writers, and perhaps most importantly, accessible, everyday people.

Hybrid writing courses emphasize spatial design because they feature physical places (the traditional classroom) and electronic places (Blackboard, Sakai, WebCT, etc.) that rely on visual rhetoric to communicate ideas about writing. Observation should play a more prominent role in composition classrooms. To restore the role of imagination in perception, Berthoff (1983) argues that perception is based on seeing, or "visual thinking" (p. 109). Hybrid courses add a visual dimension to composition classrooms because they provide instructors and students a greater range of visual tools to compose and write with including hypertext, photographs, illustrations, videos, and motion graphics. Using these tools to emphasize visual composition enhances students' perception and critical thinking skills. In many of my WRIT 300 sections, students are required, as the semester progresses, to pay more and more attention to how they present their writing. For example, students are required by the sixth week of the semester to use bolding, italics, and underlining in at least one post to enhance their ideas. By the ninth week, they are required to include visual images; by the twelfth week, they are required to include sound; and by the final week, they are required to include all of those media in at least one post.

Furthermore, instructors construct these electronic places; since no two hybrid classrooms look alike, students should be invited to examine the decisions instructors made and how they, as students, might modify their instructor's design decisions, if given the opportunity. As Wysocki (2004) writes, form is a "kind of recognition, tying us to others and to our times and places" (p. 171). The more students interrogate the visual design choices of their electronic classrooms and compare and contrast them with physical classrooms, the more likely they'll envision all pedagogical places as human constructions. Such interrogations can become an exercise in critical pedagogy, where instructors help students understand how ideologies shape places, so they can participate in influencing that construction to disrupt hegemony and take ownership of their learning. For example, one exercise in my WRIT 300 sections asks students to conduct a mini-"usability study" on our online platform and write a report detailing their findings. This assignment allows students to critique the layout and design of our digital classroom and helps students recognize the value of rhetorical thinking because they realize the importance of accounting for the needs of different audiences.

Hothem writes, "ecocomposition should inspire students to imagine their world as a text and themselves as its authors" (p. 55). Texts are not stable; instead, they can be read and re-read, interpreted and re-interpreted, just as places can be designed and redesigned. Wysocki adds that we envision "visual composition as rhetorical, as a series of choices that have much broader consequences and articulations than visual principles suggest" (p. 173). Hybrid writing courses allow students to examine those consequences and analyze the places they inhabit in the academy. Providing students such opportunities gives them ownership not only of their learning, but also of their learning environments. As Wiegand (1999) explains, the need for enhancing students' spatial literacy, or their ability to understand spatial relationships, has never been more critical because numerous entities are defining those relationships and colonizing students' spaces, most notably corporate America. As Reynolds notes, drawing upon geography is critical for compositionists because written and visual composition and geography involve "decisions about design or where things go" (p. 75). Such initiatives should be of interest to cultural geographers too, since they "want the construction of identity understood as a spatial process" (p. 57). Hybrid writing courses facilitate those drives because they allow students to identify relationships between the spatial elements of written and visual composition.

The spatial duality of hybrid courses provides students with tangible experiences of dichotomous places. However, although these dichotomies may suggest contradiction, juxtaposing two different places—the traditional and online classroom—allows students to engage in organizational patterns such as comparing, contrasting, and classifying. While students often encounter these patterns through writing, hybrid courses allow students to apply such organizational thinking to their experiences and media beyond the written word; organizing visual space, interpersonal encounters, and informational flows in effective patterns enhances students' critical thinking by expanding the opportunities they have for applying content. For example, when I ask students to write reflectively in my WRIT 300 sections about their learning experiences in the course, I ask them to describe and compare and contrast the two places they experience in the class; to examine the processes they use when preparing for both places; to identify problems and solutions they encounter in both places; and to consider the effects one place has on the other. When students engage in such reflections, they are better equipped to understand the ramifications of these dichotomous places, especially when they can read about how their classmates also relate to this unique learning experience.

More importantly, through juxtaposition—a key concept embedded in Sirc's (2004) notion of "box-logic"—students can juxtapose these electronic places and synthesize their merits into a montage of intellectual value. By emphasizing metacognition and writing about their writing, students can reflect upon how each place affects their compositional choices and become more judicious and deliberative when working in either the physical or digital classroom. Sirc suggests, "A box-logic for composition instruction allows us to think of our work as teaching English Juxtaposition" (p. 129), or the arrangement of collected artifacts that serve as traces marking the juxtaposition of students' aesthetic and material realities. Hybrid composition courses, because they can function as digital repositories for students' compositional and linguistic artifacts, provide an ideal place for collecting such artifacts and offer a collaborative forum to receive feedback about how students might arrange such artifacts.

While administering WRIT 300, one of the more puzzling student responses, which I initially heard often, was this: there was no relationship between classroom and online instruction. I wondered if this was a legitimate complaint or a sign of students' limitations. However, although relationships for many instructors and some students were obvious, some students persisted in making this claim. Something else about ecoliteracy was at work here. As Fritjof Capra (2005) suggests, ecoliteracy includes more than just knowing about ecology; ecoliteracy means acting and thinking ecologically, and this can be achieved by thinking in terms of "relationships, connectedness, and context." We must shift our perceptions "from the parts to the whole, from objects to relationships, from objective knowledge to contextual knowledge, from quantity to quality, from structure to process, from contents to patterns." Key concepts that facilitate such "perceptual shifts" include "networks, nested systems, interdependence, diversity, cycles, flows, development, and dynamic balances" (p. 18–29). Another argument for hybrid composition courses is that they promote ecoliteracy by requiring students to identify spatial relationships, information flows, and systems thinking between the places they inhabit.

I addressed this challenge by creating opportunities—and additional places—for students to analyze relationships between the physical and digital classrooms. For example, after our face-to-face session each week, as students migrated into the online portion of the course, the first exercise I assigned was a summary of what we covered in the face-to-face class, how that material related to the previous week's topics, and what they learned from the current week's topics. By activating their memory in a digital place, a location they had far more control over; by asking students to practice their summarization and application skills; and by asking students to juxtapose relationships among learning experiences, students were better able to make connections between our face-to-face and online instructional places.

However, hybrid composition courses do not stop at ecoliteracy: their ability to promote literacy—specifically digital, computer, and visual literacy—is critical. As Gee (1989) explains, literacy is the "mastery of or fluent control over a secondary discourse" (p. 486). The more secondary discourses we master beyond our primary discourse, or our "home-based sense of identity" (p. 485), the more literate we become. Hybrid courses are uniquely positioned to emphasize multiple literacies because of the dynamic textual richness they possess. This is particularly crucial because, as Samuels (2004) argues, "postmodern student literacies are most often shaped by television, movies, the Internet, and advertising, and not by the modern emphasis on books and reading. . . . In response to this binary opposition between modern print culture and postmodern electronic discourse . . . we must see how modern cultural literacies are now co-existing with multiple modes of postmodern literacy." The juxtaposition of electronic and print media allows students to gain competence in new discursive practices, a key element, Gee argues, of enhancing their literacy.

Hybrid composition courses extend students' writing experiences across multiple platforms in ways that require students to think in hyper-rhetorical ways. Since rhetorical acts should account for genre and media in addition to other traditional elements of rhetoric (audience, message, etc.), writers in hybrid courses must constantly be aware of genre, media, audience, and so forth. They must understand how genres and media function rhetorically, and providing opportunities for students to write in different media and genres for different audiences in different contexts expands those opportunities. Media may include discussion forums, chat rooms, blogs, and videos; furthermore, by requiring students to engage with such media, instructors can emphasize how concepts such as media and genre intersect and influence each other.

For example, blogs in professional settings—though their credibility is still contested in the academy—are not only a popular medium, but that popularity has morphed into a distinct written genre with unique linguistic and rhetorical conventions including a more personal, conversational style; use of first-person pronouns; brevity of content; and a purpose aimed at stimulating debate and comments. The medium of a blog has transformed blogs into a written genre, a phenomenon students should be aware of given the ubiquity of their digital writing acts. Furthermore, giving students opportunities to choose online whether a video, photograph, or other graphics or whether orthographic elements such as bolding, underlining, or italics enhance their written texts is important because it highlights the relationships between the written and visual. Understanding relationships among written and visual media and genres is a key step in expanding students' literacy.

Goodfellow and Lea (2005) also note how digital writing enhances the rhetorical demands placed on students because students often don't perceive the work they perform online as "writing"; instead, they relate these digital discursive practices to speech (note the pervasive use of the word "discussion"). Goodfellow and Lea argue that texts students produce online are typically considered subordinate to texts they produce in face-to-face settings. This subordination occurs because online texts are used for either socialization purposes; scaffolding for other more important, higher-order skills; or exposure to a broader, more diverse range of interpretations of course material. However, in hybrid composition courses, the writing students perform online should play as important a role as other types of writing. In this context, the place where writing occurs should not dictate its value, especially since the digital writing students perform in their classes and workplaces may hold significant value. Making at least some of the digital writing students perform in hybrid composition classes equal to writing they do offline improves all students' writing acts, especially when students realize their audience online is broader and more complex.

Helping students evaluate the rhetorical differences between digital and print texts is a pivotal step toward helping them understand rhetoric because writing in two different places requires students to conceptualize two different rhetorical constructs. As Dobrin notes (2001), "Writing does not begin in the self; rather, writers begin writing by situating themselves, by putting themselves in a place, by locating with in a space," which is why the word *topic* originates from the Greek word topoi, which literally means "place" (p. 18–19). For example, when working online at home, students may be communicating with classmates experiencing different social or environmental contexts: time zones, climate, community disturbances, and other factors may vary, so students must rhetorically account for those differences, all of which place overtly shapes. Requiring students to consistently write for live audiences, in different media, and for different purposes allows them to exercise their rhetorical muscles and obtain rhetorical flexibility, a key ingredient in navigating secondary discourse communities. As Cooper reminds us, purposes only "arise out of interaction" with other people (p. 369).

The dichotomy afforded in hybrid composition courses also has critical implications for the creation and ongoing maintenance of discourse communities. As Harris (1989) argues, writers gain deeper understanding of their discourse communities when they separate from them. We never genuinely leave our communities, but we never actually are fully in them either: "we are all at once both insiders and outsiders," Harris writes (p. 590). Hybrid composition courses manifest this paradox: students are part of a group, but outside it. They work communally but individually. Additionally, writers construct meaning by "repositioning" themselves against the "polyphony" of privileged discourses circulating throughout their respective communities (p. 588). Hybrid writing courses are excellent for facilitating this repositioning because they place students in multiple rhetorical and discursive positions during a semester. Additionally, not only can they expand students' literacy and rhetorical skills, but they can also extend students' conceptions of writing itself.

Because hybrid courses have two distinct places, instructors can better position specific types of writing within each. Instructors can help students delineate in one place between conventions occurring across the curriculum, then juxtapose more discipline-specific conventions in the other. For example, instructors can emphasize more WAC-oriented instruction in the face-to-face setting and more WID-oriented instruction in the digital setting (or vice versa, depending on an instructors' strengths and style). Alternatively, to help students understand writing's dynamic nature, instructors can focus on specific topics in different settings such as rhetoric in the digital setting, composition in the face-to-face setting, or other variations. Furthermore, having two distinct places allows students to better understand differences between expressivist and transactional writing. In hybrid courses, students can cultivate their private (expressivist) and public (transactional) personas because they are provided two distinct places to compose. Paradoxically, by separating the two types of writing, instructors can help students synthesize both types of writing and understand how one can complement the other. Instructors can use the face-to-face component of a hybrid course to help students write for themselves in more expressivist modes of discourse; conversely, they can use the digital component to emphasize more public, transactional writing. Obviously, a number of other variations exist, but that's the allure of hybrid composition courses: By expanding the number of writing places, they expand the opportunities for how writers perceive writing and themselves. Finally, as one of many other potential dichotomies and juxtapositions hybrid composition courses offer, Perl (1979) writes, "composing becomes the carrying forward of an implicit sense into explicit form" (p. 59). Instructors can use the face-to-face component to help students draw out their implicit meanings and the digital component to further extract the explicit. In essence, hybrid composition courses offer instructors, programs, and institutions more opportunities to advance the spectrum of written discourse's dynamics.

Another important juxtaposition hybrid composition courses offer is embedded in the texts students produce in digital and face-to-face classroom settings. In such courses, physical and virtual worlds collide, thus infusing a sense of "virtual materiality" into hybrid composition courses that bring the remoteness of fully online courses into the physical materiality of traditional classrooms. As Hass (1996) argues, students often perceive digital texts as distant, but when students have the opportunity to literally touch their texts, they invest more time in composing them and remember their arguments more clearly. This materiality helps students produce more memorable texts. Syverson (1999) also emphasizes the physicality of writing and how writing is an "embodied" act. She writes, "Writers, readers, and texts have physical bodies and consequently not only the content but the process of their interaction is dependent on, and reflective of, physical experience" (p. 12). By capitalizing on the physical experiences in traditional classrooms, hybrid courses require students to physically perform in public and private, digital and natural, and interpersonal and intrapersonal contexts and produce physical artifacts they can bring to class for further dialogue.

Furthermore, in hybrid, dichotomous, and juxtaposed contexts, students can trace migrations of their texts and experience how collaboration, audience, discourse communities, genres, and media influence textual production. These textual migrations—where for example a student posts a draft onto an online discussion board in Blackboard, receives feedback from peers, then revises the draft and brings it to class for an in-class workshop—have significant ramifications for ecocomposition. By tracing the places a text has migrated through, students can better understand how exactly those places have left their own traces and influenced that text. Cubitt (2005) suggests migration itself is an ecological medium. He writes, "Like the great migrations of animals, human migration moves not only biomass but everything that travels with animals: their pests, their dung, their diseases and their genes." Our textual and discursive values migrate and evolve, too, along with our texts, and as Cubitt argues, everything projects meaning, including migration. Animals and humans are "senders and receivers, nodes in an increasingly interwoven webwork of communication, whose mediations they perform in their bodies and their technologies" (p. 23). Texts are such nodes too, receiving information from a network of influential forces, place being just one. Prior (2009) calls these migrations "composed utterances" and urges compositionists "to analyze the chains of utterances that are woven together in a teleological project; the various ways that the composed document/ performance overtly or covertly indexes its specific history of composition; and the ways that production, reception, and use take that history into account" (p. 21). If students can identify and understand these utterances, they increase their opportunities to revise and ultimately improve their texts because sometimes places in the network produce unintended effects that may prove detrimental or beneficial. Hybrid composition courses facilitate "induced textual migrations" because they require students to compose in at least three places—at home, on campus, and online—and each is triangulated to shape and inform the other.

Conclusions

This chapter will hopefully stimulate more dialogue about administering and teaching hybrid composition courses. Given the mounting demands placed on composition instructors, including the need to teach more specialized, secondary discourses; the need to enhance students' overall literacy skills; the need to conserve resources while simultaneously improving instructional quality; and the need to meet growing enrollments, such dialogue is needed. Fortunately, the theoretical perspectives of digital writing and ecocomposition share a common ideological foundation: both value social constructionist theories of texts and discourse. Although more research needs to be conducted to learn more precisely how place shapes students' disciplinary identities, and how exactly students themselves account for those disciplinary identities, and although concepts of place can assume a range of forms, this essay has examined one specific type of place—the digital classroom found in hybrid composition courses—and its potential for enhancing students' identities as writers.

However, other academic places—writing centers, networked computer classrooms, home-schooled students' residential settings, and the workplace settings students inhabit during, for example, service learning opportunities—all warrant further investigation. How do such places affect composing and writing processes? How can hybrid composition courses leverage the unique attributes of those places and help students compose and write more effectively? And how can those places, when juxtaposed alongside the places embedded in hybrid composition courses, influence students' disciplinary identities? Moreover, ecocomposition is only one theoretical lens we can use for illuminating such relationships. Composition scholars studying service learning, public writing, and multimodal composition can all contribute to these conversations about students' identities and the hybrid composition course. The intersections where ecocomposition, hybrid courses, and WID converge may be the brightest place yet for composition's future.

Most importantly, hybrid composition courses are an ideal mechanism for enhancing students' ecological literacy and ultimately their ecological selves. This is important not only because of the environmental challenges our planet faces, but because ecological literacy is an important way of thinking and communicating found in numerous professions and disciplines. By emphasizing the value of understanding relationships, connections between places, textual migrations, compositional utterances, information flows, and systems thinking, students will be better equipped to solve the problems they encounter.

References

Berkenkotter, C. (1983). Decisions and revisions: The planning strategies of a publishing writer. In Sondra Perl (Ed.), *Landmark essays on writing process* (pp. 127–140). Davis, CA: Hermagoras Press.

Berthoff, A. E. (1983). The intelligent eye and the thinking hand. In Sondra Perl (Ed.), *Landmark essays on writing process* (pp. 107–112). Davis, CA: Hermagoras Press.

Bowden, D. (1993). The limits of containment: Text-as-container in composition studies. *College Composition and Communication, 44,* 364–379.

Brown, K. (2004). Technology: Building interaction. *TechTrends: Linking Research & Practice to Improve Learning, 48*(5), 36–38.

Capra, F. (2005). Speaking nature's language: Principles for sustainability. In M. Stone & Z. Barlow (Eds.), *Ecological literacy: Educating our children for a sustainable world* (pp. 18–29). San Francisco, CA: Sierra Club Books.

Cooper, M. (1986). The ecology of writing. *College English, 48*(4), 364–375.

Cubitt, S. (2005). *EcoMedia.* Amsterdam, The Netherlands: Rodopi.

Dobrin, S. I. (2001). Writing takes place. In S. Dobrin & C. R. Weisser (Eds.), *Ecocomposition: Theoretical and Pedagogical Perspectives* (pp. 11–25). Albany, NY: State University of New York Press.

Dobrin, S. I., & Weisser, C. R. (2002). *Natural discourse: Toward ecocomposition.* Albany, NY: State University of New York Press.

Downs, D., & Wardle, E. (2011). *Writing about writing: A college reader.* New York, NY: Bedford/St. Martin's.

Drew, J. (2001). The politics of place. In S. I. Dobrin & C. R. Weisser (Eds.), *Ecocomposition: Theoretical and pedagogical perspectives* (pp. 57–68). Albany, NY: State University of New York Press.

Eckersley, R. (1992). *Environmentalism and political theory: Towards an eco-centric approach*. Albany, NY: State University of New York Press.

Emig, J. (1971). The composing process: Review of the literature. In S. Perl (Ed.), *Landmark essays on writing proce*ss (pp. 1–22). Davis, CA: Hermagoras Press.

Gee, J. P. (1989). Literacy, discourse, and linguistics: Introduction. In E. Wardle & D. Downs (Eds.), *Writing about writing* (pp. 481–497). New York, NY: Bedford/St. Martin's.

Goodfellow, R., & Lea, M. R. (2005). Supporting writing for assessment in online learning. *Assessment & Evaluation in Higher Education, 30*(3), 261–271.

Harris, J. (1989). The idea of community in the study of writing. In E. Wardle and D. Downs (Eds.), *Writing about writing* (pp. 581–594). New York, NY: Bedford/St. Martin's.

Hawisher, G. E., LeBlanc, P., Moran, C., & Selfe, C. L. (1996). *Computers and the teaching of writing in American higher education, 1979–1994: A history*. Norwood, NJ: Ablex.

Hothem, T. (2009). Suburban studies and college writing: Applying ecocomposition. *Pedagogy: Critical Approaches to Teaching Literature, Language, Composition, and Culture, 9*(1), 35–59.

Killingsworth, M. J. (2006). Maps and towers: Metaphors in studies of ecological discourse. *Interdisciplinary Studies in Literature and Environment, 13*(1), 83–90.

Nicol, D. J., Minty, I., & Sinclair, C. (2003). The social dimensions of online learning. *Innovations in Education and Teaching International, 40*(3), 270–280.

Odell, L. (1984). *Reading and writing in the workplace*. Paper presented at the Conference on College Composition and Communication. New York City, March 31, 1984.

Perl, S. (1979). The composing processes of unskilled college writers. In Sondra Perl (Ed.), *Landmark essays on writing processes* (pp. 39–61). Davis, CA: Hermagoras Press.

Peterson, C. L., and Caverly, D. C. (2005). Techtalk: Building academic literacy through online discussion forums. *Journal of Developmental Education, 29*(2), 38–39.

Prior, P. (2009). From speech genres to mediated multimodal genre systems: Bakhtin, Voloshinov, and the question of writing. In C. Bazerman, A. Bonini, and D. Figueiredo (Eds.), *Genre in a changing world* (pp. 17–34). Fort Collins, CO: WAC Clearinghouse http://wac.colostate.edu/books/genre/chapter2.pdf

Reynolds, N. (2004). *Geographies of writing: Inhabiting places and encountering difference.* Carbondale, IL: Southern Illinois University Press.

Samuels, R. (2004). Re-inventing the modern university with WAC: Postmodern composition as cultural and intellectual history. *Across the Disciplines, 1.* Retrieved from http://wac.colostate.edu/atd/articles/samuels2004.cfm

Sirc, G. (2004). Box-logic. In *Writing new media: Theory and applications for expanding the teaching of composition* (pp. 111–146). Logan, UT: Utah State University Press.

Slovic, S. (1999). Seeking the language of solid ground: Reflections on ecocriticism and narrative. *Fourth Genre: Explorations in Narrative, 1*(2), 34–38.

Syverson, M. A. (1999). *The wealth of reality: An ecology of composition.* Carbondale, IL: Southern Illinois University Press.

Walker, P. (2010). (Un)Earthing a vocabulary of values: A discourse analysis for ecocompositionists. *Composition Studies, 38*(1), 69–87.

Weisser, C. R. (2001). Ecocomposition and the greening of identity. In S. I. Dobrin & C. R. Weisser (Eds.), *Ecocomposition: Theoretical and pedagogical perspectives* (pp. 81–95). Albany, NY: State University of New York Press.

Wiegand, P. (1999). How teachers can stop continental drift. *Topic 21,* 1–6.

Wysocki, A. F. (2004). The sticky embrace of beauty: On some formal relations in teaching about the visual aspects of texts. In *Writing new media: Theory and applications for expanding the teaching of composition* (pp. 147–197). Logan, UT: Utah State University Press.

ॐ Contributors

Chris Anson is distinguished university professor and director of the Campus Writing and Speaking Program at North Carolina State University, where he teaches graduate and undergraduate courses in language, composition, and literacy, and works with faculty across the disciplines to enhance writing and speaking instruction. He has published 15 books and over 120 articles and book chapters relating to writing and has spoken widely across the United States and in 30 other countries. He serves on the editorial boards of seven peer-reviewed journals. He has received numerous teaching awards and has participated in over $2 million in grants. He is past Chair of the Conference on College Composition and Communication and past president of the Council of Writing Program Administrators, and he was recently elected to the Steering Committee of the International Society for the Advancement of Writing Research. His full c.v. can be found at www.ansonica.net.

Patricia Webb Boyd is an associate professor at Arizona State University in Tempe, AZ where she teaches courses in rhetoric and composition studies to the full range of students (from graduate students to first-year students). Her research interests include feminist interpretations of popular culture, critiques of the use of technology in writing courses, and analyses of students' writing.

Andy Buchenot is associate professor in the department of English in the Indiana University School of Liberal Arts at IUPUI. He teaches courses in digital literacy, writing pedagogy, and first-year composition. His research, which focuses on student writing and digital technology, has appeared in the *Journal of Teaching Writing, Kairos Praxis Wiki*, and the *Journal of Consumer Health on the Internet.*

Nick Carbone began teaching writing with computers in 1989 by sneaking his class into the secretarial sciences (he is not making that up) classroom so that his students could learn WordStar. Since then he's directed a college writing program, WAC program, and writing center, and worked as a director for digital teaching and learning for a college textbook publisher. He writes about technology and teaching in addition to leading faculty development workshops.

Linda Di Desidero joined the faculty of Marine Corps University in 2012 as the director of the Leadership Communication Skills Center (LCSC). Throughout her career, she has chaired two academic departments and administered a writing center, and she has taught graduate and undergraduate courses in professional communication, composition, linguistics, literature, and education. Dr. Di Desidero holds a PhD in Linguistics (Northwestern University), an EdM in English Education (Rutgers University), and BA degrees in English and in German language and literature (Rutgers University). In addition to her projects on third space writing theory that inform the development of LCSC Studio courses, Dr. Di Desidero's most recent research uses methods associated with the ethnography of communication to investigate language and identity within specific educational and leadership contexts. Her current projects examine the ways in which leadership and gender identities are constructed and displayed both in online relational discourse and in the public discourse of executive leaders.

H. Mark Ellis is a professor of sociology in the Department of Sociology at William Paterson University in Wayne, NJ. He received his BA in Sociology from Montclair State University and his MA and PhD from Northwestern University. He studied classical piano at The Oberlin Conservatory of Music, The Manhattan School of Music, and at Peabody Institute of The Johns Hopkins University. His research and teaching interests include: effective pedagogy for the classroom; race, class and gender; complex social organizations; work and society; the sociology of music and culture; and the sociology of police work. He completed the summer, 2017 Management Development Program at Harvard Graduate School of Education and is the Faculty Director of First-Year Seminar at William Paterson University.

Phoebe Jackson is professor of English at William Paterson University. She has published work in composition studies and on American women writers including Edith Wharton, Willa Cather, Carolyn Chute, Elizabeth Strout, and Harriette Simpson Arnow. With Emily Isaacs, she co-edited the book, *Public Works: Student Writing as Public Text.*

Christopher Justice is a lecturer who teaches courses in the English, digital communications, integrated design, and university writing programs in the University of Baltimore's School of Communications Design. His research combines the environmental humanities and writing studies with a particular emphasis on alternative, animal, and ichthyologic writing systems.

Kristine Larsen is professor of astronomy at Central Connecticut State University where she teaches online, hybrid, flipped, and on-ground courses at a variety of levels. Her research focuses on the intersections between science and society, including science pedagogy. Her latest book is *The Women Who Popularized Geology in the 19th Century* (Springer 2018).

Liane Robertson is co-author of *Writing Across Contexts: Transfer, Composition, and Sites of Writing* (2014), winner of the CCCC 2015 Research Impact Award, and the Council of Writing Program Administrators 2014 Best Book Award. Her most recent research on knowledge transfer in writing has appeared in *Understanding Writing Transfer: Implications for Transformative Student Learning in Higher Education* (2017), *Critical Transitions: Writing and the Question of Transfer* (2016), *A Rhetoric of Reflection* (2016), and *Naming What We Know: Threshold Concepts of Writing Studies* (2015). She is associate professor and director of the Writing Across the Curriculum program at William Paterson University of New Jersey.

Christopher Weaver is an associate professor of English and the director of the Program in Writing and Rhetoric at William Paterson University. Dr. Weaver writes about composition theory and pedagogy. He is the co-editor of *The Theory and Practice of Grading Writing* which was chosen as the outstanding book of the year in the field of education by *Choice: Current Reviews for Academic Libraries*.

Index